INTRODUCTORY ECONOMETRICS

MARK B. STEWART AND
KENNETH F. WALLIS

Introductory Econometrics

Second Edition

BASIL BLACKWELL

First published 1981
Basil Blackwell Ltd
108 Cowley Road
Oxford OX4 1JF, UK

Reprinted 1982, 1984, 1986, 1987

British Library Cataloguing in Publication Data

Stewart, Mark B.
    Introductory econometrics. — 2nd ed.
    I. Title   II. Wallis, Kenneth Frank
    330'.01'82   HB139

    ISBN 0-631-12568-X
    ISBN 0-631-12569-8 Pbk

Printed in Great Britain
by Billing and Sons Ltd, Worcester

CONTENTS

PREFACE

This book is an introduction to econometrics for non-specialists. It aims to give a clear understanding of the problems involved in the empirical measurement of economic relationships and the techniques that can solve those problems. Having read this book economists will be in a position both to evaluate existing empirical research and to initiate research of their own.

The first edition of this book originated in a course of lectures at the London School of Economics that formed part of a taught master's degree programme in economics, and many such programmes continue to include a quantitative methods component for which the present edition remains relevant. Undergraduate programmes in economics have increasingly come to incorporate an introductory econometrics or quantitative economics component, and the present edition reflects this trend. It is based on our experience in teaching such courses both to final-year undergraduates and to master's degree students at the University of Warwick.

An appreciation of the theoretical framework within which empirical work is undertaken and evaluated is, we believe, important in any piece of applied economic research. Therefore the early part of the book discusses the elements of econometric models, both static and dynamic, their theoretical underpinnings, properties and uses. This distinguishes the present volume from most other econometrics texts, which go straight to estimation, spending little or no time explaining what is being estimated, and what for. The outstanding exception is *Econometric Models and Methods* by C. F. Christ, which has had a considerable influence on our teaching over the years and, thereby, on the present volume. Anyone familiar with Professor Christ's text will recognise that we are in his intellectual debt. We are also grateful to him for permission to make use of some of his material for the purpose of certain sections of this book.

In many universities and polytechnics a course in basic economic statistics precedes an introductory econometrics course, and this is assumed herein. A good indication of the material we presume to be contained in such a course is given by *An Introduction to Statistical Analysis for Economists* by J. J. Thomas. While such a course would undoubtedly include the theory of the simple linear regression model, this is outlined in Chapter 5 to achieve a complete and unified treatment.

An acquaintance with the basic ideas of matrix algebra will increase the amount that the reader gets out of this book, but those without such a background should not be put off. The main ideas in the book are conveyed without the use of matrix algebra, and although matrices are used as a convenient simplification at certain points, alternative arguments are always presented.

This new edition has been completely rewritten and contains much additional material. The treatment of many existing topics has been broadened and several new topics introduced, particularly on estimation and testing. This reflects the widening in the range of techniques that the reader of empirical work in economics is likely to encounter. Indeed we have had such a reader very much in mind when deciding which topics to include.

We are grateful for the comments and suggestions of many students and colleagues, in particular Mark Salmon, and for the expert secretarial assistance of Kerrie Beale, Shirley Patterson, Ann Sampson and Yvonne Slater.

I

WHAT IS ECONOMETRICS?

"Econometrics may be defined as the quantitative analysis of actual economic phenomena based on the concurrent development of theory and observation, related by appropriate methods of inference."

Samuelson, Koopmans and Stone, 1954.

Econometrics is concerned with the measurement and empirical testing of economic relationships. As this quotation indicates, the key ingredients are theory, observation, and inference. Economic theory leads to statements about the relations between economic variables under certain assumptions, statements that can often be expressed as equations or inequalities, but in which any coefficients are seldom specified numerically. While economic theory may predict the sign or direction of response of an economic variable to a specified change in relevant circumstances, it is generally unable to predict the magnitude of the response. The measurement of relations between economic variables, and their use in prediction, is the task of econometrics. Economic theory provides hypotheses, which are then confronted with observations. The actual process of observation, of collecting and presenting economic data, is the subject matter of economic statistics. The techniques used, for example in constructing index numbers or seasonally adjusting economic time series, may be very elaborate, but economic statistics is usually concerned with the measurement of variables taken one at a time. Econometrics is concerned with the measurement of relations between variables, with the confrontation of theory with evidence, and the methods used are those of statistical inference. These methods in general do not differ from one area of application to another, and the general principles governing their use in economics are the same as those in any other field in which statistical analysis is employed. Nevertheless in some instances there have been developed particular statistical techniques for dealing with empirical problems that arise in economics but have no counterpart in other fields, and these also form part of econometrics.

In the next three chapters we consider the properties of econometric models. A model provides a summary of relevant economic theory in a form that is convenient for empirical analysis, and so facilitates measurement and testing. Statistical estimation and testing, and the use of the resulting relations for analysis and prediction, are discussed in the remaining chapters.

II

INTRODUCTION TO
ECONOMETRIC MODELS

2.1 A SIMPLE NATIONAL INCOME SYSTEM

We introduce some basic concepts by means of a simple example, namely a two-equation Keynesian national income determination system.

The first element of this example is a consumption function, describing the relation between consumption and income. Using the notation for these variables that is conventional in economics we denote consumption by C and income by Y, so that the consumption function can be readily expressed as

$$C = f(Y).$$

The behaviour of consumers, Keynes argued, is such that consumption increases as income increases, but not by as much as the increase in income, and that the proportion of income consumed decreases as income increases. More formally, the first statement says that the first derivative of the function, the marginal propensity to consume, is positive but less than one, that is,

$$0 < \frac{dC}{dY} < 1,$$

and the second that

$$\frac{d(C/Y)}{dY} < 0.$$

Differentiating the consumption-income ratio with respect to income gives

$$\frac{\mathrm{d}(C/Y)}{\mathrm{d}Y} = \frac{1}{Y}\frac{\mathrm{d}C}{\mathrm{d}Y} - \frac{C}{Y^2},$$

and the statement that this quantity is negative is equivalent to the statement that the income elasticity of consumption is less than one, that is,

$$\frac{Y}{C}\frac{\mathrm{d}C}{\mathrm{d}Y} < 1.$$

Any mathematical function with these two properties is consistent with Keynes' two arguments mentioned above, and for some purposes in economic theory it is not necessary to say anything further about the function f. However, in order to use a consumption function as a framework for data analysis and as an element of a system for making quantitative predictions, it is necessary to specify a functional form. The simplest possibility, useful at least as a first approximation, is to assume that consumption is a *linear* function of income, that is,

$$C = \alpha + \beta Y.$$

The first derivative, $\mathrm{d}C/\mathrm{d}Y$, is equal to the slope coefficient β, and the proportion of income consumed decreases as income increases if the intercept term α is positive, hence this linear function is consistent with Keynes' arguments if the coefficients satisfy

$$\alpha > 0, \qquad 0 < \beta < 1.$$

The consumption function describes consumers' behaviour, and is thus an example of a *behavioural relation*. Relevant data may comprise *time series* observations on aggregate consumers' expenditure and income over time, or *cross-section* data relating to a sample of households at a given point in time. We shall variously use the subscripts t

or i to index particular observations on variables, often without reference to a specific context, although common usage might suggest that C_t and Y_t denote aggregate consumption and income at time t, while C_i and Y_i denote the consumer expenditure and income of the ith household in a cross-section sample. In either case the number of observations in the sample is denoted n, thus the range of the subscripts is indicated as $t = 1, \ldots, n$ or $i = 1, \ldots, n$. We assume that the coefficients α and β are constant across the sample of n observations, and so refer to them as *parameters*. In general parameters are denoted by Greek letters.

The present context is a national income determination system, thus an aggregate time series interpretation is relevant. We complete the system by writing the income definition or accounting identity

$$Y_t = C_t + I_t,$$

which divides income into two components of effective demand, the second being investment or autonomous expenditure. We now have a pair of equations that describe the determination of the values of the variables C and Y in terms of the values of the variable I and parameters α and β. The variables determined within the system are termed *endogenous variables*, while those determined outside the system, about which the system has nothing to say, are termed *exogenous variables*. The statement of the relations among the variables, together with a classification of variables as endogenous or exogenous, comprises the economic *model*, thus the model of our present example is

$$C_t = \alpha + \beta Y_t$$
$$Y_t = C_t + I_t$$

endogenous variables: C_t, Y_t; exogenous variable: I_t.

For the system to be consistent, that is, to have a determinate solution giving unique values of the endogenous variables in terms of parameters and exogenous variables, without redundancy, the number of equations in the model must be the same as the number of endogenous variables.

Let us consider this solution algebraically. Substituting from the income identity into the consumption function gives

$$C_t = \alpha + \beta(C_t + I_t)$$

and on rearranging we obtain

$$C_t = \frac{\alpha}{1-\beta} + \frac{\beta}{1-\beta} I_t.$$

Likewise, on eliminating C_t from the pair of equations and rearranging we obtain

$$Y_t = \frac{\alpha}{1-\beta} + \frac{1}{1-\beta} I_t.$$

We can define new parameters for these equations, and write

$$C_t = \gamma_0 + \gamma_1 I_t$$
$$Y_t = \delta_0 + \delta_1 I_t.$$

Then, if the numerical values of γ_0, γ_1, δ_0 and δ_1 were known we could use these equations to predict the values of C and Y associated with any value of I.

This last pair of equations is known as the _reduced form_ of the model. Each reduced form equation expresses a single endogenous variable in terms of exogenous variables and parameters. The reduced form describes the result of the interactions among the endogenous variables, without describing the interactions themselves: these simultaneous connections among endogenous variables are described in the original formulation of the model, known as the *structural form*. The equations of the structural form, or _structural equations_, typically comprise behavioural relations, describing the behaviour of different economic agents or sectors of the economy, and identities, which may be of an accounting, definitional or technical nature: further examples will be discussed below. The parameters of the structural equations are simply referred to as *structural parameters*. The coefficients of the reduced form equations are defined in terms of these parameters as follows:

$$\gamma_0 = \frac{\alpha}{1 - \beta} \qquad \gamma_1 = \frac{\beta}{1 - \beta}$$

$$\delta_0 = \frac{\alpha}{1 - \beta} \qquad \delta_1 = \frac{1}{1 - \beta}.$$

Since there are four reduced form coefficients but only two structural parameters we expect there to be two interrelations among the reduced form coefficients. Simple inspection reveals these to be $\gamma_0 = \delta_0$ and $\delta_1 - \gamma_1 = 1$, that is, the intercept terms of the reduced form equations for income and consumption are equal, and their slope coefficients differ by one. It is postulated that α, the intercept term of the consumption function, is positive, and that β, the marginal propensity to consume, lies between 0 and 1, and so the reduced form coefficients are all positive. These statements about the interrelations and the signs (but not the magnitude) of these coefficients are as far as theoretical reasoning will take us.

To use the reduced form equations to predict the levels of income and consumption associated with a given level of investment we need to know the numerical values of these coefficients, and we now briefly consider empirical observation and measurement. Since we have an exact linear relation, observations at two different values of I will suffice to evaluate the reduced form coefficients. Suppose that the values of I observed in two periods are 20 and 30 units, and that the associated values of Y are 120 and 160 units respectively. Then we need to solve for δ_0 and δ_1 in the equations

$$120 = \delta_0 + \delta_1 20$$

$$160 = \delta_0 + \delta_1 30.$$

On doing this, we obtain $\delta_1 = 4$ and $\delta_0 = 40$, and so the reduced form equation for income is

$$Y = 40 + 4I.$$

This equation can be used to predict the value of Y associated with any value of I, for example if $I = 25$ then $Y = 140$. The reduced form equation for consumption can be obtained similarly. Since the income identity always holds it is no surprise to learn that values of C of 100 and 130 units respectively are observed in the two periods, and on solving for γ_0 and γ_1 in the relations

$$100 = \gamma_0 + \gamma_1 20$$
$$130 = \gamma_0 + \gamma_1 30$$

the reduced form equation for consumption is obtained as

$$C = 40 + 3I.$$

This again can be used as a prediction equation: if I is increased to 35 units, consumption will increase to 145.

These separate reduced form equations can be used for prediction of C or Y without reference to the underlying structural form, but we may nevertheless be interested in the structural parameter values for their own sake. To obtain these we return to the relations between structural parameters and reduced form coefficients, and attempt to solve

$$40 = \frac{\alpha}{1 - \beta}, \quad \text{and} \quad 4 = \frac{1}{1 - \beta} \quad \text{or} \quad 3 = \frac{\beta}{1 - \beta}.$$

The last two equations are equivalent, for the estimated reduced form equations do indeed satisfy the requirement that the slope coefficients differ by one. Simple calculation gives $\beta = \frac{3}{4}$ and $\alpha = 10$ and so the consumption function is given as

$$C = 10 + \tfrac{3}{4}Y.$$

Such determination of the structural parameter values from the reduced form coefficients is not always possible, and the question of what is possible is known as the *identification* problem.

When numerical values of all structural parameters are specified, we have what is termed a *structure*. The term *model,* introduced above, refers to the situation in which these numerical parameter values are *not* known, and in general represents the end-product of economic theory or prior reasoning. We proceed from a model to a structure by means of empirical observation and measurement.

With this terminology, a *structural change* is simply a change in the structure, for instance, a change in the numerical value of a structural parameter. In our example, if consumers altered their allocation of income into consumption and saving such that the marginal propensity to consume rose from its value of 0.75 to a new value of 0.80, we would say that a structural change had occurred.

Our previous statement about the use of reduced form equations for prediction now needs qualifying. A reduced form equation, with numerical values of its coefficients known, is sufficient to predict the value of an endogenous variable associated with a given value of an exogenous variable provided that the structure is unchanged. But if a structural change occurs it is necessary to calculate new values of the reduced form coefficients before a prediction can be made, and knowledge of the structure is needed for this. For example, to consider the effect on the predictions of income of an increase in β from 0.75 to 0.80, we need to know that the coefficients in the reduced form equation are given by

$$\delta_0 = \frac{\alpha}{1 - \beta}, \quad \delta_1 = \frac{1}{1 - \beta}.$$

If the value α is unchanged at 10, then the new values of the reduced form coefficients are $\delta_0 = 50$ and $\delta_1 = 5$, and the value of Y associated with a value of I of 25 in the new structure is 175. The structural form is typically the most convenient framework for economic reasoning, while the reduced form in effect provides a summary that is adequate for prediction as long as the structure remains the same. We now have two possible reasons for seeking knowledge of structural parameter values. The first is knowledge for its own sake, for example, to answer the question, what *is* the value of the marginal propensity to consume. The second is to facilitate analysis of structural change, for example, to calculate predictions of endogenous variables after such a change. In the absence of structural change, however, reduced form coefficient values are sufficient for prediction.

2.2 A DEMAND-AND-SUPPLY EXAMPLE

A second example serves to develop further and emphasise the basic ideas. We consider a simple model of the competitive market for a commodity that is subject to an excise tax. The price of the commodity is sufficiently flexible to equate demand and supply in every period.

The behaviour of buyers of the commodity is described by a demand function, which says that Q^d, the quantity demanded, is a function of the market price of the commodity P, with a negative slope, thus

$$Q^d = f(P), \qquad \frac{dQ^d}{dP} < 0.$$

Once more for practical purposes we take this function to be linear, and so write

$$Q^d = \alpha_0 + \alpha_1 P, \quad \alpha_1 < 0.$$

The behaviour of sellers of the commodity is described by a supply function, in which Q^s, the quantity supplied, is an increasing function of the price received by sellers, namely $P - E$, the price before tax, where E is the per unit excise tax. Again assuming linearity we have

$$Q^s = \beta_0 + \beta_1(P - E), \quad \beta_1 > 0.$$

The market-clearing condition is

$$Q^d = Q^s,$$

thus we have three equations describing the determination, in terms of parameters and the excise tax variable, of the variables P, Q^d and Q^s. But these last two variables are equal by the market-clearing condition, so it is simpler to use this equation to eliminate one variable, and define Q, without superscript, as the quantity traded, giving a two-equation system. Thus our model in *structural form* is

$$Q = \alpha_0 + \alpha_1 P$$
$$Q = \beta_0 + \beta_1 (P - E)$$

endogenous variables: Q, P; exogenous variable: E.

Each of the structural equations is a *behavioural relation*, describing the behaviour of one particular group or sector in the economy. The nature of one group's response to changes in the values of variables is not affected by the behaviour of the other group. For example, the demand equation says that buyers are influenced by the market price of the product, but not by the breakdown of this price into the pre-tax price plus the tax. It is the pre-tax price that influences sellers, according to the supply equation, but again this equation is not affected by buyers' behaviour: a change in the elasticity of demand for the commodity, reflected in the parameter α_1, has no effect on sellers' response to changes in price. The structural equations are sometimes called autonomous relations: they have the property of *autonomy*, being affected only by the behaviour of one group or sector in the economy.

Solving the demand and supply equations simultaneously for Q and P gives the *reduced form*. On equating the right-hand sides we have

$$\alpha_0 + \alpha_1 P = \beta_0 + \beta_1 (P - E)$$

and on rearranging we have the reduced form equation for price:

$$P = \frac{\alpha_0 - \beta_0}{\beta_1 - \alpha_1} + \frac{\beta_1}{\beta_1 - \alpha_1} E.$$

Then substituting for P in either of the structural equations gives

$$Q = \frac{\alpha_0 \beta_1 - \alpha_1 \beta_0}{\beta_1 - \alpha_1} + \frac{\alpha_1 \beta_1}{\beta_1 - \alpha_1} E.$$

Again, each reduced form equation expresses a single endogenous variable in terms of exogenous variables (only one, in our examples) and parameters. These equations do not have the property of autonomy, for both are affected by any change in the behaviour of either buyers or sellers, for example, by a change in the numerical value of a structural parameter. On rewriting the reduced form equations by using new symbols for their coefficients we have

$$P = \gamma_0 + \gamma_1 E$$

$$Q = \delta_0 + \delta_1 E.$$

Once the numerical values of the coefficients γ_0, γ_1, δ_0 and δ_1 are known, these equations can be used to predict the price of the commodity and the quantity traded at any level of the excise tax, provided that the structure does not change. Knowledge of the reduced form coefficients comes from observation of the values of P and Q associated with different values of E, and again in this context of exact linear relations observations at two different values of E are enough to determine the values of γ_0, γ_1, δ_0 and δ_1. Of course if the value of E never changes then this will not be possible, but in such a situation it would no longer be appropriate to speak of E as a *variable*.

The expressions for the reduced form coefficients in terms of the structural parameters are

$$\gamma_0 = \frac{\alpha_0 - \beta_0}{\beta_1 - \alpha_1} \qquad \gamma_1 = \frac{\beta_1}{\beta_1 - \alpha_1}$$

$$\delta_0 = \frac{\alpha_0 \beta_1 - \alpha_1 \beta_0}{\beta_1 - \alpha_1} \qquad \delta_1 = \frac{\alpha_1 \beta_1}{\beta_1 - \alpha_1}.$$

Given the original restrictions $\alpha_1 < 0$ and $\beta_1 > 0$ it is clear that the denominator $\beta_1 - \alpha_1$ is positive, and so $\gamma_1 > 0$ and $\delta_1 < 0$, that is, as the tax increases, price increases and quantity decreases. Further restrictions arise from the requirement that both price and quantity must be positive. Considering first the structural equations and sketching these in the usual Marshallian price-quantity diagram with price on the vertical axis, as in Figure 2.1, we require the two lines to intersect in the positive quadrant, as sketched. For this to occur it is necessary that, at their intersections with the horizontal axis, the supply function is to the left of the demand function, and at their intersections with the vertical axis, the supply function is below the demand

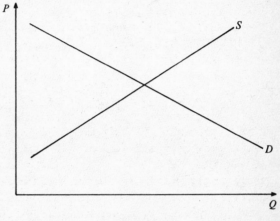

Figure 2.1

function. The first requirement is that $\beta_0 < \alpha_0$ with $\alpha_0 > 0$, and the second that $-\beta_0/\beta_1 < -\alpha_0/\alpha_1$ with $-\alpha_0/\alpha_1 > 0$, which on rearrangement gives $\alpha_0\beta_1 - \alpha_1\beta_0 > 0$. These imply that $\gamma_0 > 0$ and $\delta_0 > 0$, which could equivalently be obtained directly by noting that the intercepts of the reduced form equations, giving the values of price and quantity at zero tax, must be positive. Unlike the national income example, here there are no further restrictions on the reduced form coefficients: the four coefficients are functions of four structural parameters, and so no interrelations are implied.

As in the previous example, we can solve back from the reduced form coefficients to the structural parameters, if we wish to know the structural parameters either for their own interest (for example to use demand and supply elasticities in other exercises) or to enable predictions under structural change to be made. The algebraic solution is

$$\alpha_0 = \delta_0 - \frac{\delta_1 \gamma_0}{\gamma_1} \qquad \alpha_1 = \frac{\delta_1}{\gamma_1}$$

$$\beta_0 = \delta_0 - \frac{\delta_1 \gamma_0}{\gamma_1 - 1} \qquad \beta_1 = \frac{\delta_1}{\gamma_1 - 1} \,.$$

Thus, having obtained numerical values of the reduced form coefficients from data, unique values of the structural parameters could be deduced and we say that the structural parameters are *identified*. As already noted, this is not always possible. For example, suppose that there is no excise tax. Then the observed values of P and Q give the values of γ_0 and δ_0, but this is insufficient information to yield the values of α_0, α_1, β_0 and β_1, so these are not identified. This matter is explored further in chapter 4.

2.3 STOCHASTIC MODELS

The exact equations of our two examples often provide a convenient framework for theoretical analysis, but seldom correspond to observable behaviour. While a relationship such as the simple linear consumption function may fit data on C and Y reasonably well over a period of time or across a cross-section sample, it will not do so exactly: discrepancies occur year-by-year, or household-by-household. Of course a perfect explanation can be obtained by adopting a polynomial function whose degree increases as more observations are obtained. We saw in the national income example that two observations on Y and I are sufficient to evaluate the reduced form coefficients, and the resulting reduced form equation clearly fits these data perfectly. In practice we do not anticipate that a third observed pair of Y-I values will lie on the calculated line, but an exact fit can be obtained by considering the quadratic

$$Y_t = \delta_0 + \delta_1 I_t + \delta_2 I_t^2$$

and using the three observations to determine the values of δ_0, δ_1 and δ_2. Again, a fourth *Y-I* observation is unlikely to satisfy the resulting equation, but can be accommodated by appropriate values of the coefficients of the cubic

$$Y_t = \delta_0 + \delta_1 I_t + \delta_2 I_t^2 + \delta_3 I_t^3,$$

and so on. However such increasing complexity is generally impractical, and economists have learned to mistrust explanations of economic behaviour that are made to fit the facts exactly.

In practice we relax not the linearity assumption but the assumption of exact behavioural relations. We do this by regarding the relation as having two parts. The first part, the right-hand side of the exact equations discussed so far, is the *systematic* part of the relation. To this we add a *non-systematic* part, which serves to connect the systematic part to the real world. The influences on the left-hand-side variable that are important and can be observed are included in the systematic part, and these are often few in number. However there are other factors, each with small and possibly unpredictable influence, factors that possibly cannot be identified or measured, that taken together form the non-systematic part. Some of these may have only a fleeting influence: there may be only one political crisis, exceptionally cold winter, epidemic, change in fashion or taste in our observation period. But in general there are more such influences than we can list, and their total effect corresponds to the non-systematic part of the relationship.

We represent the non-systematic part by adding a *disturbance term* to the relation and treating this as a *random* or *stochastic* variable, as in statistical theory. That is, it is a variable that takes on different values as described by a probability distribution. Conventionally the disturbance term, also called the random error term, is denoted by the symbol u, so we now write the consumption function, for example, as

$$C_t = \alpha + \beta Y_t + u_t.$$

We assume that the disturbance term at time t has an expected value of zero:

$$E(u_t) = 0.$$

If the mean value were anything other than zero, then the disturbance term could be said to contain a systematic effect, contradicting the distinction we have just drawn. Often we do not need to specify the probability distribution of the disturbance term, but we shall discuss in later chapters the situations in which such a specification is necessary. Then it is typically assumed that the disturbance term has a normal probability distribution with mean zero and variance denoted by σ^2, and this assumption is written

$$u \sim N(0, \sigma^2).$$

As before we complete the system with the income identity, and having introduced the random error term we speak of the resulting equations as a *stochastic model*, which now is

$$C_t = \alpha + \beta Y_t + u_t$$
$$Y_t = C_t + I_t$$

endogenous variables: C_t, Y_t: exogenous variable: I_t.

An exogenous variable was previously defined as a variable determined outside the model, and the extension of this idea to the stochastic case requires that the variable be unaffected by the random influences on consumption represented by the disturbance term. To be precise, an *exogenous variable* is a variable whose value in any period is independent of the values of the disturbance terms in the model in any period. We write disturbance terms in the plural to look beyond our simple example which contains only one behavioural relation and hence only one disturbance term.

We do not attach random disturbances to identities. In general definitions, accounting identities, technical relations, equilibrium conditions, and so forth hold exactly. For example, profit equals total revenue less total costs, tax revenue equals the tax rate times the tax base, the balance of trade equals exports minus imports, and so on. Sometimes there are errors of measurement of economic variables, or "statistical discrepancies" and "balancing items" in national accounts. However exact measurement can eliminate such *errors in variables*, and they are not our main concern: no exact measurement can ensure that the consumption function perfectly fits data on C and Y year after year, and we concentrate on *errors in equations*, the disturbance terms in behavioural relations.

Continuing with the national income example, we next derive the reduced form of the stochastic model, analogous to that obtained in section 2.1. By the same procedure we obtain

$$C_t = \frac{\alpha}{1-\beta} + \frac{\beta}{1-\beta} I_t + \frac{1}{1-\beta} u_t$$

$$Y_t = \frac{\alpha}{1-\beta} + \frac{1}{1-\beta} I_t + \frac{1}{1-\beta} u_t$$

in which each reduced form equation now contains a random error term. Each endogenous variable is thus a random variable, and we can again regard the equations as having systematic and non-systematic parts. (As can be seen, in this simple example the non-systematic parts of consumption and income are equal.) Given the numerical values of the reduced form coefficients, it is not possible to predict exactly the values of consumption and income associated with a given value of investment, because of the random nature of the variables. Predictions based on the systematic parts of the reduced form equation will be subject to error, although the errors will have expected values of zero. For example, taking the values used in the numerical illustration of section 2.1 and denoting the reduced form random error $u_t/(1-\beta)$ as v_t, the reduced form equation for income is

$$Y_t = 40 + 4I_t + v_t.$$

The predicted value of Y associated with a value of I of 25 is 140, but the actual value will deviate from this as a result of the random disturbance term. But since u_t has a mean of zero so does v_t, and the prediction errors will average out at zero. Additionally, if the variance of the reduced form disturbance were known, then we could say something about the likely size of the error.

The demand-and-supply example of section 2.2 allows us to discuss a further aspect of stochastic models. Again we add random disturbance terms to the behavioural equations, and so write the stochastic model as

$$\text{demand:} \quad Q = \alpha_0 + \alpha_1 P + u^d$$

$$\text{supply:} \quad Q = \beta_0 + \beta_1(P - E) + u^s$$

endogenous variables: Q, P; exogenous variable: E.

The random disturbance u^d is the non-systematic part of the demand function, representing the influence on buyer's behaviour of all factors other than price. Likewise the error term in the supply function, u^s, captures the effect of omitted factors on sellers' behaviour. Each non-systematic part has an expected value of zero:

$$E(u^d) = E(u^s) = 0.$$

In general we might expect that some of the factors that have a small, accidental influence on buyers' behaviour also influence sellers in some way. For example, climatic factors might affect both the demand for and the supply of an agricultural commodity, but of course if particular weather variables that have a regular substantial effect can be identified then they should be included in the systematic part of the appropriate function. The possibility that some random factors influence both disturbance terms implies that the disturbances will be correlated, positively or negatively, and the methods of analysis and estimation that we use allow for this possibility. We typically do not assume that the random disturbances are uncorrelated. The general definition of the covariance of two random variables is the expected value of the cross-product of their mean deviations, that is,

$$\text{cov}(u^d, u^s) = E\{u^d - E(u^d)\}\{u^s - E(u^s)\} ,$$

but since the disturbances have zero means, this reduces to the expected value of their cross-product,

$$\text{cov}(u^d, u^s) = E(u^d u^s).$$

Likewise the definition of the variance is simplified by the zero mean condition:

$$\text{var}(u^d) = E(u^d)^2, \qquad \text{var}(u^s) = E(u^s)^2.$$

The coefficient of correlation between the two variables is given by the covariance divided by the product of their standard deviations, that is,

$$\frac{\text{cov}(u^d, u^s)}{\sqrt{\text{var}(u^d)\,\text{var}(u^s)}}$$

and this quantity lies between -1 and 1, and in general is non-zero.

The reduced form of the model is

$$P = \frac{\alpha_0 - \beta_0}{\beta_1 - \alpha_1} + \frac{\beta_1}{\beta_1 - \alpha_1}E + \frac{u^d - u^s}{\beta_1 - \alpha_1}$$

$$Q = \frac{\alpha_0\beta_1 - \alpha_1\beta_0}{\beta_1 - \alpha_1} + \frac{\alpha_1\beta_1}{\beta_1 - \alpha_1}E + \frac{\beta_1 u^d - \alpha_1 u^s}{\beta_1 - \alpha_1},$$

and on rewriting these equations compactly by using new symbols we have

$$P = \gamma_0 + \gamma_1 E + v_1$$

$$Q = \delta_0 + \delta_1 E + v_2.$$

The reduced form disturbances, denoted v_1 and v_2, are related to the structural disturbances as follows:

$$v_1 = \frac{u^d - u^s}{\beta_1 - \alpha_1}, \qquad v_2 = \frac{\beta_1 u^d - \alpha_1 u^s}{\beta_1 - \alpha_1}.$$

Each reduced form disturbance is a function of both structural disturbances, that is, the random influences on either demand or supply affect both the market-clearing price and the quantity traded. Since the structural disturbances have mean values of zero, so do the reduced form disturbances:

$$E(v_1) = \frac{E(u^d) - E(u^s)}{\beta_1 - \alpha_1} = 0, \qquad E(v_2) = \frac{\beta_1 E(u^d) - \alpha_1 E(u^s)}{\beta_1 - \alpha_1} = 0.$$

The covariance between the reduced form disturbances is in general non-zero, irrespective of any covariance between the structural disturbances, because a given structural disturbance affects both reduced form disturbances. For example, a random upward shift in the demand function, caused by a positive value of u^d, leads to a random increase in price ($v_1 > 0$) and quantity ($v_2 > 0$). As an exercise, we can relate the covariances of v_1 and v_2 to the covariance and variances of u^d and u^s:

$$
\begin{aligned}
\mathrm{cov}(v_1, v_2) &= E(v_1 v_2) \\[2mm]
&= E\left(\frac{u^d - u^s}{\beta_1 - \alpha_1}\right)\left(\frac{\beta_1 u^d - \alpha_1 u^s}{\beta_1 - \alpha_1}\right) \\[3mm]
&= \frac{\beta_1 E(u^d)^2 - (\beta_1 + \alpha_1)\, E(u^d u^s) + \alpha_1 E(u^s)^2}{(\beta_1 - \alpha_1)^2} \\[3mm]
&= \frac{\beta_1 \,\mathrm{var}(u^d) - (\beta_1 + \alpha_1)\, \mathrm{cov}(u^d, u^s) + \alpha_1 \,\mathrm{var}(u^s)}{(\beta_1 - \alpha_1)^2}.
\end{aligned}
$$

Remembering that $\beta_1 > 0$ and $\alpha_1 < 0$, it is clear that this covariance could be either positive or negative. Random shifts in the demand function cause price and quantity to move in the same direction, while random shifts in the supply function cause price and quantity to move in opposite directions, so which random shift dominates (has the greater variance) will tend to determine the sign of this covariance.

2.4 GENERAL REPRESENTATIONS OF SIMULTANEOUS EQUATION MODELS

To be able to discuss general matters away from the context of specific examples we present a general notation for linear models. There are some standard conventions that we now describe.

The model is linear, with G equations that hold simultaneously. Endogenous variables are denoted by y's, exogenous variables by x's and disturbances by u's. There are G endogenous variables and K exogenous variables in the model; these variables are observable, while the disturbances are not. Thus the tth observation on the ith endogenous variable is denoted y_{it}, $i = 1, \ldots, G$, $t = 1, \ldots, n$ and the tth observation on the kth exogenous variable is x_{kt}, $k = 1, \ldots, K$, $t = 1, \ldots, n$. The structural parameters are the coefficients in the equations, coefficients of endogenous and exogenous variables being denoted by β's and γ's respectively. The coefficients are written with two subscripts, the first indicating the equation in question and the second the particular variable to which the coefficient is attached. One of the x's, say the first, may be a dummy variable whose value is always equal to 1, so that its coefficient γ_{g1} represents a constant term in the gth equation. With this notation we can write out the G structural equations as follows, collecting all terms involving observable variables on the left-hand side:

$$\beta_{11}y_{1t} + \beta_{12}y_{2t} + \ldots + \beta_{1G}y_{Gt} + \gamma_{11}x_{1t} + \gamma_{12}x_{2t} + \ldots + \gamma_{1K}x_{Kt} = u_{1t}$$
$$\beta_{21}y_{1t} + \beta_{22}y_{2t} + \ldots + \beta_{2G}y_{Gt} + \gamma_{21}x_{1t} + \gamma_{22}x_{2t} + \ldots + \gamma_{2K}x_{Kt} = u_{2t}$$
$$\vdots$$
$$\beta_{G1}y_{1t} + \beta_{G2}y_{2t} + \ldots + \beta_{GG}y_{Gt} + \gamma_{G1}x_{1t} + \gamma_{G2}x_{2t} + \ldots + \gamma_{GK}x_{Kt} = u_{Gt}.$$

The use of summation notation allows the equations to be written more compactly:

$$\sum_{i=1}^{G} \beta_{gi}y_{it} + \sum_{k=1}^{K} \gamma_{gk}x_{kt} = u_{gt}, \quad g = 1, \ldots, G.$$

Alternatively, the model can be written in matrix terms as

$$\begin{bmatrix} \beta_{11} & \beta_{12} \ldots \beta_{1G} \\ \beta_{21} & \beta_{22} \ldots \beta_{2G} \\ \vdots & \vdots \quad \vdots \\ \beta_{G1} & \beta_{G2} \ldots \beta_{GG} \end{bmatrix} \begin{bmatrix} y_{1t} \\ y_{2t} \\ \vdots \\ y_{Gt} \end{bmatrix} + \begin{bmatrix} \gamma_{11} & \gamma_{12} \ldots \gamma_{1K} \\ \gamma_{21} & \gamma_{22} \ldots \gamma_{2K} \\ \vdots & \vdots \quad \vdots \\ \gamma_{G1} & \gamma_{G2} \ldots \gamma_{GK} \end{bmatrix} \begin{bmatrix} x_{1t} \\ x_{2t} \\ \vdots \\ x_{Kt} \end{bmatrix} = \begin{bmatrix} u_{1t} \\ u_{2t} \\ \vdots \\ u_{Gt} \end{bmatrix}.$$

Defining **B** and Γ as the above matrices of coefficients, using the convention that a bold-face (heavy type) capital letter denotes a matrix whose elements are denoted by the corresponding small letter, and y_t, x_t and u_t as the column vectors of variables and disturbances, we can finally write the model as

$$By_t + \Gamma x_i = u_t.$$

Since the number of equations is equal to the number of endogenous variables the matrix B is square, of dimension $G \times G$. The matrix Γ has dimension $G \times K$, and there is no necessary connection between these two numbers.

In each equation one of the β-coefficients is assigned the value of 1. This *normalization rule* could be thought of as indicating the particular y-variable regarded as the dependent variable in that equation, but this term is slightly inappropriate because in the simultaneous equation context all the y's are *jointly dependent* variables. Sometimes the normalization rule is implemented by assigning the value of 1 to the diagonal elements of B, then if the gth equation is a behavioural relation we might consider it to be the equation primarily concerned with the determination of the gth endogenous variable. There is no need for the rule to be implemented in this way, however, as we shall see in our examples.

Specific content is given to this general framework by imposing restrictions on it. Some of the β's and γ's may be assigned zero values, indicating that the corresponding variables do not appear in particular equations. Typically economic reasoning suggests which variables should enter a particular behavioural relation, but by implication it also suggests which variables should not. Such restrictions are termed *exclusion restrictions*; for example the restriction $\beta_{12} = 0$ serves to exclude the second endogenous variable of the model from the first equation. Additionally, an equation that is an *identity* has the numerical values of its coefficients specified (typically 1 or -1), and its disturbance is always zero.

We can illustrate these points by casting our previous examples into this new framework. Retaining the original symbols, but rearranging the equations into the matrix format, the national income example can be written as

$$\begin{bmatrix} 1 & -\beta \\ -1 & 1 \end{bmatrix} \begin{bmatrix} C_t \\ Y_t \end{bmatrix} + \begin{bmatrix} -\alpha & 0 \\ 0 & -1 \end{bmatrix} \begin{bmatrix} 1 \\ I_t \end{bmatrix} = \begin{bmatrix} u_t \\ 0 \end{bmatrix}.$$

The vector of endogenous variables has two components, and the first element of the exogenous variable vector is the dummy variable, always equal to 1, its coefficient being the intercept term in the consumption function. Each row of the matrix **B** contains a unit element: the normalization rule. Our consumption function says that consumption is a function of income, but not of investment, hence the coefficient γ_{12} is set equal to zero. The second equation is an identity: the second rows of the matrices **B** and Γ contain no unknown coefficients, and the second element of the disturbance vector is zero.

Similarly the demand-and-supply example can be written as

$$\begin{bmatrix} -\alpha_1 & 1 \\ -\beta_1 & 1 \end{bmatrix} \begin{bmatrix} P \\ Q \end{bmatrix} + \begin{bmatrix} -\alpha_0 & 0 \\ -\beta_0 & \beta_1 \end{bmatrix} \begin{bmatrix} 1 \\ E \end{bmatrix} = \begin{bmatrix} u^d \\ u^s \end{bmatrix}.$$

Since both the demand and supply functions were initially written with Q on the left-hand side, the unit elements in each row of the matrix **B** now appear in the same column. There is one exclusion restriction: the excise tax variable does not enter the demand function, and so there is a zero in the top right corner of the matrix Γ. The second equation is also subject to a restriction, of a slightly more general kind. Since the quantity supplied is a function of the price before tax, $P - E$, the separate variables P and E appear with coefficients that are equal but opposite in sign. This is indicated by the presence of the structural parameter β_1 in two places in the coefficient matrices, and in terms of the general notation the restriction is $\beta_{21} + \gamma_{22} = 0$. This is an example of a *homogeneous linear restriction*, that is, a linear combination of the structural parameters must equal zero. While exclusion restrictions are the most common way of incorporating theoretical information on a particular context into the general model framework, they can be seen as special cases of the more general homogeneous linear restriction, for such a special case is precisely what we have when we write $\gamma_{12} = 0$ in the present example.

Returning to the general representation we next consider the *reduced form* of the model. The general reduced form of G equations, each expressing an endogenous variable in terms of exogenous variables and disturbances, can be written as

$$y_{1t} = \pi_{11}x_{1t} + \pi_{12}x_{2t} + \ldots + \pi_{1K}x_{Kt} + v_{1t}$$

$$y_{2t} = \pi_{21}x_{1t} + \pi_{22}x_{2t} + \ldots + \pi_{2K}x_{Kt} + v_{2t}$$

$$\vdots$$

$$y_{Gt} = \pi_{G1}x_{1t} + \pi_{G2}x_{2t} + \ldots + \pi_{GK}x_{Kt} + v_{Gt}.$$

The π's represent the reduced form coefficients and the v's the reduced form disturbances. Again these equations can be written in matrix terms as

$$
\begin{bmatrix} y_{1t} \\ y_{2t} \\ \vdots \\ y_{Gt} \end{bmatrix} =
\begin{bmatrix} \pi_{11} & \pi_{12} \ldots \pi_{1K} \\ \pi_{21} & \pi_{22} \ldots \pi_{2K} \\ \vdots & \vdots \quad \vdots \\ \pi_{G1} & \pi_{G2} \cdots \pi_{GK} \end{bmatrix}
\begin{bmatrix} x_{1t} \\ x_{2t} \\ \vdots \\ x_{Kt} \end{bmatrix} +
\begin{bmatrix} v_{1t} \\ v_{2t} \\ \vdots \\ v_{Gt} \end{bmatrix}.
$$

Defining Π as the above $G \times K$ matrix of coefficients, and $\mathbf{v}_t$ as the column vector of reduced form error terms, we can write the reduced form as

$$\mathbf{y}_t = \Pi\mathbf{x}_t + \mathbf{v}_t.$$

The relation between the structural form and the reduced form can be obtained explicitly by solving the structural form as follows. First take the terms involving exogenous variables to the right-hand side, to give

$$\mathbf{B}\mathbf{y}_t = -\Gamma\mathbf{x}_t + \mathbf{u}_t.$$

Next assume that the $G \times G$ matrix $\mathbf{B}$ is non-singular, that is, its determinant is non-zero, so that its inverse exists, and multiply through by $\mathbf{B}^{-1}$:

$$\mathbf{B}^{-1}\mathbf{B}\mathbf{y}_t = -\mathbf{B}^{-1}\Gamma\mathbf{x}_t + \mathbf{B}^{-1}\mathbf{u}_t.$$

Then on simplifying slightly we have the unique solution for $\mathbf{y}_t$:

$$\mathbf{y}_t = -\mathbf{B}^{-1}\Gamma\mathbf{x}_t + \mathbf{B}^{-1}\mathbf{u}_t,$$

and this is the reduced form. Thus the reduced form coefficients are related to the structural parameters by the equation

$$\Pi = -\mathbf{B}^{-1}\Gamma,$$

and the reduced form disturbances are related to the structural disturbances by

$$\mathbf{v}_t = \mathbf{B}^{-1}\mathbf{u}_t.$$

Although some elements of the matrices $\mathbf{B}$ and Γ will be assigned zero values, as we have discussed, in general these will not lead to zero values for any π-coefficients, so that every exogenous variable enters each reduced form equation. Similarly each reduced form disturbance is a linear combination of all the structural disturbances, and since the u's have zero means so do the v's. The endogenous variables are themselves random variables, and the systematic part of a reduced form equation gives the conditional expectation of an endogenous variable (conditional upon the values of the x's, that is), which we write as

$$E(y_{it}\mid x_{1t},x_{2t},\ldots,x_{Kt}) = \sum_{k=1}^{K} \pi_{ik}x_{kt}.$$

This last statement has implicitly made use of our previous definition of exogeneity, namely that x_{kt} and u_{gs} are independent for every k, g, s and t, so that the conditional mean of v_{it} is zero. That is, the disturbances have zero mean whatever the values of the exogenous variables. Conditional expectations of endogenous variables are what we calculate in prediction exercises: these may be genuine forecasting exercises, if the index t refers to a future point in time, or hypothetical analyses of economic policy options, if some of the exogenous variables are policy instruments controlled by an economic policy-maker.

We finally look at the reduced forms of our examples in this new setting. The reduced form of the national income system is

$$\begin{bmatrix} C_t \\ Y_t \end{bmatrix} = \begin{bmatrix} \pi_{11} & \pi_{12} \\ \pi_{21} & \pi_{22} \end{bmatrix} \begin{bmatrix} 1 \\ I_t \end{bmatrix} + \begin{bmatrix} v_{1t} \\ v_{2t} \end{bmatrix}$$

where the reduced form coefficients are given as

$$\begin{bmatrix} \pi_{11} & \pi_{12} \\ \pi_{21} & \pi_{22} \end{bmatrix} = -\mathbf{B}^{-1}\Gamma = -\begin{bmatrix} 1 & -\beta \\ -1 & 1 \end{bmatrix}^{-1}\begin{bmatrix} -\alpha & 0 \\ 0 & -1 \end{bmatrix}$$

$$= -\frac{1}{1-\beta}\begin{bmatrix} 1 & \beta \\ 1 & 1 \end{bmatrix}\begin{bmatrix} -a & 0 \\ 0 & -1 \end{bmatrix}$$

$$= \frac{1}{1-\beta}\begin{bmatrix} \alpha & \beta \\ \alpha & 1 \end{bmatrix}$$

and the reduced form disturbances as

$$\begin{bmatrix} v_{1t} \\ v_{2t} \end{bmatrix} = \mathbf{B}^{-1}\begin{bmatrix} u_t \\ 0 \end{bmatrix} = \frac{1}{1-\beta}\begin{bmatrix} 1 & \beta \\ 1 & 1 \end{bmatrix}\begin{bmatrix} u_t \\ 0 \end{bmatrix} = \frac{1}{1-\beta}\begin{bmatrix} u_t \\ u_t \end{bmatrix}.$$

Of course these results correspond to those given previously. Similarly the demand-and-supply example has reduced form

$$\begin{bmatrix} P \\ Q \end{bmatrix} = \begin{bmatrix} \pi_{11} & \pi_{12} \\ \pi_{21} & \pi_{22} \end{bmatrix}\begin{bmatrix} 1 \\ E \end{bmatrix} + \begin{bmatrix} v_1 \\ v_2 \end{bmatrix}$$

with coefficients given in terms of structural parameters as

$$\begin{bmatrix} \pi_{11} & \pi_{12} \\ \pi_{21} & \pi_{22} \end{bmatrix} = -\mathbf{B}^{-1}\Gamma = -\begin{bmatrix} -\alpha_1 & 1 \\ -\beta_1 & 1 \end{bmatrix}^{-1}\begin{bmatrix} -\alpha_0 & 0 \\ -\beta_0 & \beta_1 \end{bmatrix}$$

$$= -\frac{1}{\beta_1-\alpha_1}\begin{bmatrix} 1 & -1 \\ \beta_1 & -\alpha_1 \end{bmatrix}\begin{bmatrix} -\alpha_0 & 0 \\ -\beta_0 & \beta_1 \end{bmatrix}$$

$$= \frac{1}{\beta_1-\alpha_1}\begin{bmatrix} \alpha_0 - \beta_0 & \beta_1 \\ \alpha_0\beta_1 - \alpha_1\beta_0 & \alpha_1\beta_1 \end{bmatrix},$$

and disturbances related to the structural disturbances by

$$\begin{bmatrix} v_1 \\ v_2 \end{bmatrix} = \mathbf{B}^{-1}\begin{bmatrix} u^d \\ u^s \end{bmatrix} = \frac{1}{\beta_1-\alpha_1}\begin{bmatrix} 1 & -1 \\ \beta_1 & -\alpha_1 \end{bmatrix}\begin{bmatrix} u^d \\ u^s \end{bmatrix} = \frac{1}{\beta_1-\alpha_1}\begin{bmatrix} u^d - u^s \\ \beta_1 u^d - \alpha_1 u^s \end{bmatrix}.$$

again as before.

The final question raised in the discussion of these examples in sections 2.1 and 2.2 was whether, given numerical values of the reduced form coefficients, unique values of the structural parameters could be deduced. In the present framework it is convenient to express the relations between the two sets of coefficients by taking the equation

$$\Pi = -\mathbf{B}^{-1}\Gamma$$

and multiplying back by $\mathbf{B}$ to obtain

$$\mathbf{B}\Pi + \Gamma = \mathbf{0}$$

for, given the π's, these equations are linear in the β's and γ's. For example in the latter case the question is whether, given the four π-coefficients, the relations

$$\begin{bmatrix} -\alpha_1 & 1 \\ -\beta_1 & 1 \end{bmatrix}\begin{bmatrix} \pi_{11} & \pi_{12} \\ \pi_{21} & \pi_{22} \end{bmatrix} + \begin{bmatrix} -\alpha_0 & 0 \\ -\beta_0 & \beta_1 \end{bmatrix} = \begin{bmatrix} 0 & 0 \\ 0 & 0 \end{bmatrix}$$

can be solved for α_0, α_1, β_0 and β_1. Reiterating the previous answer is left as an exercise to the reader, and discussion of the general case is held over until chapter 4.

EXERCISES

2.1 Obtain the reduced form of the following demand and supply model:

demand function: $Q = \alpha_0 + \alpha_1 P + \alpha_2 Y + u_1$

supply function: $Q = \beta_0 + \beta_1 P + u_2$

endogenous variables: Q, P; exogenous variable: Y.

2.2 Obtain the reduced form of the model

$$C_t = \alpha + \beta(Y_t - T_t)$$
$$Y_t = C_t + I_t + G_t$$

endogenous variables: C_t, Y_t; exogenous variables: I_t, T_t, G_t.

Suppose that the policy makers choose a target level for Y, assign T exogenously, and set G to achieve the target level of Y for given I and T. What is the required value of G? Is Y now exogenous and G endogenous? What light is cast on your answer to this last question by the addition of a disturbance term to the consumption function, so that the model becomes stochastic?

2.3 Consider the following model,

$$C_t = \alpha + \beta Y_t + u_{1t}$$
$$Y_t = C_t + I_t + G_t$$
$$I_t = \gamma + \delta Y_t + u_{2t}$$

endogenous variables: C_t, Y_t, I_t; exogenous variable: G_t.

Set up this model in matrix terms using the conventions described in section 2.4 and obtain the reduced form. (If you wish, check that your expressions for the reduced form coefficients obtained by matrix inversion correspond to those obtained by conventional substitution methods applied to the above equations.) How many restrictions are there on the six reduced form coefficients (compare with the examples discussed on pp. 7 and 13), and what are these restrictions? Show that, given numerical values of the reduced form coefficients, unique values of α, β, γ and δ can be deduced, that is, given the π's, the equations

$$\mathbf{B\Pi + \Gamma = 0}$$

have a unique solution for the unknown elements of $\mathbf{B}$ and $\mathbf{\Gamma}$.

III

DYNAMIC MODELS

3.1 INTRODUCTION

In this chapter we consider models designed to describe the behaviour of economic variables over time. Thus attention is restricted to time series data, and the subscript t that indexes different sample observations on a given variable refers only to time. In many areas of economics time plays an important role: firms and households do not react instantly to changed circumstances, but take time to adjust their decisions and habits; often it takes time to recognise that circumstances have changed; there are institutional constraints and social conventions that dictate that certain economic events occur at certain times of year; the manufacture of goods takes time, which may be several years in the case of large capital investment projects; in many economic decisions the conditions prevailing at the moment of decision are less important than those expected to prevail at some future times; for some problems important variables may be the rates of change of economic magnitudes, such as the rate of change of prices, or inflation rate in common parlance.

The consumption function example of the previous chapter

$$C_t = \alpha + \beta Y_t + u_t$$

now provides an example of a *static* equation. The only determinant of current consumption is current income, all adjustments are assumed to be completed in a single period, and if income changes suddenly next period, consumers' expenditure changes suddenly too. A simple example of a *dynamic* equation is obtained if it is postulated that there is a one-period delay before consumption responds to income, that is, that consumption depends on income with a one period lag:

$$C_t = \alpha + \beta Y_{t-1} + u_t.$$

A further example arises if consumers' expenditure responds to current income, but the previous level of expenditure also exerts an influence, since consumers' habits are slow to change:

$$C_t = \alpha + \beta Y_t + \gamma C_{t-1} + u_t.$$

This equation relates the current value of the left-hand side variable to, among other things, the previous value of that variable, and is a simple example of a difference equation.

The term *difference equation* applies generally to a relation among the values of a variable at various points in time. The term itself might suggest that it should apply to a relation among the differences of the variable, that is, the changes in the value of the variable in moving from one period to the next. The change $y_t - y_{t-1}$ is denoted Δy_t, where the symbol Δ denotes the *difference operator,* which simply indicates that the variable y_t is to be operated on, or transformed, to give the new variable Δy_t. The first difference operator can, if necessary, be applied repeatedly, thus $\Delta(\Delta y_t)$ is given as $\Delta y_t - \Delta y_{t-1}$, which is the second difference of y_t, denoted $\Delta^2 y_t$. By substitution this can be expressed in terms of the values of y at different points in time:

$$\Delta^2 y_t = \Delta y_t - \Delta y_{t-1}$$
$$= (y_t - y_{t-1}) - (y_{t-1} - y_{t-2})$$
$$= y_t - 2y_{t-1} + y_{t-2}.$$

Similarly the third difference of y can be defined as $\Delta^3 y_t = \Delta(\Delta^2 y_t)$ and in turn expressed in terms of y_t, y_{t-1}, y_{t-2} and y_{t-3}. Strictly speaking, a difference equation relates the value y_t to one or more of its differences Δy_t, $\Delta^2 y_t$, . . . , but it is clear that by using the above definitions such an equation can be expressed as a relation between y_t and $y_{t-1}, y_{t-2}, \ldots$, and this is the sense in which we shall use the term.

The difference operator Δ is always defined over a single time interval, whatever the interval of observation of the variable. Thus if we have a series of annual observations, the first difference gives the change in the value of the variable over a year; with quarterly data, the first difference is the change from one quarter to the next, and so on.

The only situation in which we are likely to depart from this is that in which a variable is observed more frequently than once a year, and we wish to consider the annual change in the variable. To do this we define the *seasonal difference* $\Delta_s y_t = y_t - y_{t-s}$, where s is the number of observations per year: $s = 4$ (quarterly data) and $s = 12$ (monthly data) are the two values we might meet in practice. Thus with quarterly data $\Delta_4 y_t$ gives the difference in the value of the variable between one quarter and the corresponding quarter of the preceding year. If the data contain a fixed seasonal pattern superimposed on any other variation, then the difference between values of the variable in the same quarter of successive years will be free of this seasonal pattern.

Explicit use of higher differences $\Delta^j y_t$ is relatively rare in economics, at least for $j > 2$. If y_t is a stock variable, then Δy_t is the corresponding flow and $\Delta^2 y_t$ its rate of change. A convenient device for expressing the *proportionate* rate of change of a variable is given by considering the difference of its logarithm:

$$\Delta(\log y_t) = \log y_t - \log y_{t-1} = \log (y_t/y_{t-1})$$

$$= \log \left(1 + \frac{y_t - y_{t-1}}{y_{t-1}}\right).$$

If the proportionate growth $(y_t - y_{t-1})/y_{t-1} = g_t$, say, is relatively small, for example $g_t = 0.03$ corresponds to 3% growth per unit time, then we can use the approximation $\log (1 + g) \simeq g$, hence $\Delta(\log y_t) \simeq g_t$. This provides a discrete-time approximation to the corresponding continuous-time quantity, obtained by differentiation:

$$\frac{d \log y(t)}{dt} = \frac{1}{y(t)} \frac{dy}{dt}.$$

If the variable y_t is the general price level then $100 \times \Delta(\log y_t)$ approximates the rate of inflation, measured as a percentage. The second difference $100 \times \Delta^2(\log y_t)$ approximates the increase or decrease in the inflation rate, measured in percentage points per unit time. The accuracy of these approximations decreases at higher rates of inflation.

In the remainder of this chapter we discuss the formulation and analysis of dynamic relations between economic variables, and the properties of systems of such relations. First we consider distributed lag relations, as general devices for describing the dynamic response of one variable to changes in another variable. Then we describe some economic models that have been put forward to account for such relations, paying particular attention to the modelling of unobservable expectations variables. Finally we consider various possible forms of "solution" of dynamic systems, and associated questions of stability.

3.2. DISTRIBUTED LAGS

The variable y is related to the variable x with a *distributed lag* if the relationship can be written, in linear form, as

$$y_t = \alpha + \beta_0 x_t + \beta_1 x_{t-1} + \beta_2 x_{t-2} + \ldots + \beta_m x_{t-m} + u_t$$

$$= \alpha + \sum_{j=0}^{m} \beta_j x_{t-j} + u_t.$$

In the remainder of this section we neglect the random disturbance term u_t, and focus on the systematic part of the relationship. The static models of the previous chapter are obtained if β_0 is non-zero but $\beta_1, \beta_2, \ldots, \beta_m$ are all zero; y responds to x with a *fixed delay* of k periods, say, if β_k is non-zero and all the other β-coefficients are zero. In the general distributed lag model above, the coefficient β_j is the partial derivative $\partial y_t / \partial x_{t-j}$, and the whole set of coefficients, $j = 0, 1, \ldots, m$, show how the reaction of y to a change in x is distributed over time. A simple sketch of this reaction can be drawn by assuming that the x-variable has a constant value in all time periods except time t_0, when it is one unit greater than this constant value. Then y has a constant value until time t_0, when it responds to the unit impulse in x, and it continues to be displaced from its long-run level for a further m periods, as illustrated in Figure 3.1. In this diagram the displacement at time $t_0 + j$ from the long-run level of y is given by the coefficient β_j. (Strictly speaking this should be shown as a bar chart, rather than a continuous line, since we are working with discrete time.)

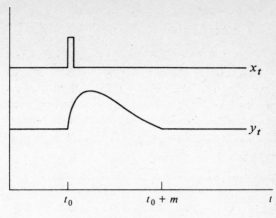

Figure 3.1

For an alternative representation we consider the response of y to a maintained increase or unit step in x, occurring at time t_0. Then the immediate reaction of y is again given by β_0, but in the next period the response of y is given by $\beta_0 + \beta_1$, since x remains at its new level, and in general the change in y after k periods is given by the partial sum $\beta_0 + \beta_1 + \ldots + \beta_{k-1}$, counting the period in which the change occurs as period 1. If the β-coefficients are all positive, as in Figure 3.1, then y increases steadily until it attains its new long-run value at time $t_0 + m$, as illustrated in Figure 3.2. The difference between the "old" and "new" constant values is given by the complete sum $\beta_0 + \beta_1 + \ldots + \beta_m$, which is termed the *long-run multiplier*, and β_0 is the *impact multiplier*. In some distributed lag models the maximum lag m is set equal to infinity for mathematical convenience. Of course it is required that the long-run multiplier be finite, that is,

$$\sum_{j=0}^{\infty} \beta_j < \infty,$$

which in general requires, not implausibly, that $\beta_j \to 0$ as $j \to \infty$.

There is no general requirement that the β-coefficients should all have the same sign: it is possible that y initially overreacts to a

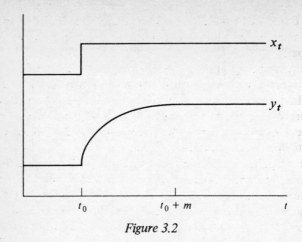

Figure 3.2

change in x, and compensating adjustments are subsequently needed. When the coefficients do have the same sign it is conventional to define them positively, thus if an increase in x causes a long-run decrease in y we take the negative sign outside the summation so that the β_j's represent the positive weights measuring the importance of the j-period lag. The analogy with probability distributions or relative frequency distributions then suggests that summary measures such as the mean or the median might be calculated. The mean lag is simply the weighted average of the lags, in which the lag of j periods enters with weight β_j, or with relative weight $\beta_j/\Sigma\beta_j$, thus

$$\text{mean lag} = \frac{\displaystyle\sum_{j=0}^{\infty} j\beta_j}{\displaystyle\sum_{j=0}^{\infty} \beta_j}.$$

Similarly the median lag is the number of periods required for the long-run adjustment to be one-half complete. In the cumulative adjustment illustration of Figure 3.2 it is the number of periods required for the value of y to be halfway between its "old" and "new" constant values.

In the distributed lag functions sketched in Figure 3.3, the median lag is that value of j at which the area under the curve is divided into two equal parts.

The general distributed lag function may be impractical for empirical work, for the number of coefficients $m+1$ may be unmanageably large. In practice we seek to express the β_j's as functions of a small number of parameters, and then devise convenient ways of estimating these parameters. Once this is done the β_j-values implied by the estimated parameters can be calculated.

The simplification introduced by Koyck in his work *Distributed Lags and Investment Analysis* (1954) has had a substantial impact, for it leads to a regression equation which can be readily estimated, and has also been shown to have a meaningful interpretation in terms of economic behavioural hypotheses, as discussed below. Koyck assumed that, after some point, the coefficients decline *geometrically*. We may not wish to specify how the first few β_j's behave, but the simplest form (which is a perfectly good illustration of the technique) is obtained if we assume that the geometric decline does start at the beginning. Then we have

$$\beta_j = \lambda^j \beta, \qquad j = 0, 1, \ldots, \qquad 0 < \lambda < 1$$

where β and λ are constants, and the requirement that λ is between 0 and 1 ensures that the β_j's converge smoothly to zero. Thus the β_j's are functions of just two parameters, and the distributed lag equation is

$$y_t = \alpha + \beta(x_t + \lambda x_{t-1} + \lambda^2 x_{t-2} + \ldots)$$

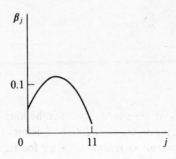
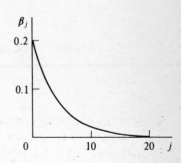

Figure 3.3

(An example of the geometric lag distribution is sketched in the right-hand panel of Figure 3.3.) The impact multiplier, measuring the instantaneous effect of x on y, is equal to β, and the long-run multiplier, measuring the change in the long-run value of y caused by a unit increase in the level of x, is equal to

$$\sum_{j=0}^{\infty} \beta_j = \beta \sum_{j=0}^{\infty} \lambda^j = \frac{\beta}{1-\lambda},$$

recalling the expression for the sum of a geometric series. The mean lag is given as

$$\frac{\sum_{j=0}^{\infty} j\beta_j}{\sum_{j=0}^{\infty} \beta_j} = \frac{\beta \sum_{j=0}^{\infty} j\lambda^j}{\beta \sum_{j=0}^{\infty} \lambda^j},$$

and to calculate this in terms of β and λ we first need to evaluate the sum

$$S = \sum_{j=0}^{\infty} j\lambda^j = \lambda + 2\lambda^2 + 3\lambda^3 + 4\lambda^4 + \dots.$$

Multiplying both sides by λ gives

$$\lambda S = \lambda^2 + 2\lambda^3 + 3\lambda^4 + 4\lambda^5 + \dots,$$

and then on subtracting we obtain

$$S - \lambda S = \lambda + \lambda^2 + \lambda^3 + \lambda^4 + \dots,$$

which is another geometric series with sum $\lambda/(1-\lambda)$. Thus $S = \lambda/(1-\lambda)^2$, and we have

$$\text{mean lag} = \frac{\beta\lambda/(1-\lambda)^2}{\beta/(1-\lambda)} = \frac{\lambda}{1-\lambda}.$$

It may seem that the assumption of a geometric distributed lag has made little progress towards a regression equation that can be estimated from a finite sample of data because the infinite past of the x-series still appears on the right-hand side of the equation. To make further progress we introduce the *Koyck transformation*, a neat device that gives a directly estimable equation. At time t we have

$$y_t = \alpha + \beta(x_t + \lambda x_{t-1} + \lambda^2 x_{t-2} + \ldots),$$

and similarly at time $t-1$

$$y_{t-1} = \alpha + \beta(x_{t-1} + \lambda x_{t-2} + \lambda^2 x_{t-3} + \ldots).$$

Multiplying both sides of this latter equation by λ gives

$$\lambda y_{t-1} = \alpha\lambda + \beta(\lambda x_{t-1} + \lambda^2 x_{t-2} + \lambda^3 x_{t-3} + \ldots),$$

and we see that the terms involving $x_{t-1}, x_{t-2}, \ldots$ on the right-hand side of this equation are identical to those appearing in the equation for y_t. So if we subtract one from the other everything but the constant term and the term involving x_t cancels, giving

$$y_t - \lambda y_{t-1} = \alpha(1 - \lambda) + \beta x_t.$$

The infinite past of the x-series has disappeared, and we have a final equation whose coefficients can be estimated by regression methods:

$$y_t = \alpha(1 - \lambda) + \beta x_t + \lambda y_{t-1}.$$

Thus the parameters β and λ of the geometric distributed lag are estimated directly as the coefficients in a regression of y on x and the lagged value of y, and the intercept term is an estimate of $\alpha(1 - \lambda)$, from which an estimate of α can be deduced.

The expression for the long-run multiplier may be obtained directly from this last equation. Suppose that x has a constant value over time. Then once all the lagged adjustments have been completed, the value of y will also be constant, and the relation between these *equilibrium* values of y and x will be described by

$$y = \alpha(1 - \lambda) + \beta x + \lambda y.$$

That is, when the constant y-value is entered as the lagged dependent variable on the right-hand side of the equation together with the constant x-value, the same y-value is given as the "next period" observation in equilibrium. Collecting the terms in y, we see that the derivative $\partial y / \partial x$, describing the relation between the long-run steady-state values of the variables, is given as $\beta/(1 - \lambda)$, as obtained previously.

3.3 THE PARTIAL ADJUSTMENT HYPOTHESIS

Now we consider what sort of behaviour by economic agents might give rise to these distributed lags. In this section we describe the partial adjustment or stock adjustment hypothesis.

Suppose that there is a desired or planned level of some variable that an economic agent would like to achieve at time t, and denote this as y_t^*. For example, this might represent a firm's optimum capital stock. But assume that there are frictions, delays, costs of doing business, habit persistence and so forth, such that the desired level cannot be entirely achieved in a single period. Starting from the previously existing level y_{t-1} the change required to attain the desired level is $y_t^* - y_{t-1}$, but the actual change $y_t - y_{t-1}$ is only a fraction of this. Assuming that the proportion achieved is $(1 - \gamma)$, where $0 < \gamma < 1$, the partial adjustment hypothesis can be written

$$y_t - y_{t-1} = (1 - \gamma)(y_t^* - y_{t-1})$$

or

$$y_t = (1 - \gamma)y_t^* + \gamma y_{t-1}.$$

Small values of γ imply relatively quick adjustment, and if $\gamma = 0$ adjustment is complete, not partial, in a single period. Larger values of γ imply that the past value of the variable exerts a greater influence, and if $\gamma = 1$ nothing ever changes.

So far little has been said about the desired value y_t^*. If data on this are available, then the above equation can be estimated. But this is very rare, and the economic modeller generally requires an explanation for the determination of the unobservable y_t^*. For example, a firm's optimum capital stock might depend on the prices of its output and the factors of production, which can be observed. As a simple illustration, suppose that the desired level depends on a single explanatory variable x_t as follows:

$$y_t^* = \alpha + \beta x_t.$$

Then on substituting this expression for y_t^* in the preceding equation we obtain the relation between observable variables as

$$y_t = \alpha(1 - \gamma) + \beta(1 - \gamma)x_t + \gamma y_{t-1},$$

which is of the same form as the estimating equation obtained under the geometric distributed lag assumption. Although this equation has been obtained directly, rather than via the Koyck transformation, its equivalence to the geometric distributed lag can be seen by repeated substitution for the lagged y term:

$$y_t = \alpha(1 - \gamma) + \beta(1 - \gamma)x_t + \gamma\{\alpha(1 - \gamma) + \beta(1 - \gamma)x_{t-1} + \gamma y_{t-2}\}$$

$$= \alpha(1 - \gamma)(1 + \gamma) + \beta(1 - \gamma)(x_t + \gamma x_{t-1})$$
$$+ \gamma^2\{\alpha(1 - \gamma) + \beta(1 - \gamma)x_{t-2} + \gamma y_{t-3}\}$$

$$= \ldots$$

$$= \alpha(1 - \gamma)\sum_{j=0}^{\infty}\gamma^j + \beta(1 - \gamma)\sum_{j=0}^{\infty}\gamma^j x_{t-j},$$

the term $\gamma^n y_{t-n}$ tending to zero since $0 < \gamma < 1$. Thus the relation

$$y_t = \alpha + \beta(1 - \gamma)\sum_{j=0}^{\infty}\gamma^j x_{t-j}$$

is implied by the partial adjustment hypothesis, and this repeated substitution has in effect reversed the Koyck transformation.

Again we might calculate the mean lag as $\gamma/(1 - \gamma)$. Alternatively we might calculate how many periods are required to accomplish a given proportion p of the desired adjustment (noting that adjustment is 100% complete only asymptotically, in this model). After one period $(1 - \gamma)$ of the desired change is accomplished, so a fraction γ of the change is remaining. In the second period, $(1 - \gamma)$ of this is eliminated so after two periods, a total of $(1 - \gamma) + \gamma(1 - \gamma) = (1 - \gamma^2)$ is accomplished and γ^2 remains. By the end of the third period $(1 - \gamma)$ of this is achieved and γ of it remains, i.e. γ^3 of the original desired change remains. In general we have that after n periods

$$1 - \gamma^n$$

of the change is accomplished. If we set this expression equal to some value p we may solve for n to give the number of periods required for adjustment to be a proportion p complete:

$$p = 1 - \gamma^n$$

therefore

$$n = \frac{\log (1 - p)}{\log \gamma}.$$

As an illustration let us ask when the change will be 90% complete ($p = 0.9$) for various values of γ. If $\gamma = 0.1$ then the actual change is 0.9 of the desired change and the number of periods required is of course one. If $\gamma = 0.5$, then the number of periods required is

$$n = \frac{\log 0.1}{\log 0.5} = 3.32.$$

If $\gamma = 0.9$ (a high value of the coefficient of the lagged dependent variable, implying slow adjustment) we have

$$n = \frac{\log 0.1}{\log 0.9} = 21.85.$$

which, with quarterly data, would imply that 5½ years are required for a desired change to be 90% complete. Setting $p = 0.5$ in the above expression gives the median lag.

It is often said that the partial adjustment hypothesis is rather *ad hoc*, but a justification can be provided in terms of a cost minimisation procedure. Suppose that a firm selects the value of the variable y_t so as to minimise the weighted sum of "disequilibrium" and "adjustment" costs:

$$C_t = a_1(y_t - y_t^*)^2 + a_2(y_t - y_{t-1})^2.$$

The first term on the right-hand side represents the costs incurred by being away from the optimum or desired position y_t^*, and the second term represents the costs of changing y, for example, hiring and firing costs if y represents the size of the firm's labour force. The cost function is quadratic, and implies that over-shooting is as costly as under-shooting, and that upward and downward adjustments are equally expensive. To find the value of y_t that minimises C_t we equate the first partial derivative to zero:

$$\frac{\partial C_t}{\partial y_t} = 2a_1(y_t - y_t^*) + 2a_2(y_t - y_{t-1}) = 0.$$

On rearranging, this gives

$$y_t = \frac{a_1}{a_1 + a_2} y_t^* + \frac{a_2}{a_1 + a_2} y_{t-1},$$

and on setting $\gamma = a_2/(a_1 + a_2)$, so that $1 - \gamma = a_1/(a_1 + a_2)$, we have

$$y_t - y_{t-1} = (1 - \gamma)(y_t^* - y_{t-1}),$$

the partial adjustment hypothesis. If adjustment costs are relatively important the coefficient a_2 will be relatively large, which implies a value of γ near to 1 and relatively slow adjustment. Clearly if $a_2 = 0$ there are no costs of adjustment and the firm moves immediately to the desired position y_t^*.

3.4 EXPECTATIONS MODELS

The key element in a second group of models that give rise to dynamic equations is the expectations or anticipations of future variables. We assume that behaviour with respect to a particular dependent vairable is influenced by expected or anticipated values of an exogenous explanatory variable. The expectations might relate to such variables as sales, prices, incomes, or interest rates according to the particular problem in hand. For example, a retailer's inventories may depend on the sales he expects to make in the following period, money balances may react to expected interest rates, consumers' expenditure to expected income, raw material stocks to expected future prices, and so on. Although actual observations on the expectational variables might be available from, say, surveys on sales anticipations or business investment intentions, these are relatively rare, and in most cases anticipations remain unobservable. Then to obtain a model in terms of observable variables it is necessary to add an assumption about the formation of expectations.

To focus on the modelling of expectations we postulate a simple behavioural relation

$$y_t = \alpha + \beta \hat{x}_{t+1},$$

where $\hat{x}_{t+1}$ denotes the forecast or expected value of x_{t+1}, formed at time t. For example y_t might denote current inventories and $\hat{x}_{t+1}$ forecast sales. Other timing relationships are possible, for example $\hat{x}_t$ might appear as the explanatory variable, being interpreted as a forecast calculated at time $t-1$ or as the "expected normal level" of x. However few of the substantive conclusions are changed by altering the timings, and the formulation that we use may be intuitively clearer, with its direct forecasting interpretation.

A simple assumption is that currently observed conditions are expected to prevail in the next period, giving "naive" or "no-change" expectations: $\hat{x}_{t+1} = x_t$. Clearly, if the assumption of naive expectations is incorporated in the above behavioural relation, the result is indistinguishable from a simple static relation between the observed values of y and x. A less simple assumption is the "same-change" forecasting rule, in which the next period's value is anticipated to differ from the current value by the same amount that the current value has been observed to differ from the previous value: $\hat{x}_{t+1} - x_t = x_t - x_{t-1}$.

More generally it might be assumed that, when calculating forecasts based on past data, economic agents use their knowledge of the behaviour of the variable over time. If successive x-values are correlated with one another, this *autocorrelation* indicates the extent to which current and past values are helpful in forecasting future values. To be precise, we assume that economic agents have information about the data generation process of the x-variable, and that they use this information optimally. To do this a statistical model of the x-variable is constructed, then the forecast that has minimum mean squared error is calculated. A building block of such models is a purely random variable, which we denote ϵ_t. This has zero expected value:

$$E(\epsilon_t) = 0;$$

its variance is constant over time:

$$E(\epsilon_t^2) = \sigma^2;$$

and there is zero covariance between its values at different points of time:

$$E(\epsilon_t \epsilon_s) = 0, \qquad t \neq s.$$

A sample of observations on such a variable is plotted in Figure 3.4. The fact that there is no correlation between any pair of values implies that current and past data contain no information that is useful in forecasting the next value, so the best estimate is simply the mean value, namely zero. Of course economic time series typically have non-zero autocorrelation, but the non-autocorrelated nature of ϵ_t makes it convenient to work with when constructing more general models.

Example 1 Suppose x_t obeys the *first-order autoregression*

$$x_t = \rho x_{t-1} + \epsilon_t, \qquad |\rho| < 1.$$

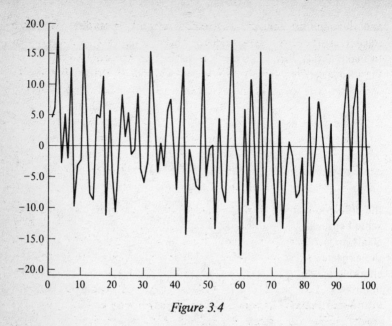

Figure 3.4

This has the form of a regression of x_t on its own past value, hence the term autoregression, and it is of first order because only a one-period lagged value of x appears on the right-hand side. The value that we seek to forecast will also be generated in the same way,

$$x_{t+1} = \rho x_t + \epsilon_{t+1},$$

and since we have no information at time t that is useful in forecasting ϵ_{t+1}, apart from its mean value, but x_t is known, a sensible forecast would seem to be

$$\hat{x}_{t+1} = \rho x_t.$$

We can demonstrate that this forecast is "best" by setting up a general forecasting rule in terms of current and past data,

$$\hat{x}_{t+1} = \sum_{j=0}^{\infty} a_j x_{t-j}$$

and then finding the set of a-coefficients that minimises the mean squared error of forecast. The forecast error is $x_{t+1} - \hat{x}_{t+1}$, and we wish to make $E(x_{t+1} - \hat{x}_{t+1})^2$ as small as possible. Substituting for x_{t+1} from the autoregressive model and for $\hat{x}_{t+1}$ from the forecasting rule gives

$$E(x_{t+1} - \hat{x}_{t+1})^2 = E(\rho x_t + \epsilon_{t+1} - \sum_{j=0}^{\infty} a_j x_{t-j})^2$$

$$= E(\epsilon_{t+1})^2 + E(\rho x_t - \sum_{j=0}^{\infty} a_j x_{t-j})^2,$$

the cross-product between ϵ_{t+1} and the terms in x having zero expected value because ϵ_{t+1} is uncorrelated with any previous data. The a-coefficients appear only in the second term on the right-hand side, which is the expected value of a square, and so is clearly non-negative. However choosing $a_0 = \rho$, $a_1 = a_2 = \ldots = 0$ makes its value zero, so this choice minimises the forecast error variance, and the "sensible" forecast introduced initially is seen to be the best forecast in this sense. The result implies that, given the current value x_t, previous data x_{t-1}, $x_{t-2}, \ldots$ convey no additional information that helps in forecasting x_{t+1}.

In the limit as $\rho \to 1$, the autoregressive model becomes

$$\Delta x_t = \epsilon_t,$$

called the *random walk* model, in which the first difference of the x-series is purely random. Such models have been extensively applied to share prices in studies of stock exchange behaviour, and a sample from a random walk series is plotted in Figure 3.5. The above forecasting rule now gives $\hat{x}_{t+1} = x_t$, and so we see that the "naive" forecast is actually the best forecast if the series being predicted follows a random walk.

Example 2 We now modify the first-order autoregression by making its error term a moving average of two successive random shocks:

$$x_t = \rho x_{t-1} + \epsilon_t - \theta \epsilon_{t-1}, \qquad |\theta| < 1,$$

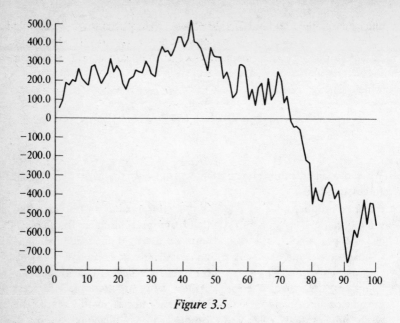

Figure 3.5

giving an *autoregressive-moving average* model. Thus a given random shock has an effect that persists for two periods, since it affects the contemporaneous x-value and also the following value. Rearranging the equation to give an expression for ϵ_t, and repeatedly substituting from this expression in lagged form gives

$$
\begin{aligned}
x_t &= \epsilon_t + \rho x_{t-1} - \theta(x_{t-1} - \rho x_{t-2} + \theta \epsilon_{t-2}) \\
&= \epsilon_t + (\rho - \theta)x_{t-1} + \theta \rho x_{t-2} - \theta^2(x_{t-2} - \rho x_{t-3} + \theta \epsilon_{t-3}) \\
&= \epsilon_t + (\rho - \theta)(x_{t-1} + \theta x_{t-2}) + \theta^2 \rho x_{t-3} - \theta^3(x_{t-3} - \rho x_{t-4} + \theta \epsilon_{t-4}) \\
&= \epsilon_t + (\rho - \theta)(x_{t-1} + \theta x_{t-2} + \theta^2 x_{t-3}) + \theta^3 \rho x_{t-4} - \theta^4 \epsilon_{t-4} \\
&= \ldots \\
&= \epsilon_t + (\rho - \theta)(x_{t-1} + \theta x_{t-2} + \theta^2 x_{t-3} + \theta^3 x_{t-4} + \ldots),
\end{aligned}
$$

the term $\theta^n \epsilon_{t-n}$ tending to zero as n increases. This is a more convenient representation for determining the optimal forecasting rule, since advancing it by one period gives the representation of x_{t+1} as

$$x_{t+1} = \epsilon_{t+1} + (\rho - \theta)(x_t + \theta x_{t-1} + \theta^2 x_{t-2} + \ldots),$$

which suggests, as a sensible forecast,

$$\hat{x}_{t+1} = (\rho - \theta) \sum_{j=0}^{\infty} \theta^j x_{t-j}.$$

We can again demonstrate that this is the best forecast. The general forecasting rule is

$$\hat{x}_{t+1} = \sum_{j=0}^{\infty} a_j x_{t-j}$$

and the mean squared forecast error is

$$E(x_{t+1} - \hat{x}_{t+1})^2 = E(\epsilon_{t+1} + (\rho - \theta) \sum_{j=0}^{\infty} \theta^j x_{t-j} - \sum_{j=0}^{\infty} a_j x_{t-j})^2$$

$$= E(\epsilon_{t+1})^2 + E\left[(\rho - \theta) \sum_{j=0}^{\infty} \theta^j x_{t-j} - \sum_{j=0}^{\infty} a_j x_{t-j}\right]^2.$$

Again the minimum mean squared forecast error is achieved when the second term is zero, that is, when the coefficients in the forecasting rule are given by $a_j = (\rho - \theta)\theta^j$. Hence the best forecast is

$$\hat{x}_{t+1} = (\rho - \theta) \sum_{j=0}^{\infty} \theta^j x_{t-j},$$

giving the forecast as an infinite distributed lag of observed x-values. A convenient formula for updating the forecast is obtained by writing

$$\hat{x}_{t+1} = (\rho - \theta)x_t + (\rho - \theta)(\theta x_{t-1} + \theta^2 x_{t-2} + \theta^3 x_{t-3} + \ldots)$$

and noting that the second term on the right-hand side is $\theta\hat{x}_t$, where $\hat{x}_t$ is the forecast of x_t calculated at time $t-1$ from the same forecasting rule. (Note that this amounts to an application of the Koyck transformation.) Thus

$$\hat{x}_{t+1} = (\rho - \theta)x_t + \theta\hat{x}_t,$$

and if $\rho = 1$ this gives the form widely known in economics as *adaptive expectations*:

$$\hat{x}_{t+1} = (1 - \theta)x_t + \theta\hat{x}_t$$

or

$$\hat{x}_{t+1} = \hat{x}_t + (1 - \theta)(x_t - \hat{x}_t).$$

The adaptive expectations hypothesis saw successful application in empirical work in the mid-1950's, being first employed by Phillip Cagan in his study of hyperinflation and by Marc Nerlove in his study of the dynamics of agricultural supply, and subsequently in scores of applications. It is simply postulated that expectations are amended or adapted in proportion to past forecasting errors, the next period's forecast $\hat{x}_{t+1}$ being given by the forecast of the current level, $\hat{x}_t$, amended by a proportion of the current forecast error $x_t - \hat{x}_t$. If θ is close to zero expectations adapt rather rapidly to recent data, while if θ is near one expectations are slow to change: in this latter case note that the coefficients in the distributed lag form decline rather slowly, so that data from the more distant past influence current expectations. Like the partial adjustment hypothesis, the adaptive expectations hypothesis has often been criticised for its apparent *ad hoc* nature, but the foregoing argument (which was developed after the hypothesis had been employed in the early applied studies) shows that the hypothesis is sensible if we believe that the exogenous variable is generated according to $\Delta x_t = \epsilon_t - \theta\epsilon_{t-1}$ and that agents' expectations are optimal forecasts in this framework. (Of course for other data generation processes adaptive expectations may be far from optimal.)

Returning to the original behavioural relation

$$y_t = \alpha + \beta \hat{x}_{t+1},$$

and incorporating adaptive expectations in either of its forms,

$$\hat{x}_{t+1} = (1 - \theta) \sum_{j=0}^{\infty} \theta^j x_{t-j}$$

or

$$\hat{x}_{t+1} = \theta \hat{x}_t + (1 - \theta) x_t,$$

we have a further justification for the geometric distributed lag model:

$$y_t = \alpha + \beta(1 - \theta) \sum_{j=0}^{\infty} \theta^j x_{t-j}.$$

Again the infinite distributed lag can be eliminated by the Koyck transformation:

$$
\begin{aligned}
y_t - \theta y_{t-1} &= \alpha + \beta(1 - \theta)(x_t + \theta x_{t-1} + \theta^2 x_{t-2} + \ldots) \\
&\quad - [\alpha\theta + \beta(1 - \theta)(\theta x_{t-1} + \theta^2 x_{t-2} + \theta^3 x_{t-3} + \ldots)] \\
&= \alpha(1 - \theta) + \beta(1 - \theta) x_t,
\end{aligned}
$$

or, equivalently, the unobservable expectations variable can be eliminated from the behavioural relation by using the second adaptive expectations form above:

$$
\begin{aligned}
y_t - \theta y_{t-1} &= \alpha + \beta \hat{x}_{t+1} - \theta(\alpha + \beta \hat{x}_t) \\
&= \alpha(1 - \theta) + \beta(\hat{x}_{t+1} - \theta \hat{x}_t)
\end{aligned}
$$

hence

$$y_t = \alpha(1 - \theta) + \beta(1 - \theta) x_t + \theta y_{t-1}.$$

Notice that this is precisely the same final equation as that obtained from the partial adjustment hypothesis, showing the duality between the adaptive expectations and partial adjustment hypotheses, at least in these simple cases. Thus if we find that a regression equation of this form provides a satisfactory explanation of y_t, it is open to argument whether lags in adjustment or expectational variables are at work. Regression analysis cannot distinguish the two hypotheses, although we shall return to this problem below.

3.5 DYNAMIC SYSTEMS

In this section we consider systems of equations that explain the behaviour of a number of endogenous variables, as in chapter 2, but in which some equations now contain dynamic elements, as discussed earlier in this chapter. Such dynamic systems describe the behaviour over time of the endogenous variables, and we shall be interested in studying the nature of the *time path*, together with such questions as whether the path converges to an *equilibrium* position. Again the main ideas are developed in the context of a simple example.

The example is the two-equation national income determination system with which chapter 2 began, now incorporating a one-period delay in the consumption function:

$$C_t = \alpha + \beta Y_{t-1}$$

$$Y_t = C_t + I_t$$

endogenous variables: C_t, Y_t; exogenous variable: I_t.

Suppose that investment is equal to the constant value I in every time period, and let us ask what is the nature of the equilibrium position. The equilibrium values of the endogenous variables are defined as the values that, once achieved, are continuously maintained. Hence the equilibrium values of consumption and income, denoted C^e and Y^e, can be obtained by solving the pair of equations

$$C^e = \alpha + \beta Y^e$$

$$Y^e = C^e + I.$$

The time subscripts have been removed from the model: in equilibrium the lagged value of income is equal to the current value. The solution of these static equations is

$$C^e = \frac{1}{1 - \beta} (\alpha + \beta I)$$

$$Y^e = \frac{1}{1 - \beta} (\alpha + I).$$

Note that this solution is exactly as obtained in the static case (p. 6 above). The equilibrium position of the dynamic system has thus been found as the solution of a static model obtained from the dynamic system by ignoring differences in the time subscripts.

This statement generalises: for every dynamic system having an equilibrium position there is a corresponding static system which describes that position — a simple form of correspondence principle. However, one static system can serve for a number of dynamic systems, so that this relationship is not one-to-one. A simple and trivial illustration of this point is provided in our model, by lagging the income term in the consumption function by two periods, or three periods, and so on. Though each case would provide a different dynamic system the corresponding static system would remain the same.

Now we consider the time path of the variables and, in particular, whether this equilibrium position can be reached. The starting point of the path is denoted by the values C_0 and Y_0, termed *initial conditions*. The dynamic system then gives the time path of C_t and Y_t in terms of initial conditions, parameter values and values of exogenous variables. If, whatever the initial conditions, these paths tend to equilibrium, the system is said to be *stable*.

It is convenient to distinguish the income variable in the two forms in which it appears in this system: Y_{t-1} in the consumption function and Y_t in the income identity. We call Y_{t-1} a *lagged endogenous* variable and Y_t (and C_t) *current endogenous* variables. The two equations of the model then describe the determination of the two current endogenous variables in terms of lagged endogenous (Y_{t-1}) and exogenous (I_t) variables, and these latter are referred to together as *predetermined* variables. At time t, the value of Y_{t-1} is known – it is predetermined as of time t – and the system gives the values of C_t and Y_t. The explicit solution for these values is given by the *reduced form* of the model, thus the previous definition of a reduced form equation requires a slight extension in the dynamic case: it describes the determination of a current endogenous variable in terms of parameters and predetermined variables. Note that with this definition the consumption function is already a reduced form equation, and the complete reduced form is

$$C_t = \alpha + \beta Y_{t-1}$$
$$Y_t = \alpha + \beta Y_{t-1} + I_t.$$

The reduced form allows us to calculate a time path step-by-step: given an initial condition Y_0 and the value I_1, the reduced form gives C_1 and Y_1; then C_2 and Y_2 in terms of Y_1 and I_2; next C_3 and Y_3 in terms of Y_2 and I_3; and so on.

The reduced form may not be the most convenient solution form if we wish to describe the evolution of a single endogenous variable. For example, to obtain the consumption path it is necessary to solve both reduced form equations period-by-period. This need is eliminated by introducing the notion of a *final equation*, which expresses a current endogenous variable in terms of exogenous variables and lagged values of itself but of no other endogenous variable. With this definition the reduced form equation for income is already a final equation: it describes the evolution of income without reference to the behaviour of consumption. However in the consumption reduced form equation we need to eliminate Y_{t-1} to obtain a final equation, which we do by using the identity $Y_{t-1} = C_{t-1} + I_{t-1}$. So the final equations are

$$C_t = \alpha + \beta C_{t-1} + \beta I_{t-1}$$
$$Y_t = \alpha + \beta Y_{t-1} + I_t,$$

and these can be used independently of one another to describe the time path of the respective endogenous variables. Each is a difference equation in a single endogenous variable.

A final equation allows the calculation of the time path of an endogenous variable period-by-period, but for some purposes it may be more convenient to have a general expression for the value of the variable at any point in time, as a function of time (and exogenous variables, initial conditions and structural parameters). The solution of the difference equation provides such an expression, and we now briefly review the solution of first-order difference equations in a general context.

The linear first-order non-homogeneous difference equation with constant coefficients a and b is

$$y_t = a + by_{t-1}.$$

As above, let y^e be the equilibrium value of y, that is, the value such that if y is fixed at y^e then it will remain there for evermore. Hence

$$y^e = a + by^e$$

or

$$y^e = \frac{a}{1-b}, \qquad (b \neq 1).$$

Substituting this into the original difference equation gives

$$y_t = (1 - b)y^e + by_{t-1},$$

and rearranging gives a homogeneous difference equation in the deviation of y from y^e:

$$y_t - y^e = b(y_{t-1} - y^e).$$

Given an initial condition y_0, we have

$$y_1 - y^e = b(y_0 - y^e),$$

then

$$y_2 - y^e = b(y_1 - y^e) = b^2(y_0 - y^e),$$
$$y_3 - y^e = b(y_2 - y^e) = b^3(y_0 - y^e),$$

and so on. The general solution, applicable for any value of t, is

$$y_t - y^e = b^t(y_0 - y^e).$$

Thus y_t approaches y^e if and only if the right-hand side goes to zero as t increases, and this requires $b^t \to 0$ as $t \to \infty$ (assuming that the system didn't actually start out in equilibrium, with $y_0 = y^e$). The necessary and sufficient condition for $b^t \to 0$ is $|b| < 1$, which gives us the *stability condition*. So in this first-order case, whether a dynamic system converges to an equilibrium depends on the magnitude of the coefficient of the lagged dependent variable in the final equation. If $|b| < 1$, the values y_t approach the equilibrium value y^e; if $|b| > 1$, the system diverges or explodes. If $b < 0$, the path is oscillatory; if $b > 0$ the path is smooth or monotonic. If $b = 1$, y_t has a linear trend *ad infinitum*; if $b = -1$, y_t oscillates around y^e with constant amplitude.

Returning to our model, the final equation for consumption is

$$C_t = \alpha + \beta C_{t-1} + \beta I_{t-1},$$

and assuming that $I_t = I$, constant over time, we had obtained the equilibrium position as

$$C^e = \frac{1}{1 - \beta}(\alpha + \beta I).$$

Now we know that the general solution for C_t is

$$C_t - C^e = \beta^t(C_0 - C^e).$$

The stability condition is $|\beta| < 1$, and we expect to have a stable solution since β is the marginal propensity to consume. The two convergent solutions are sketched in Figure 3.6, assuming that $C_0 < C^e$ (The assumption that I_t is constant implies a fixed equilibrium value C^e; if we were to specify that I_t varied over time in some way, following a linear trend, say, then the equilibrium position would be a moving

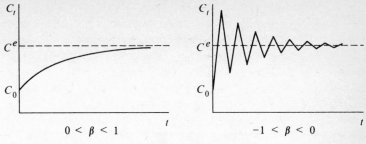

$$0 < \beta < 1 \qquad\qquad -1 < \beta < 0$$

Figure 3.6

one, and the path of C_t would approach this equilibrium path rather than the horizontal line in the diagram.)

Notice that the same stability condition, $|\beta| < 1$, is obtained by examining the final equation for income. In fact, both final equations have the same autoregressive structure — the number of lagged values of the dependent variable that appear on the right-hand side, and the coefficients with which they appear, are the same. In other words, the homogeneous parts of the different equations are identical. This is a general result. Intuitively, it does not make sense for one variable of a model to have a divergent solution path while another variable converges to equilibrium, and the result not only confirms this intuition but also says that convergence or divergence takes place at the same rate for every variable. There is no necessary correspondence between the remaining parts of the final equations, that is, the terms involving current and/or lagged exogenous variables, but the importance of the result is that in order to obtain the stability condition of the model, it is only necessary to examine a single final equation. In practice we examine whichever final equation is easiest to derive, but should other final equations be required for other purposes, then the knowledge that they all have the same autoregressive structure may ease the burden of their derivation.

3.6. FURTHER EXAMPLES OF DYNAMIC MODELS

In this section we develop a further application of stability analysis and at the same time illustrate the proposition that, while there exists a corresponding static model describing an equilibrium position for every dynamic model, nevertheless the same static model can serve for more than one dynamic model. The static three equation model that we work with is as follows:

$$C = \alpha + \beta Y$$
$$Y = C + I$$
$$I = \gamma Y + A$$

endogenous variables: C, Y, I; exogenous variable: A.

Investment now has a component that depends on income, together with an autonomous component A. Two simple examples of dynamic systems are considered.

Example 1 We first retain the consumption function of the preceding sections in which consumption depends on income with a one period lag:

$$C_t = \alpha + \beta Y_{t-1}.$$

The model is completed by adding the remaining two equations with current dated variables:

$$Y_t = C_t + I_t$$
$$I_t = \gamma Y_t + A.$$

It is simpler to assume that the exogenous variable has a constant value A say, so that there is a single equilibrium position given as a function of A rather than a moving equilibrium position which is a function of A_t. Substituting into the income identity gives

$$Y_t = \alpha + \beta Y_{t-1} + \gamma Y_t + A$$

and on rearranging we obtain the reduced form equation for income as

$$Y_t = \frac{\alpha + A}{1 - \gamma} + \left[\frac{\beta}{1 - \gamma} \right] Y_{t-1}.$$

This equation is already a final equation: it contains no lagged endogenous variables other than lagged values of Y_t, the dependent variable. The first term on the right-hand side corresponds to the constant a of the foregoing non-homogeneous difference equation, and the expression in square brackets to the coefficient b, required to be less than one in absolute value for stability. A general solution for Y_t in terms of an initial condition, an equilibrium value (itself a function of α, β, γ and A) and time can then be readily derived. For our present purposes we simply require the stability condition, which examination of the final equation shows to be

$$-1 < \frac{\beta}{1-\gamma} < 1.$$

If this condition is satisfied then the system is stable, and converges towards the equilibrium position obtained as the solution of the static model.

The value of $\beta/(1-\gamma)$ determines the stability properties of all three endogenous variables, as stated above, but if the final equations for consumption or investment are required for other purposes then the knowledge of the autoregressive structure of the final equation for income is helpful. For example, the consumption function has no current endogenous variable on the right-hand side, and so is already a reduced form equation. To obtain the final equation we need to express the right-hand side in terms of the exogenous variable and lagged values of consumption, not income or investment. Thus substitution from the lagged income identity does not help, since it introduces the lagged value of another endogenous variable. However subtracting $\beta/(1-\gamma)$ times the lagged value of the equation produces an expression in Y_{t-1} and Y_{t-2} which, according to the income final equation, is equal to a function of parameters and the exogenous variable, and this does the trick:

$$C_t - \frac{\beta}{1-\gamma} C_{t-1} = \alpha + \beta Y_{t-1} - \frac{\beta}{1-\gamma}(\alpha + \beta Y_{t-2})$$

$$= \alpha\left(1 - \frac{\beta}{1-\gamma}\right) + \beta\left(Y_{t-1} - \frac{\beta}{1-\gamma} Y_{t-2}\right)$$

$$= \alpha\left(1 - \frac{\beta}{1-\gamma}\right) + \beta\left(\frac{\alpha+A}{1-\gamma}\right).$$

Therefore the final equation for consumption is

$$C_t = \left(\alpha + \frac{\beta A}{1 - \gamma}\right) + \left(\frac{\beta}{1 - \gamma}\right) C_{t-1}$$

Again the bracketed expressions correspond to the coefficients a and b of the general first-order difference equation, and $a/(1 - b)$ gives the static equilibrium level of consumption.

We now analyse the stability condition to determine which combinations of values of the structural parameters β and γ give rise to stable situations, and which do not. A pair of values of β and γ can be denoted by a point on a plane, and we seek to divide the plane into regions in which the inequality

$$-1 < \frac{\beta}{1 - \gamma} < 1$$

is satisfied, and those in which it is not. First, when manipulating this inequality we must pay attention to the sign of the denominator, since multiplying through an inequality by a negative number reverses the direction of the inequality. Thus if $1 - \gamma > 0$, that is, $\gamma < 1$, the condition becomes

$$-(1 - \gamma) < \beta < 1 - \gamma,$$

while if $1 - \gamma < 0$, that is, $\gamma > 1$, stability requires

$$-(1 - \gamma) > \beta > 1 - \gamma.$$

We first consider the case $\gamma < 1$, and so in Figure 3.7 restrict attention to the half-plane lying to the left of the dotted line. For stability the two inequalities

$$-(1 - \gamma) < \beta, \qquad \beta < (1 - \gamma)$$

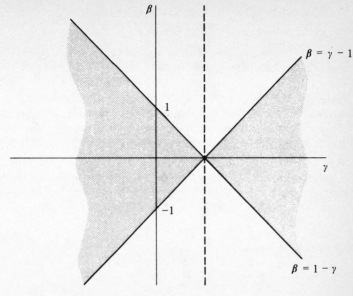

Figure 3.7

must be satisfied, and we take the left-hand one first. The diagram is divided into areas in which β is greater than or less than $-(1 - \gamma)$ by the line $\beta = -(1 - \gamma)$, so we plot this line, and then (β, γ) values such that $\beta > -(1 - \gamma)$ are represented by points lying above the line. Likewise, taking the right-hand inequality, we plot the line $\beta = 1 - \gamma$, then the inequality $\beta < 1 - \gamma$ is satisfied at all points lying below it. Thus the double inequality is satisfied at points between the two lines, that is, in the shaded area. Now considering the case $\gamma > 1$, that is, the half-plane to the right of the dotted line, for stability we require

$$-(1 - \gamma) > \beta, \qquad \beta > 1 - \gamma.$$

The boundary lines that divide the half-plane into stable and unstable regions are again $\beta = -(1 - \gamma)$ and $\beta = 1 - \gamma$, but now stable pairs of values are represented by points lying below the first line, that is, satisfying $\beta < -(1 - \gamma)$, and above the second line ($\beta > 1 - \gamma$), giving the right-hand shaded area. Hence the system is stable if the parameters β and γ fall anywhere in the shaded area of Figure 3.7.

Example 2 A second dynamic example illustrates both that one can use a given static system to represent equilibrium positions for more than one dynamic system and again that restrictions on parameter values may be derived from the requirements of stability. We revert to an unlagged consumption function, and assume that current investment depends on last period's income, so our model is now

$$C_t = \alpha + \beta Y_t$$

$$Y_t = C_t + I_t$$

$$I_t = \gamma Y_{t-1} + A$$

endogenous variables: C_t, Y_t, I_t; exogenous variable: A.

The reduced form equation for Y_t is

$$Y_t = \frac{1}{1 - \beta} (\gamma Y_{t-1} + \alpha + A),$$

which is already a final equation. The stability condition is therefore

$$-1 < \frac{\gamma}{1 - \beta} < 1.$$

If $1 - \beta > 0$, we require

$$-(1 - \beta) < \gamma < 1 - \beta$$

while if $1 - \beta < 0$, the inequalities become

$$-(1 - \beta) > \gamma > 1 - \beta.$$

Following the same procedure as before gives Figure 3.8, in which the shaded area represents pairs of values yielding stable solutions.

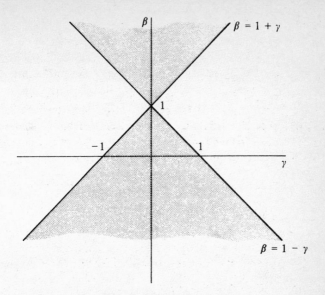

Figure 3.8

Not all parts of this diagram are interesting from the point of view of the economic system. Since β and γ are marginal propensities to consume and invest attention is restricted to the positive quadrant. Further, if it is reasonably assumed that $0 < \beta < 1$, then the system is stable only if the point (β, γ) lies inside the triangle whose apexes are $(0, 0), (0, 1)$ and $(1, 0)$, that is, if $0 < \beta + \gamma < 1$.

Having derived operative stability conditions, we can use these as further prior restrictions on parameter values, since economic systems typically are stable. (In practice the only exception that we meet is that in which certain variables exhibit steady exponential growth, which would arise if the coefficient b in our first-order difference equation was slightly greater than one.) It then becomes an empirical question whether the dynamic behaviour implied by parameter values corresponds to the observed behaviour of endogenous variables. In particular if estimates of parameters fall outside the stability region then a common conclusion would be that the estimated system does not adequately describe the real world. Thus an examination of the stability implications of an estimated dynamic system provides a validation procedure for that system. In models that are more complex than our examples the stability condition will involve a more complicated function of structural parameters that will often make the above diagrammatic analysis impracticable, nevertheless the condition can clearly be expressed algebraically, and these general arguments of course continue to apply.

3.7. STOCHASTIC DYNAMIC MODELS

At the beginning of this chapter we wrote down a dynamic consumption function that included a random disturbance term, but in the subsequent sections this term has been neglected, in order to focus on other aspects of dynamic models. We now consider the consequences of reintroducing the random disturbance term. The reasons for the inclusion of a random disturbance term in a dynamic behavioural relation are exactly the same as those discussed in a static context in chapter 2. The random error represents the effect on the dependent variable of a host of omitted influences that are unobserved or unidentified.

For example, we now write the partial adjustment hypothesis as

$$y_t = (1 - \gamma)y_t^* + \gamma y_{t-1} + u_t$$

where u_t is a random element of the observable variable y_t additional to the contribution of the partial adjustment hypothesis itself. On substituting the simple relation given by the hypothesis that the desired level is determined by the exogenous variable x_t,

$$y_t^* = \alpha + \beta x_t,$$

the relation between observable variables now contains the random disturbance term:

$$y_t = \alpha(1 - \gamma) + \beta(1 - \gamma)x_t + \gamma y_{t-1} + u_t.$$

In the same spirit we could add a random disturbance term to the equation for y_t^* to represent influences other than x on the desired level of y, in which case the disturbance term in this last equation is a composite of both random shocks. As in static models, the disturbance term is interpreted as the non-systematic part of the relation, and hence has zero mean, $E(u_t) = 0$.

The systematic part of this equation describes the determination of the current endogenous variable y_t by the exogenous variable x_t and the lagged endogenous variable y_{t-1}, that is, by the predetermined variables, using the term introduced earlier in this chapter. In static models the definition of an exogenous variable as a variable determined outside the system was formalised by the requirement that such a variable be independent of the random errors in the model in all time periods, and this requirement is maintained in dynamic models. In the present context the statement that x is an exogenous variable implies that the condition $E(x_t u_s) = 0$ for all t and s is satisfied. However, this condition does not provide a definition of a predetermined variable, for lagged endogenous variables clearly fail to satisfy it. At time t, y_{t-1} is a predetermined variable, but the model states that at time $t-1$ y_{t-1} is directly influenced by the random disturbance u_{t-1}. Moreover, y_{t-1} depends on y_{t-2}, which itself depends on u_{t-2}, and so on: by repeated substitution we see that y_{t-1} depends on all past disturbances. Hence the definition we adopt is that a variable is *predetermined* at time t if it is independent of all current and future disturbances in the model. Denoting such a variable by z_t, we require $E(z_t u_s) = 0$ for $s \geqslant t$. To put it another way, we require the current and past values of the variable to be independent of the current disturbance.

Difficulties arise in this framework if the disturbance term is autocorrelated. If u_t is independent of its own past values $u_{t-1}, u_{t-2}, \ldots$, then although y_{t-1} depends on u_{t-1} it will be independent of u_t and can be regarded as predetermined. However if u_t is correlated with u_{t-1}, then y_{t-1} and u_t will be correlated via their common link with u_{t-1}, and y_{t-1} fails to be predetermined. In later chapters we discuss the problems that this presents for estimation.

The reintroduction of random disturbances allows us to begin to weaken our previous statement that the partial adjustment and adaptive expectations models are observationally indistinguishable. Adding an error term to the behavioural relation in the expectations model gives

$$y_t = \alpha + \beta \hat{x}_{t+1} + u_t.$$

Assuming that the unobservable $\hat{x}_{t+1}$ obeys

$$\hat{x}_{t+1} - \theta \hat{x}_t = (1 - \theta)x_t$$

we obtain a relation between observable variables by transforming in a manner equivalent to that used above (p. 49), as follows:

$$y_t - \theta y_{t-1} = (\alpha + \beta \hat{x}_{t+1} + u_t) - \theta(\alpha + \beta \hat{x}_t + u_{t-1})$$
$$= \alpha(1 - \theta) + \beta(\hat{x}_{t+1} - \theta \hat{x}_t) + (u_t - \theta u_{t-1}),$$

hence we have the relation

$$y_t = \alpha(1 - \theta) + \beta(1 - \theta)x_t + \theta y_{t-1} + v_t,$$

where the disturbance term v_t is given by $v_t = u_t - \theta u_{t-1}$. If the original disturbances u are not autocorrelated, in particular $E(u_t u_{t-1}) = 0$, the new disturbances are composed of two successive u-values, and hence do exhibit autocorrelation. We have

$$E(v_t) = E(u_t - \theta u_{t-1}) = E(u_t) - \theta E(u_{t-1}) = 0$$
$$E(v_t v_{t-1}) = E(u_t - \theta u_{t-1})(u_{t-1} - \theta u_{t-2})$$
$$= E(u_t u_{t-1} - \theta u_{t-1}^2 - \theta u_t u_{t-2} + \theta^2 u_{t-1} u_{t-2})$$
$$= E(u_t u_{t-1}) - \theta E(u_{t-1}^2) - \theta E(u_t u_{t-2}) + \theta^2 E(u_{t-1} u_{t-2}).$$

The first, third and fourth terms involve the covariances between u-values at different points of time and so are zero if u is non-autocorrelated, but the second term involves the variance of u, which is clearly non-zero. Then successive values of the v-series are negatively correlated:

$$E(v_t v_{t-1}) = -\theta \, \text{var}(u).$$

This result provides a contrast to the partial adjustment model: if the random disturbances in the behavioural equations of each model are free of autocorrelation, so is the disturbance term in the final equation of the partial adjustment model, but not of the adaptive expectations model. The error term in the final equation of the partial adjustment model is simply the disturbance term introduced into the partial adjustment hypothesis, whereas the error term in the final equation of the adaptive expectations model is a moving average of the original disturbance, as a result of the transformation undertaken to eliminate the unobservable variable, and hence is in general autocorrelated. Although the systematic parts of the final equations are identical in these simple cases, the correlation pattern of the disturbances is not, and this can be exploited in empirical work.

3.8 THE RATIONAL EXPECTATIONS HYPOTHESIS

In section 3.4 we considered one approach to the modelling of unobservable expectations variables which was based on the assumption that expectations are formed by extrapolating from past experience, thus forecasts of the future value of a variable were calculated from its current and past values, in various ways. In this section we consider an alternative approach, based on the rational expectations hypothesis, which assumes that expectations are essentially the same as the predictions of the relevant economic theory. The previous approach remains the appropriate one if the variable about which expectations are formed is an exogenous variable, since by definition our theories and models do not describe the determination of the values of exogenous variables. But if the variable about which expectations are formed is an endogenous variable, then it may be more appropriate to assume that expectations are formed as if agents anticipate the workings of the model that determines the value of the variable. For example, a change in the level of excise tax on a commodity will have an effect on the price of the commodity, and if either suppliers or consumers wish to predict this effect they will do better to consider relevant demand and supply factors than to base a prediction on past prices. Our discussion proceeds in the context of a simple example, namely that of the market for an agricultural commodity.

The farmers who produce this commodity must make their planting decisions before they know the price that they will receive for the crop at harvest-time. If a high price for the crop is anticipated, then a substantial harvest will be planned, but if a low price is expected to prevail, then planting will be reduced. Using a linear approximation, we can represent the farmers' supply function as

$$Q_t = \beta_0 + \beta_1 \hat{P}_t, \qquad \beta_1 > 0,$$

where Q_t is the quantity supplied to the market, $\hat{P}_t$ is the expectation, formed at the time of planting, of the market-clearing price P_t, and we are ignoring random disturbances and other exogenous influences on supply (such as climatic factors) for the moment. These ignored factors contribute to uncertainty about price, but the state of demand for the product may also be uncertain. If, in the face of this uncertainty, the price is predicted by looking at past prices, then the framework of section 3.4 is relevant: for example, the naive prediction rule $\hat{P}_t = P_{t-1}$ might be used, in which case we obtain the supply function of the simple cobweb model (compare Exercise 3.4). However, the rational expectations hypothesis postulates that price expectations are essentially the same as the predictions of the relevant demand-and-supply model. Let us complete the model with the simple demand function

$$Q_t = \alpha_0 + \alpha_1 P_t, \qquad \alpha_1 < 0, \qquad \alpha_0 > \beta_0,$$

and assume that price adjusts so as to clear the market. Then the rationally expected price $\hat{P}_t$ is the value that leads to the supply of a quantity which is such that the market-clearing price is exactly what was expected. The hypothesis is that expectations are formed as if farmers correctly anticipate the operation of the market. An expression for the required value of $\hat{P}_t$ can be readily deduced. Equating demand and supply gives

$$\alpha_0 + \alpha_1 P_t = \beta_0 + \beta_1 \hat{P}_t,$$

hence the relation between actual and expected price is

$$P_t = \frac{\beta_0 - \alpha_0}{\alpha_1} + \frac{\beta_1}{\alpha_1} \hat{P}_t.$$

The value of $\hat{P}_t$ such that this expectation is fulfilled, $\hat{P}_t = P_t$, is given by solving

$$\hat{P}_t = \frac{\beta_0 - \alpha_0}{\alpha_1} + \frac{\beta_1}{\alpha_1} \hat{P}_t,$$

so the rational expectation of price is

$$\hat{P}_t = \frac{\alpha_0 - \beta_0}{\beta_1 - \alpha_1}.$$

This price expectation leads to the supply of the quantity

$$Q_t = \beta_0 + \beta_1 \frac{\alpha_0 - \beta_0}{\beta_1 - \alpha_1} = \frac{\alpha_0 \beta_1 - \alpha_1 \beta_0}{\beta_1 - \alpha_1},$$

and the buyers' demand function tells us that, when faced with this quantity, the market will clear at a price given by

$$\frac{\alpha_0 \beta_1 - \alpha_1 \beta_0}{\beta_1 - \alpha_1} = \alpha_0 + \alpha_1 P_t.$$

On rearranging this expression, the market-clearing price is seen to be

$$P_t = \frac{\alpha_0 - \beta_0}{\beta_1 - \alpha_1},$$

exactly what it was (rationally) expected to be.

This exact self-fulfilling nature of rational expectations is modified once random disturbances enter the model. The stochastic version of our model is

$$Q_t = \alpha_0 + \alpha_1 P_t + u_{1t}$$
$$Q_t = \beta_0 + \beta_1 \hat{P}_t + u_{2t},$$

and so the relation between actual and expected price becomes

$$P_t = \frac{\beta_0 - \alpha_0}{\alpha_1} + \frac{\beta_1}{\alpha_1} \hat{P}_t + \frac{u_{2t} - u_{1t}}{\alpha_1}.$$

Expectations formed at time $t - 1$ consistent with this relation satisfy

$$\hat{P}_t = \frac{\beta_0 - \alpha_0}{\alpha_1} + \frac{\beta_1}{\alpha_1} \hat{P}_t + \frac{\hat{u}_{2t} - \hat{u}_{1t}}{\alpha_1},$$

where $\hat{u}_{1t}$ and $\hat{u}_{2t}$ are the predicted values of the disturbance terms. If the disturbances are non-autocorrelated, so that information up to time $t - 1$ does not help in forecasting their values at time t, then the best forecasts of u_{1t} and u_{2t} are simply their mean values, namely zero, and the same expression as above is obtained:

$$\hat{P}_t = \frac{\alpha_0 - \beta_0}{\beta_1 - \alpha_1}.$$

Now, however, the actual price deviates from this expectation as a result of these unanticipated random shocks, since the preceding relations give

$$P_t = \hat{P}_t + \frac{u_{2t} - u_{1t}}{\alpha_1}.$$

For example, if weather conditions are unusually bad and the harvest is reduced ($u_{2t} < 0$), then the market-clearing price is higher than anticipated ($u_{2t}/\alpha_1 > 0$, remembering $\alpha_1 < 0$). Thus there will be errors in the price forecasts, but these will be purely random, and exhibit no systematic pattern. Having observed this higher-than-anticipated price, rational farmers' behaviour in the following period will not change. Of course if one year's bad weather influences the forecast of the following year's weather, then this should be incorporated in price expectations, but this takes us away from price-quantity models with purely random disturbances, and requires the introduction of additional variables.

In general we might expect both the demand and the supply functions of a more realistic model to contain further variables, but the consequences are illustrated perfectly well by adding a single exogenous variable. Let us assume that the level of demand is affected by the variable X_t, which might represent consumers' income or the price of an imported substitute for the commodity, for example. Now the model is

$$Q_t = \alpha_0 + \alpha_1 P_t + \alpha_2 X_t + u_{1t}$$

$$Q_t = \beta_0 + \beta_1 \hat{P}_t + u_{2t}.$$

Equating the right-hand sides leads to the relation

$$P_t = \frac{\beta_0 - \alpha_0}{\alpha_1} + \frac{\beta_1}{\alpha_1} \hat{P}_t - \frac{\alpha_2}{\alpha_1} X_t + \frac{u_{2t} - u_{1t}}{\alpha_1}.$$

This would be the reduced form equation for P_t if $\hat{P}_t$ were an observable exogenous variable, but under the rational expectations hypothesis we simply use it to tell us how the unobservable variable $\hat{P}_t$ is formed. Again assuming that the random disturbances are non-autocorrelated, expectations consistent with the model satisfy

$$\hat{P}_t = \frac{\beta_0 - \alpha_0}{\alpha_1} + \frac{\beta_1}{\alpha_1} \hat{P}_t - \frac{\alpha_2}{\alpha_1} \hat{X}_t,$$

where $\hat{X}_t$ denotes the expectation of X_t formed at time $t-1$. Rearrangement gives

$$\hat{P}_t = \frac{\alpha_0 - \beta_0}{\beta_1 - \alpha_1} + \frac{\alpha_2}{\beta_1 - \alpha_1} \hat{X}_t.$$

Knowing that demand, and hence the market price, is influenced by the variable X, it is rational for farmers to take this into account when forming price expectations, by attempting to predict X_t. It might appear that the rational expectations hypothesis has simply transferred the problem from forecasting an endogenous variable to forecasting an exogenous variable, but the key ingredient is the information about the structure of the relevant system describing the market, that is, about the links between endogenous and exogenous variables.

Errors in forecasting the exogenous variable contribute an additional component to the error in the rational expectation, for we have

$$P_t = \hat{P}_t - \frac{\alpha_2}{\alpha_1}(X_t - \hat{X}_t) + \frac{u_{2t} - u_{1t}}{\alpha_1}.$$

However, the error $P_t - \hat{P}_t$ will again be purely random if past information on X is used in an optimal way, so that its forecast error $X_t - \hat{X}_t$ is purely random. For example, if X_t follows a first-order autoregression

$$X_t = \rho X_{t-1} + \epsilon_t,$$

then, as shown in section 3.4, the best forecast calculated at time $t - 1$ is $\hat{X}_t = \rho X_{t-1}$ and the error in this forecast is ϵ_t. On substituting for $\hat{X}_t$ we obtain an expression for $\hat{P}_t$ in terms of X_{t-1} and various parameters, and substituting this in turn into the "reduced form" equation for P_t gives a distributed lag equation between P and X:

$$P_t = \frac{\beta_0 - \alpha_0}{\alpha_1} + \frac{\beta_1}{\alpha_1}\left(\frac{\alpha_0 - \beta_0}{\beta_1 - \alpha_1} + \frac{\alpha_2}{\beta_1 - \alpha_1}\rho X_{t-1}\right) - \frac{\alpha_2}{\alpha_1}X_t + \frac{u_{2t} - u_{1t}}{\alpha_1}$$

$$= \frac{\alpha_0 - \beta_0}{\beta_1 - \alpha_1} - \frac{\alpha_2}{\alpha_1}X_t + \frac{\alpha_2\beta_1\rho}{\alpha_1(\beta_1 - \alpha_1)}X_{t-1} + \frac{u_{2t} - u_{1t}}{\alpha_1}.$$

There is no apparent dynamic element in the original model, such as lags in adjustment, merely the passage of time between the formation of price expectations and the realisation of actual price, but this is sufficient to give another potential source of distributed lag models.

Notice that the lag function depends on the structure of the forecast of the exogenous variable, which in turn depends on the behaviour of the X-series itself: if more lagged X-values become relevant in forecasting, because the behaviour of the X-series changes, then the form of the distributed lag model also changes. In practice it is important to distinguish the two potential sources of distributed lags, namely the structure of the economic model and the behaviour of the exogenous variables.

EXERCISES

3.1 For the following distributed lag models, calculate the impact multiplier, the long-run multiplier, and the mean lag, if possible.

(a) $y_t = 0.75x_t + 0.5x_{t-1} + 0.25x_{t-2}$

(b) $y_t = 0.1x_{t-1} + 0.2x_{t-2} + 0.3x_{t-3} + 0.2x_{t-4} + 0.1x_{t-5}$

(c) $y_t = 1.5x_t + 0.75x_{t-1} - 0.25x_{t-2}$.

3.2 In his capacity-output studies, Koyck estimated an equation of the form

$$y_t = \alpha + \beta_1 x_t + \beta_2 x_{t-1} + \beta_2 \lambda x_{t-2} + \beta_2 \lambda^2 x_{t-3} + \ldots.$$

Transform this equation into an equation containing a finite number of x-values, and hence show how the four parameters may be estimated. Show that a final equation containing the same variables may be derived from a partial adjustment hypothesis, where the "desired" level of y_t depends on x_t and x_{t-1}.

3.3 Suppose that the desired level of y depends on next period's forecast value of x:

$$y_t^* = \alpha + \beta \hat{x}_{t+1}$$

where the forecast is formed according to the adaptive expectations hypothesis:

$$\hat{x}_{t+1} = \theta \hat{x}_t + (1 - \theta)x_t.$$

The actual level of y adjusts to the desired level according to

$$y_t - y_{t-1} = (1 - \gamma)(y_t^* - y_{t-1}).$$

Obtain an equation expressing y_t as a function of a finite number of observed values of x and y. From estimates of this equation, could you obtain separate estimates of γ and θ? Compare the implication of your answer with previous remarks about the duality between the adaptive expectations and partial adjustment hypotheses (p. 50).

3.4 Consider the market for a commodity produced in an annual crop. The quantity demanded depends on the current price:

$$Q_t = \alpha_0 + \alpha_1 P_t,$$

the quantity supplied this year is a function of last year's price:

$$Q_t = \beta_0 + \beta_1 P_{t-1},$$

and the market is cleared in every year. Under what conditions on the parameters is the system stable?

Now suppose that the quantity supplied is a function of this year's expected price, where price expectations are formed according to the adaptive expectations hypothesis. Show that, for certain values of the adaptive expectations parameter, this change will stabilize a previously unstable system.

3.5 Obtain the reduced form and final equation for Y_t, and the stability condition for the following model:

$$C_t = \alpha + \beta Y_t + \gamma C_{t-1}$$
$$Y_t = C_t + I_t$$

endogenous variables: C_t, Y_t; exogenous variable: I_t.

3.6 Obtain the final equation for Y_t and the stability condition for the following model:

$$C_t = \alpha + \beta Y_t$$
$$Y_t = C_t + I_t$$
$$I_t = \gamma \Delta Y_t + G_t$$

endogenous variables: C_t, Y_t, I_t; exogenous variable: G_t.

3.7 Consider the following model of the market for a commodity:

demand: $\qquad X_t = \alpha_0 + \alpha_1 P_t + u_{1t}$ $\qquad \alpha_1 < 0$

supply: $\qquad Q_t = \beta_0 + \beta_1 P_t + u_{2t}$ $\qquad \beta_1 > 0$

price adjustment: $\Delta P_t = \gamma \Delta S_{t-1} + u_{3t}$

stock level: $\qquad S_t = S_{t-1} + Q_t - X_t$

where X_t, Q_t, P_t and S_t are sales, output, price and end-period stock level respectively, and $\Delta P_t = P_t - P_{t-1}$.

(a) Obtain the static equilibrium values of price and quantity (ignoring the disturbance terms). What further restrictions on the parameters of the model are suggested by these values?

(b) By deriving the final equation for P_t, or otherwise, obtain the range of values of γ for which the system is stable. Does your answer have a sensible economic interpretation in the context of the price adjustment equation?

3.8 Adding a disturbance term u_t to the consumption function, derive the final equation for C_t in stochastic versions of the models in exercises 3.5 and 3.6. Check that in each case the final equation for C_t has the same autoregressive structure as that for Y_t (note the discussion on p. 55). In each case, is the lagged dependent variable independent of the error term in the final equation?

IV

THE IDENTIFICATION PROBLEM

4.1 INTRODUCTION

Let us first recap some earlier discussion to put the identification problem in context. We said that *a priori* economic theorising can tell us very little about the actual magnitudes of the parameters of behavioural relations, and that estimation of the structural parameters is necessary if we wish to test hypotheses about the underlying behaviour or simply to obtain numerical values as ends in themselves. On the other hand, if all we are interested in is prediction, then there is a case in which we do not need to know structural parameters at all, and the sequence that we follow is:

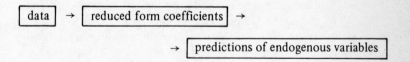

This is valid when there is no intervening change of structure between the observation and prediction periods (pp. 8–9 above), although we shall in due course find a situation in which knowledge of the structural parameters improves the predictions even in the absence of structural change. In the presence of structural change, however, we need to know or estimate the parameters of behavioural relationships in the observation period, so that the effect of the change can be assessed before moving to predictions, and the sequence is as follows:

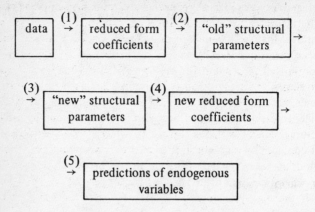

Knowledge of the structural change is incorporated at stage (3), and stages (4) and (5) are straightforward algebraic operations as discussed in chapter 2. Stages (1) and (2) will be our concern for the remainder of this book. Whether stage (2) is possible, that is, whether numerical values of the structural parameters can be deduced from a given (estimated) reduced form is the *identification* problem, and the *estimation* problem arises at stage (1). The identification problem is logically prior, and is treated first, because if it is not possible to infer structural parameter values from reduced form coefficient values, there is no point in estimating the reduced form (except for prediction under unchanged structure). Although the estimation problem is presented here as the problem of obtaining reduced form coefficient estimates from data on the endogenous and exogenous variables during the observation period, we shall see in chapter 10 that there are ways of estimating the structural parameters directly from the data, provided that the model is identified, that is, that stage (2) is possible. So even here it is necessary to check the identifiability of the model, or its equations, or their parameters, before attempting any estimation.

To concentrate attention on the identification problem, we assume in this chapter that we have perfect knowledge of the reduced form and that such stage (1) problems as sampling variability in estimates can be ignored. One way of looking at this is to assume that we have an infinite sample of data. Thus we collapse the first link in the above chain, and use "data" and "reduced form" as equivalent concepts.

The identification problem arises because there may be a number of structures that will generate the same reduced form, or the same observations. Equivalently, given a set of data, many hypotheses could be formulated to account for the observations. What we attempt to do is to eliminate as many of these hypotheses as possible on *a priori* grounds, arguing that they are inconsistent with economic theory, and the identification problem is solved when exactly one hypothesis (or structure) remains which is consistent with both data and theory. The most common way in which prior restrictions are imposed on a general relationship as a result of theoretical reasoning is by specifying particular values for parameters — typically we specify that a parameter is zero if the theory leads us to believe that the variable to which the parameter is attached does not influence the particular economic behaviour in question. Here we shall not be considering situations in which the theory leads to statements concerning the behaviour of the error terms, and so we shall proceed by considering the exact equivalents of the stochastic models we are interested in analysing. That is, we consider that the "data" give us a perfectly known exact reduced form.

To introduce a more formal treatment, we call the set of structures that are consistent with the data the *data-admissible* structures. For an equation to be consistent with the data we mean that the given values of the predetermined variables and the corresponding values of the endogenous variables given by the reduced form satisfy the equation exactly. Recall that the use of the term "structure" implies that numerical values of parameters are specified (p. 9). Thus the data-admissible structures are those whose reduced forms are identical (having identical coefficient values) with the given data or reduced form. Alternatively, data-admissible structures can be described as *observationally equivalent*.

Somewhat more trivially, the set of structures consistent with the model, obeying the restrictions imposed by the model, are said to be *model-admissible*. To go back to our earliest example on p. 5, any equation that contains only consumption and income and excludes

investment is model-admissible as a consumption function: it satisfies
the restrictions of the theory.

We can now use these two notions to define exactly what we mean
by identifiability. A *structure* is *identified* with respect to a given model
and given data if there is one and only one structure that is both model-
and data-admissible. That is, there is only one set of numerical values of
the structural parameters corresponding to the reduced form given by
the data that also satisfies the prior restrictions imposed by the model.
This definition can be disaggregated to apply to the identifiability of
a single structural equation or even of a single parameter value. Thus,
again, a structural equation is identified if there are *unique* values of
its parameters corresponding to the given reduced form and satisfying
the prior restrictions. We may have a model in which some equations
are identified and other equations are not. Similarly some parameter
values of a single equation in a model may be identified while other
parameter values are not, but this is less common.

4.2 A DEMAND-AND-SUPPLY ILLUSTRATION

Case 1.   Let us start with a very simple form of demand-and-supply
model. The behavioural equations specify that the quantities bought
and sold are functions of the price of a commodity. We ignore the
error terms as noted above, and substitute $Q_t = Q_t^s = Q_t^d$ from the
market clearing condition, and so have:

$$D: \qquad Q_t = \alpha_0 + \alpha_1 P_t \qquad \alpha_1 < 0$$

$$S: \qquad Q_t = \beta_0 + \beta_1 P_t \qquad \beta_1 > 0$$

We are interested in the numerical values of the parameters and let us
suppose that some economist knows what the actual parameter values
are. He then takes the demand equation and multiplies it by some constant (say 3/5) and the supply equation by another (2/5) and adds them
together. He claims that the resulting equation

$$D': \qquad Q_t = \frac{3\alpha_0 + 2\beta_0}{5} + \frac{3\alpha_1 + 2\beta_1}{5} P_t$$

is the demand equation: no other economist could discover what had happened by looking at the data. Similarly, he might multiply the demand equation by 1/3 and the supply equation by 2/3, add the two together and call the result the supply equation:

$$S': \quad Q_t = \frac{\alpha_0 + 2\beta_0}{3} + \frac{\alpha_1 + 2\beta_1}{3} P_t.$$

The point is that there would be no data which could reveal what our deceitful economist had done, provided that the restrictions imposed by the theory were still met. The requirement on the slopes of the lines become

$$\frac{3\alpha_1 + 2\beta_1}{5} < 0, \qquad \frac{\alpha_1 + 2\beta_1}{3} > 0$$

and so long as these hold the deceit is undetected.

The original demand and supply equations are not identified: they have the same reduced form as the equations that are derived as linear combinations of them. Thus data satisfying D and S will also satisfy D' and S' because both pairs of equations have the same reduced form. Moreover it is possible to construct D' and S' so that their slopes have the required signs, using weights different from 3/5, 2/5 and 1/3, 2/3 if necessary. Then we have more than one set of model-admissible equations that satisfy the data. Hence the model is not identified.

An early paper on this subject is that by Working*, who observed that with the above pair of demand and supply curves there are no possible P–Q observations that will enable us to pick out a relation which we can call the demand curve and a relation which we can call the supply curve. A P–Q observation fixes the intersection of D and S, but not their slopes. Even if we have errors in each equation all the data will lie around this intersection, and any two lines intersecting at this point could be the "correct" demand and supply relations, as illustrated in Figure 4.1.

---

*E. J. Working, "What Do Statistical 'Demand Curves' Show?" Q.J.E., 1927. Reprinted in A.E.A. *Readings in Price Theory*, pp. 97–115.

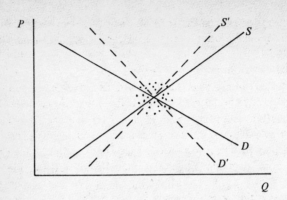

Figure 4.1

Working observed, however, that if one curve shifts systematically while the other remains fixed, then the P–Q observations given by the intersections of the curves will all lie on the curve which does not shift, which is hence identified. This gives us our next case.

Case 2. We now introduce income into the demand function:

$$D: \quad Q_t = \alpha_0 + \alpha_1 P_t + \alpha_2 Y_t \qquad \alpha_1 < 0, \qquad \alpha_2 > 0$$

$$S: \quad Q_t = \beta_0 + \beta_1 P_t \qquad\qquad \beta_1 > 0,$$

We expect that demand depends negatively on price and positively on income. Any P, Q and Y observations generated by this model, and so satisfying this pair of equations, will also satisfy any linear combination of these equations. Hence we can obtain sets of data-admissible equations simply by taking linear combinations of the equations. Let us now be slightly more general by multiplying the demand equation by $(1 - h)$ and the supply equation by h, where $0 \leqslant h \leqslant 1$. Then we can say that

$$Q_t = [(1 - h)\alpha_0 + h\beta_0] + [(1 - h)\alpha_1 + h\beta_1]P_t + (1 - h)\alpha_2 Y_t$$

is a data-admissible equation. Is it model-admissible, either as a supply curve or as a demand curve or as neither? We know it fits the data. Next we must decide whether we can pass it off as a particular equation of the model.

It certainly cannot do as a supply equation because it contains income, and our model says that supply does not depend upon income. There is only one special case in which the equation would look like a supply equation according to the restriction and that is when $h = 1$ and income is excluded. But this gives the original supply equation, and so we conclude that it is identified: there is one and only one equation which is both data-admissible and model-admissible as the supply equation.

When $h \neq 1$ the equation certainly could be the demand equation (because it would then contain income with a positive coefficient), provided that the price coefficient remained negative, that is,

$$(1 - h)\alpha_1 + h\beta_1 < 0.$$

This implies a restriction on h, namely that

$$0 \leqslant h < \frac{\alpha_1}{\alpha_1 - \beta_1}.$$

However, with α_1 negative and β_1 positive there are many values of h satisfying this restriction. There are therefore lots of data-admissible equations that satisfy the restrictions imposed by the theory and are thereby model-admissible as the demand equation, which is therefore not identified.

In terms of the simple diagrammatic representation we have a supply equation relating P and Q but, for every different income level, the demand equation gives a different $P-Q$ relation. As income varies the demand curve in the $P-Q$ plane shifts and the observations on P and Q will lie along the supply curve, which is thereby identified, as illustrated in Figure 4.2. The demand function is not identified: any other set of three parallel lines intersecting the supply curve at the same points could equally well represent the demand function.

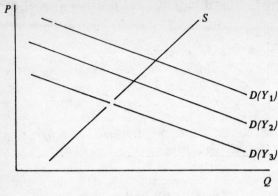

Figure 4.2

Case 3. We can identify the demand curve similarly, that is, by a shifting supply curve. A model in which this is true is

$$D: \quad Q_t = \alpha_0 + \alpha_1 P_t$$
$$S: \quad Q_t = \beta_0 + \beta_1 P_t + \beta_3 W_t$$

where W might be the wage rate or the weather. Again, there is no linear combination of the two equations that satisfies the restriction imposed on the demand curve, that is, that excludes W. In this situation the $P-Q$ data obtained as W varies show us the demand curve, which is thereby identified, as illustrated in Figure 4.3.

Case 4. Putting the last two cases together we can take a final case where both demand and supply curves shift.

$$D: \quad Q_t = \alpha_0 + \alpha_1 P_t + \alpha_2 Y_t$$
$$S: \quad Q_t = \beta_0 + \beta_1 P_t \quad\quad + \beta_3 W_t$$

In this case we cannot readily represent the situation diagrammatically since both $P-Q$ relations are shifting and so the observations in the price and quantity plane will not lie on any particular curve. But this

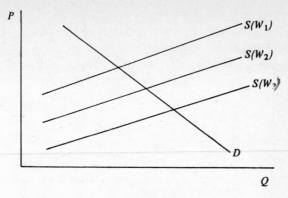

Figure 4.3

fact tells us nothing about identification. Let us set up a data-admissible linear combination of the demand and supply structure equations and see whether it is model-admissible in each case. Multiplying the demand equation by the factor $(1 - h)$ and the supply equation by h and summing the results gives the following equation satisfied by any data generated by the above structure:

$$Q_t = (1 - h)\alpha_0 + h\beta_0 + [(1 - h)\alpha_1 + h\beta_1]P_t + (1 - h)\alpha_2 Y_t + h\beta_3 W_t.$$

However no general equation of this kind can satisfy the restrictions of the model. Only if $h = 1$, so that income is excluded, is the restriction on the supply equation satisfied, and only if $h = 0$, so that W is excluded, can the equation serve as a demand equation. But these cases give the demand and supply functions themselves and so both are identified: in each case there is one and only one equation that satisfies both the data and the restrictions imposed by the theory.

So we begin to see that an equation is made identifiable by the *exclusion* of one variable from it, and the specification of a zero coefficient that we spoke about in discussing general notation (p. 22) appears to have some purpose. Any equation that includes all the variables appearing in the model is unidentified. If we were to construct a fifth case by putting Y and W into both demand and supply equations then they would both have the same form and neither would be identified in the absence of further restrictions.

We began this chapter by saying that identification is necessary for us to be able to evaluate structural parameters from reduced form coefficients. Let us return to this question in terms of these illustrations. Take the example of case 4. The two endogenous variables are P and Q, and the reduced form is

$$P_t = \frac{\alpha_0 - \beta_0}{\beta_1 - \alpha_1} + \frac{\alpha_2}{\beta_1 - \alpha_1} Y_t - \frac{\beta_3}{\beta_1 - \alpha_1} W_t$$

$$Q_t = \frac{\alpha_0 \beta_1 - \alpha_1 \beta_0}{\beta_1 - \alpha_1} + \frac{\alpha_2 \beta_1}{\beta_1 - \alpha_1} Y_t - \frac{\alpha_1 \beta_3}{\beta_1 - \alpha_1} W_t.$$

Using the generalised representation for the reduced form, we may write

$$P_t = \pi_{11} + \pi_{12} Y_t + \pi_{13} W_t$$

$$Q_t = \pi_{21} + \pi_{22} Y_t + \pi_{23} W_t,$$

where the reduced form coefficients are given in terms of structural parameters as

$$\pi_{11} = \frac{\alpha_0 - \beta_0}{\beta_1 - \alpha_1}, \qquad \pi_{12} = \frac{\alpha_2}{\beta_1 - \alpha_1}, \qquad \pi_{13} = -\frac{\beta_3}{\beta_1 - \alpha_1},$$

$$\pi_{21} = \frac{\alpha_0 \beta_1 - \alpha_1 \beta_0}{\beta_1 - \alpha_1}, \qquad \pi_{22} = \frac{\alpha_2 \beta_1}{\beta_1 - \alpha_1}, \qquad \pi_{23} = -\frac{\alpha_1 \beta_3}{\beta_1 - \alpha_1}.$$

Now we assume that actual numerical values of the π's are given to us and ask whether we can work back to the actual numerical values of the structural parameters, α's and β's. In this particular case, of course, we expect that we can do so because we have already established that both demand and supply equations are identified, and we note that here we have six equations involving six unknown α's and β's. We first take these equations pair-by-pair, and arrange them into a more convenient form. Starting with the coefficients of W_t, we see that

$$\pi_{23} - \alpha_1\pi_{13} = 0, \tag{1}$$

$$\pi_{23} - \beta_1\pi_{13} = -\frac{\alpha_1\beta_3}{\beta_1 - \alpha_1} + \frac{\beta_1\beta_3}{\beta_1 - \alpha_1} = \beta_3. \tag{2}$$

Similarly, from the coefficients of Y_t we obtain

$$\pi_{22} - \alpha_1\pi_{12} = \frac{\alpha_2\beta_1}{\beta_1 - \alpha_1} - \frac{\alpha_1\alpha_2}{\beta_1 - \alpha_1} = \alpha_2, \tag{3}$$

$$\pi_{22} - \beta_1\pi_{12} = 0. \tag{4}$$

Finally, from the intercept terms we have

$$\pi_{21} - \alpha_1\pi_{11} = \frac{\alpha_0\beta_1 - \alpha_1\beta_0}{\beta_1 - \alpha_1} - \frac{\alpha_0\alpha_1 - \alpha_1\beta_0}{\beta_1 - \alpha_1} = \alpha_0, \tag{5}$$

$$\pi_{21} - \beta_1\pi_{11} = \frac{\alpha_0\beta_1 - \alpha_1\beta_0}{\beta_1 - \alpha_1} - \frac{\alpha_0\beta_1 - \beta_1\beta_0}{\beta_1 - \alpha_1} = \beta_0. \tag{6}$$

These six equations readily yield the values of the α's and β's, the odd-numbered equations giving the α's and the even-numbered ones the β's. Equation (1) gives $\alpha_1 = \pi_{23}/\pi_{13}$ and then with this value of α_1 equations (3) and (5) give α_2 and α_0 respectively. Equation (4) gives $\beta_1 = \pi_{22}/\pi_{12}$ and then with this value of β_1 equations (2) and (6) give β_3 and β_0 respectively. Thus, given the numerical values of the reduced form coefficients, the structural parameter values can be obtained.

In an unidentified system we are not able to solve out all the structural parameters that appear in the model. In *Case 2* considered above (p. 80) the supply curve did not shift (W was absent), but the demand function did (as a function of Y). We can represent that situation in our present framework by setting $\beta_3 = 0$ so that the wage variable disappears from the model. The reduced form then simply has

P and Q as a function of one exogenous variable, Y:

$$P_t = \pi_{11} + \pi_{12}Y_t$$
$$Q_t = \pi_{21} + \pi_{22}Y_t.$$

These four reduced form coefficients are the same functions of the α's and β's as above; setting $\beta_3 = 0$ simply implies $\pi_{13} = \pi_{23} = 0$. Now we have five structural parameters and only four reduced form coefficients, which necessarily means that we cannot deduce unique values of α's and β's from given π-values, and so the complete structure is not identified. Let us see in what sense this is so. Of the rearranged equations we have now lost (1) and (2) as a result of the deletion of W from the list of variables, but (3), (4), (5) and (6) remain. Again equation (4) gives $\beta_1 = \pi_{22}/\pi_{12}$ and then (6) gives β_0, so the supply equation is identified. However in equations (3) and (5) we have only two equations in three unknown α's and so the demand equation is not identified. Although there is an infinite range of values of α_0, α_1 and α_2 satisfying these two equations once any one of them is specified the other two follow immediately. For example, if we could specify a particular value for the income elasticity of demand (α_2) from somewhere beyond our model, α_0 and α_1 would follow. Effectively, then, we are short of just one piece of information, or one restriction, without which the demand function is unidentified.

4.3   ORDER AND RANK CONDITIONS

In the previous section, we formed a set of data-admissible equations by taking linear combinations of the true structure equations (with the correct parameter values specified, that is). We now show for the general linear model both that any linear combination of the structure equations is data-admissible and also that no linear equation that is not formed in that way is data-admissible. On the one hand this is a useful general way of forming sets of data-admissible equations and on the other hand it gives *all* the data-admissible equations. Consider the general representation

$$\sum_{i=1}^{G} \beta_{gi} y_{it} + \sum_{k=1}^{K} \gamma_{gk} x_{kt} = 0 \qquad g = 1, \ldots, G$$

(continuing to work with the exact case for convenience). Each of these equations, with specified β- and γ-values, is true for every set of observed y- and x-values. It remains true when multiplied through by some constant h_g, and when all equations, multiplied by constants $h_1, h_2, \ldots, h_G$, are added together, we still get an equation that is satisfied by the y_i and x_k values. (Since this equation remains true if it is multiplied or divided through by any constant, we can without loss of generality take $\Sigma h_g = 1$.) So when we take linear combinations with weights h_g, all resulting equations remain data-admissible. Of course, if only one such weight, say h_j, is non-zero, then we get the jth structure equation back again.

Now what we need to show is that any linear equation satisfying the data must in fact be obtained in this way. Suppose the following linear equation fits the data

$$\sum_{i=1}^{G} \alpha_i y_{it} + \sum_{k=1}^{K} \delta_k x_{kt} = 0.$$

Assuming that det $\mathbf{B}$ is non-zero, the model has a unique reduced form

$$y_{it} = \sum_{k=1}^{K} \pi_{ik} x_{kt}, \qquad i = 1, \ldots, G$$

and the numerical values of the π-coefficients are given by the data. Thus these are the only expressions for each endogenous variable, taken one-at-a-time, that satisfy the data. So if the previous equation satisfies the data it must be obtained by taking α_1 times the first reduced form equation plus α_2 times the second equation plus α_3 times the third, and so on, with the δ-coefficients obeying $\delta_k = -\Sigma \alpha_i \pi_{ik}$. That is, it must be a linear combination of reduced form equations. But each reduced form equation is itself a linear combination of the structure equations, constructed so as to eliminate all y's but one. Hence any linear equation satisfying the data must be a linear combination of the true structure equations.

This helps considerably because it means that we need only consider equations that are linear combinations of the true structural equations in the model. The problem then becomes whether such an equation is model-admissible as one of the structural equations, in the sense that it satisfies the restrictions imposed by the model. Let us continue to assume for the time being that the only restrictions we have to deal with are zero restrictions. Then what we need to check is whether any linear combinations of the structural equations contain exactly the same variables as the structural equation of interest, no more, no less. If so, then the structural equation is not identified, for there is more than one data-admissible equation satisfying the exclusion restrictions.

Proceeding in small steps, we next consider a three-equation example, based on a model of the joint demand for two commodities. We get by with only three equations by assuming that the supply of the second commodity is completely inelastic, so that the quantity traded, Q_2, is a given constant. The model is

$$D_1: \quad Q_{1t} = \quad \alpha_0 \quad + \alpha_1 P_{1t} + \alpha_2 P_{2t} + \alpha_3 Y_t$$

$$S_1: \quad Q_{1t} = \quad \beta_0 \quad + \beta_1 P_{1t} \quad + \beta_4 W_t$$

$$D_2: \quad 0 = (\gamma_0 - Q_2) + \gamma_1 P_{1t} + \gamma_2 P_{2t} + \gamma_3 Y_t$$

endogenous variables: Q_{1t}, P_{1t}, P_{2t}; exogenous variables: Y_t, W_t.

The prices of the two goods are denoted P_1 and P_2 respectively, and Q_1 is the quantity traded of the first good. The third equation is written in this form to emphasise that Q_2 is constant, but the behaviour of buyers influences the price at which this quantity is traded. We could alternatively represent this by writing a demand equation for the second good as $Q_{2t}^d = \gamma_0 + \gamma_1 P_{1t} + \dots$, a supply equation as $Q_{2t}^s = \delta_0$(constant), and a market clearing condition $Q_{2t}^d = Q_{2t}^s$, but after substitution the net effect is the same. We now ask is each equation identified, or are there linear combinations of all three equations of identical form?

First, look at the supply equation. It will be identified if there is no linear combination of the other equations which excludes both P_2 and Y. To exclude P_2 we have to form a linear combination of the two demand equations with weights in inverse proportion to the coefficients of P_2, that is, γ_2 times the D_1 equation less α_2 times the D_2 equation will give us a linear combination that excludes P_2. What about Y? We can similarly exclude it with weights inversely proportional to the coefficients of Y, that is, γ_3 times the D_1 equation less α_3 times the D_2 equation yields an equation from which income has disappeared. But can we exclude both P_2 and Y at the same time? If we cannot do so we can say that the supply equation is identified. We cannot exclude both unless the weights we have established above turn out to be the same in both cases, so that excluding P_2 will automatically exclude Y and vice versa. This will happen if the weights are in the same proportion, that is, if $\gamma_2/\alpha_2 = \gamma_3/\alpha_3$. If this equation establishing proportionality among the required weights does not hold then it is impossible to establish a linear combination (which would also include S_1) that "looks like" the supply equation, which is thereby identified. Hence we have in practice established an identifiability condition in terms of some coefficients appearing in the other equations of the model, namely those of variables excluded from the equation whose identifiability is in question. Unless $\alpha_2\gamma_3 - \alpha_3\gamma_2 = 0$ the supply equation is identified. Such an absolute equality among unknown parameter values is extremely unlikely and the possibility would in practice be ignored. Nonetheless this condition must in principle be satisfied for the equation to be identified. An alternative expression of this identifiability condition is in terms of the determinant:

$$\begin{vmatrix} \alpha_2 & \alpha_3 \\ \gamma_2 & \gamma_3 \end{vmatrix} \neq 0.$$

What of the first equation? It excludes W so its specification cannot be matched by a linear combination which includes the supply equation, for this would introduce W. But any linear combination which has a zero weight for equation S_1 and is thus based only on D_1 and D_2 will exclude W, and will therefore be of the same form as D_1 (remember Q_2 is a constant). Hence D_1 is not identified.

Checking that the third equation is identified is left as an exercise for the reader.

Let us conjecture that a general rule is emerging. In the two-equation model we found that for an equation to be identified it must exclude at least one variable appearing in the model. In the three-equation example one exclusion is not enough, at least two variables must be excluded for identifiability. Indeed, there is a general rule — the *order condition* for identifiability:

> *In a model of G linear equations, to be identified an equation must exclude at least $G - 1$ of the variables appearing in the model.*

We typically distinguish between a *just-identified* equation, from which exactly $G - 1$ variables are excluded, and an *overidentified* equation, which excludes more than $G - 1$ variables. However, this is by no means the whole story. One might guess that the order condition is necessary but not sufficient, for in the above three-equation case the supply equation satisfied the order condition but we also required a particular two-by-two determinant to be non-zero. So we could satisfy the order condition (exclude $G - 1 = 2$ variables) yet have an unidentified equation through this determinant being equal to zero. This suggests that we can state a condition for identifiability that is both necessary and sufficient in terms of the appropriate determinant. This gives us the *rank condition*:

> *In a model of G linear equations, an equation is identified if and only if at least one non-zero $(G - 1) \times (G - 1)$ determinant is contained in the array of coefficients with which those variables excluded from the equation in question appear in the other equations.*

If the rank condition is satisfied the order condition is automatically satisfied but not vice versa, so the order condition is necessary but not sufficient. (Recall that the rank of a matrix is the order of the largest non-zero determinant that it contains.)

Our procedure in applying the rank condition to a system is, first, to inspect a particular equation and see what variables of the model, either endogenous or predetermined, are excluded from it. We then look at the coefficients of those excluded variables in the remaining equations. That array of coefficients will certainly have $G - 1$ rows because there are obviously that number of other equations in the system, and it will have as many columns as there are excluded variables. If there are fewer than $G - 1$ variables excluded, so that the order condition is not satisfied, then there clearly cannot be a $(G - 1) \times (G - 1)$ determinant in this array. If the order condition indicates just-identification then the array is $(G - 1) \times (G - 1)$, and we must examine its determinant. For our previous example the relevant array is

$$\begin{bmatrix} \alpha_2 & \alpha_3 \\ \gamma_2 & \gamma_3 \end{bmatrix}$$

which is 2×2 as the order condition is just satisfied. If the order condition indicates overidentification then the array has more than $G - 1$ columns and so contains more than one $(G - 1) \times (G - 1)$ determinant, and if any one of these is non-zero then the rank condition is satisfied.

As a final example, let us take one more step and construct a four-equation model. Note that we have been aligning variables in columns so that the system can be quickly written in matrix form, preserving our columns of coefficients with zeros in places where variables are excluded. We make Q_2 an endogenous variable, inserting a supply function for the second good.

$$
\begin{aligned}
D_1: \quad & Q_{1t} = \alpha_0 + \alpha_1 P_{1t} + \alpha_2 P_{2t} + \alpha_3 Y_t \\
S_1: \quad & Q_{1t} = \beta_0 + \beta_1 P_{1t} \qquad\qquad\qquad + \beta_4 W_t \\
D_2: \quad & Q_{2t} = \gamma_0 + \gamma_1 P_{1t} + \gamma_2 P_{2t} + \gamma_3 Y_t \\
S_2: \quad & Q_{2t} = \delta_0 \qquad\quad + \delta_2 P_{2t}
\end{aligned}
$$

endogenous variables: $Q_{1t}, Q_{2t}, P_{1t}, P_{2t}$; exogenous variables: Y_t, W_t.

We can write out the elements of the coefficient matrices $\mathbf{B}$ and $\boldsymbol{\Gamma}$ to simplify matters, ignoring the sign change that occurs when all terms are collected on the left-hand side. In the following table the column heading indicates the variable to which a coefficient is attached, the constant terms being regarded as the coefficients of a dummy exogenous variable which always takes the value 1.

	Q_1	Q_2	1	P_1	P_2	Y	W
D_1	1	0	α_0	α_1	α_2	α_3	0
S_1	1	0	β_0	β_1	0	0	β_4
D_2	0	1	γ_0	γ_1	γ_2	γ_3	0
S_2	0	1	δ_0	0	δ_2	0	0

Let us check out the order condition. We count the variables excluded from each equation by counting the zeros in each row, compare with $G - 1 = 3$, and note whether the equation satisfies the order condition.

Equation	No. of zeros	Order condition
D_1	2	not identified
S_1	3	just identified
D_2	2	not identified
S_2	4	over identified

The provisional conclusions are given above. Where the verdict is that an equation is not identified the provisional conclusion is also the final one. This is because, as we have said, fulfilment of the order condition is necessary for identification. It is impossible that we should find the first and third equations identified using the rank condition.

Applying the rank condition to the second equation we get the following array of coefficients of excluded variables (Q_2, P_2, Y):

$$\begin{bmatrix} 0 & \alpha_2 & \alpha_3 \\ 1 & \gamma_2 & \gamma_3 \\ 1 & \delta_2 & 0 \end{bmatrix}$$

Since the equation is just-identified by the order condition this array has only three columns, the minimum necessary for identification. Is the matrix of rank three — does it contain a 3×3 non-vanishing determinant? The determinant is equal to

$$\alpha_2\gamma_3 + \alpha_3(\delta_2 - \gamma_2).$$

Unless this is zero, and there is no reason to believe that it is, the equation is identified. If this determinant proved to be zero it would of course mean that there was a linear combination of these three equations which would exclude Q_2, P_2 and Y. We may in practice be able to sign elements in this expression on the basis of prior reasoning, but of course we will not know the actual numerical values. Nevertheless, it is extremely unlikely that this function of the five parameters would turn out to be zero, and so we proceed on the assumption that it is not and therefore the rank condition is satisfied.

The relevant array of coefficients for the fourth equation is

$$\begin{bmatrix} 1 & \alpha_1 & \alpha_3 & 0 \\ 1 & \beta_1 & 0 & \beta_4 \\ 0 & \gamma_1 & \gamma_3 & 0 \end{bmatrix}$$

Does this matrix have rank 3? We can get four 3×3 determinants, and so long as any one of them is non-zero, we have an identified equation. One of the 3×3 determinants is obtained by dropping the second column, and is $-\gamma_3\beta_4$. We have assumed *a priori* that neither of these coefficients is zero, and so the rank condition is satisfied. (Note that if $\beta_4 = 0$, so that W disappears from the model, there is still a non-zero determinant in the first three columns. In this case, this equation ceases to be over-identified and becomes just identified.)

In many situations the rank condition will in this way merely underline the order condition, for we usually simply assume that it is safe to proceed as if the relevant function of structural parameters is non-zero. But there are cases where it will throw up a different answer — there are examples of this in Exercises 4.1 and 4.2.

We have made no mention so far of the treatment of *identities* in the context of identifiability of parameter values, equations, and structures. Indeed our illustrative models have not contained identities. Clearly no question of identification arises for any identities that a model might contain. The numerical values of the coefficients of an identity are known from the beginning (typically 1 or −1), and so there is no need to ask whether they can be rediscovered from reduced form coefficient values. Although the order and rank conditions are quite irrelevant to an identity, the identities must of course be included when the identifiability of other equations of the model is being considered. An identity represents a relationship among variables, the existence of which must be acknowledged when it is being asked whether some relationship is the only one that is both data-admissible and model-admissible as a particular behavioural relation. An alternative way of handling identities, namely using them to substitute out particular variables and so to reduce the number of equations and variables, is discussed in the final section of this chapter.

4.4 AN EQUIVALENT ORDER CONDITION AND THE REDUCED FORM

Now we return to the general linear form

$$\sum_{i=1}^{G} \beta_{gi} y_{it} + \sum_{k=1}^{K} \gamma_{gk} x_{kt} = 0, \qquad g = 1, \ldots, G$$

continuing with the exact case, and with prior information expressed in terms of zero restrictions on the parameters. From considering this general case we can state the order condition for identification in a slightly more usable form. We can without loss of generality write the structural equation in which we are interested as the first equation of the system, and denote the variable on which the equation is normalized as y_1. In applying the order condition we have so far made no distinction between endogenous and predetermined variables. Let us now separate these out, and say that in this equation H endogenous variables appear, so that $G-H$ y's are excluded or have zero coefficients, and that J predetermined variables are included, so that $K-J$ x's are excluded. We may renumber the endogenous variables so that the included variables are the first ones $(y_1, \ldots, y_H)$ and the excluded ones are the remainder $(y_{H+1}, \ldots, y_G)$. Similarly the predetermined variables appearing in the structural equation are $x_1, \ldots, x_J$ and those numbered $J+1, \ldots, K$ are the excluded ones. The equation then appears as follows:

$$y_{1t} + \beta_{12}y_{2t} + \ldots + \beta_{1H}y_{Ht} + 0 + \ldots + 0$$

$$+ \gamma_{11}x_{1t} + \ldots + \gamma_{1J}x_{Jt} + 0 + \ldots + 0 = 0.$$

The first set of zeros corresponds to the $G-H$ omitted endogenous variables and the second to the $K-J$ omitted predetermined variables.

The order condition states that the number of excluded variables should be at least as great as the number of equations less one. Given that we now have a specific expression for the number of excluded variables we can write the condition as

$$(G-H) + (K-J) \geqslant G - 1.$$

The only reference to the size of the model in this inequality cancels out, and we can restate the order condition as

$$K-J \geqslant H - 1,$$

that is, the number of predetermined variables in the model excluded from this equation must be not less than the number of included endogenous variables, less one. Hence we can assess identifiability without actually going ahead and spelling out the remainder of the model — we do not need to know how many equations it contains to check this identifiability condition, for our criterion no longer contains G. In practice therefore all we need do to apply the order condition to a structural equation is simply to count up the number of endogenous variables appearing in it (H) and argue that there are a certain number $(K-J)$ of predetermined variables in the model but excluded from the equation, by considering what the variables themselves might be. We do not necessarily have to specify the complete system in order to assess whether an individual equation satisfies the order condition. Nor do we need to know how many predetermined variables the total system contains as long as we have located enough of them to satisfy $K-J \geqslant H-1$.

Now let us look at this from the point of view of estimating or identifying the parameter values of the structural equation from the *reduced form*. Equivalent order and rank conditions can be obtained in this framework. First we seek a convenient way of expressing the connections between the reduced form coefficients, assumed known, and the parameters of our structural equation. One way to do this is to use the fact that, since the reduced form is known from the data, and the structure equation satisfies the data, the latter must continue to hold on substituting for $y_1, \ldots, y_H$ from the reduced form equations. Moreover, it holds irrespective of the particular values of the predetermined variables. The relevant reduced form equations are the first H, that is, those relating to the included endogenous variables, namely

$$y_{1t} = \pi_{11}x_{1t} + \ldots + \pi_{1J}x_{Jt} + \pi_{1,J+1}x_{J+1,t} + \ldots + \pi_{1K}x_{Kt}$$

$$y_{2t} = \pi_{21}x_{1t} + \ldots + \pi_{2J}x_{Jt} + \pi_{2,J+1}x_{J+1,t} + \ldots + \pi_{2K}x_{Kt}$$

$$\vdots$$

$$y_{Ht} = \pi_{H1}x_{1t} + \ldots + \pi_{HJ}x_{Jt} + \pi_{H,J+1}x_{J+1,t} + \ldots + \pi_{HK}x_{Kt}$$

Of course these include all K predetermined variables. On substituting the right-hand sides for $y_{1t}, \ldots, y_{Ht}$ in the structural equation we obtain an expression involving H linear combinations of x's together with the original terms in $x_{1t}, \ldots, x_{Jt}$, which is equal to zero. This can only be true irrespective of the particular x-values if the coefficient of each separate predetermined variable is zero. Picking out from this expression coefficients of the individual predetermined variables one-by-one, then gives the following relations:

(coeff. of x_{1t}) $\qquad \pi_{11} + \beta_{12}\pi_{21} + \ldots + \beta_{1H}\pi_{H1} + \gamma_{11} = 0$

$$\vdots$$

(coeff. of x_{Jt}) $\qquad \pi_{1J} + \beta_{12}\pi_{2J} + \ldots + \beta_{1H}\pi_{HJ} + \gamma_{1J} = 0$

(coeff. of $x_{J+1,t}$) $\qquad \pi_{1,J+1} + \beta_{12}\pi_{2,J+1} + \ldots + \beta_{1H}\pi_{H,J+1} = 0$

$$\vdots$$

(coeff. of x_{Kt}) $\qquad \pi_{1K} + \beta_{12}\pi_{2K} + \ldots + \beta_{1H}\pi_{HK} = 0$

Alternatively, these relations between the π's, β's and γ's can be obtained directly from the general relation $\mathbf{B\Pi} + \mathbf{\Gamma} = \mathbf{0}$: they are the elements of the first row of this $G \times K$ matrix equation. The first row of $\mathbf{B}$ is $(1, \beta_{12}, \ldots, \beta_{1H}, 0, \ldots, 0)$, and these K relations are obtained by multiplying this into the columns of Π, adding the first row of Γ, which is $(\gamma_{11}, \gamma_{12}, \ldots, \gamma_{1J}, 0, \ldots, 0)$, and equating to the first row of the zero matrix. Note that in the example discussed on pp. 84–85 we have $G = 2$ and $K = 3$, and the rearranged equations numbered (1) to (6) are the six elements of the matrix equation $\mathbf{B\Pi} + \mathbf{\Gamma} = \mathbf{0}$, the odd-numbered ones being the first row and the even-numbered ones the second.

Now the question is, given numerical values of the π's, can these equations be solved for the β- and γ-values? There is no difficulty in solving the first J equations for the γ's provided that the β's are known, for these equations give $\gamma_{11}, \ldots, \gamma_{1J}$ in terms of β's and π's. But can we solve for the β-values? That question is resolved by the second block of $K-J$ equations. The number of equations is $K-J$ and the number of unknown β's is $H-1$, and immediately we have a reappearance of the order condition. A solution for the β's is only possible if the number of equations $(K-J)$ is at least as great as the number of unknowns $(H-1)$, that is $K-J \geqslant H-1$, and this is a necessary condition. It is not sufficient because, if it is just satisfied $(K-J = H-1)$

but the determinant of the coefficients of the unknown β's is zero, then we have a singular set of equations which cannot be solved. So we have an equivalent rank condition, that the rank of the matrix of coefficients in the $K-J$ equations for the $H-1$ unknown β's be $H-1$. That is, we require the rank of the $(K-J) \times (H-1)$ matrix

$$\begin{bmatrix} \pi_{2,J+1} \cdots \pi_{H,J+1} \\ \cdot \qquad \cdot \\ \cdot \qquad \cdot \\ \cdot \qquad \cdot \\ \pi_{2K} \quad \cdots \pi_{HK} \end{bmatrix}$$

to be $H-1$. This is again the necessary and sufficient condition – the rank of the matrix cannot be $H-1$ unless it also has at least $H-1$ rows, so the order condition is automatically satisfied whenever the rank condition is satisfied. When this is the case the second block of equations is solved for the values of $\beta_{12}, \ldots, \beta_{1H}$, and the values of $\gamma_{11}, \ldots, \gamma_{1J}$ immediately follow from the first block of equations.

So we have derived precisely equivalent identifiability conditions. And with the order condition written as $K-J \geqslant H-1$ we have reinterpreted the right-hand side as the number of unknown β-coefficients in the equation. In practice the new rank condition is much more difficult to implement because it is first necessary to obtain the reduced form. The rank condition as formulated earlier (p. 90) does not require this exercise – we need only to look at particular matrices of structural parameters to assess identifiability, which is somewhat easier. (For a demonstration of the equivalence of the two rank conditions see, for example, J. Johnston, *Econometric Methods,* 1st ed., pp. 251–2.)

4.5 IDENTIFICATION BY HOMOGENEOUS LINEAR RESTRICTIONS ON PARAMETERS

Up to this point we have considered identification obtained by excluding variables from an equation, that is, by assigning the value zero to particular parameters in the system. Though zero restrictions are common ways of incorporating theoretical information, they are merely special cases of homogenous linear restrictions, and the order condition is easily extended to cover this more general restriction. For the structural equation

$$\sum_{i=1}^{G} \beta_{gi} y_{it} + \sum_{k=1}^{K} \gamma_{gk} x_{kt} = u_{gt}$$

the general homogenous linear restriction on its parameters is

$$\sum_{i=1}^{G} \lambda_i \beta_{gi} + \sum_{k=1}^{K} \theta_k \gamma_{gk} = 0$$

where the λ's and θ's are specified *a priori*. Thus $\beta_{g2} = 0$, excluding y_2 from the gth equation, is the simplest example. If we specify that y_2 and y_3 appear with the same coefficient in the first equation, we have the restriction $\beta_{12} - \beta_{13} = 0$. Similarly, if y_1 and x_2 appear with equal and opposite coefficients in the second equation we have $\beta_{21} + \gamma_{22} = 0$ (recall the example presented on p. 23). Note that if three variables, say x_1, x_2, and x_3, are all to appear with the same coefficient in the first equation, we have two restrictions, say $\gamma_{11} - \gamma_{12} = 0$ and $\gamma_{11} - \gamma_{13} = 0$: the third restriction $\gamma_{12} - \gamma_{13} = 0$ is not required, it is not independent of the other two, being implied by them.

The order condition for identifiability can be extended as follows:

> *In a G-equation linear model a necessary condition for the identification of a single equation is that there are at least $G - 1$ independent homogeneous linear restrictions on the parameters of the equation.*

This order condition is slightly more general, for it contains the previous one as the special case in which the restrictions considered are all zero restrictions. Although a homogeneous linear restriction equates a linear combination of parameters to zero, and so apparently does not allow such a combination to be equated to a non-zero value, this can allow such a combination to be equated to a non-zero value, this can be overcome by using the coefficient on which the equation is normalised. For example, if we wish to specify that the coefficients of y_2 and y_3 in the first equation sum to one then we write $\beta_{11} - \beta_{12} - \beta_{13} = 0$, a homogeneous linear restriction, which together with the normalisation $\beta_{11} = 1$ achieves the desired result.

The new order condition is frequently required when *identities* have been substituted into an equation system, for eliminating particular variables typically introduces homogeneous linear restrictions into the other equations. In the example of section 2.2, the assumption that supply depends on the price before tax could have been incorporated by defining a separate pre-tax price, P°, and writing the model as

$$Q = \alpha_0 + \alpha_1 P$$

$$Q = \beta_0 + \beta_1 P^{\circ}$$

$$P^{\circ} = P - E$$

endogenous variables: Q, P, P°; exogenous variable: E.

In this formulation each behavioural equation excludes two variables of the model, and so satisfies the original order condition, and the identity raises no question of identifiability. The previous formulation can then be obtained by substituting for P° from the identity, reducing the number of equations and variables by one:

$$Q = \alpha_0 + \alpha_1 P$$

$$Q = \beta_0 + \beta_1 (P-E)$$

endogenous variables: Q, P; exogenous variable: E.

The first equation excludes one variable and the second has one homogeneous linear restriction (that the coefficients of P and E sum to zero) so on applying the new order condition the conclusion about identifiability is unaltered.

In general such substitutions do not change the identifiability of a model, for the information content is not changed, but merely presented in a different way. The reduced form can be viewed as a representation in which, by substitution, all endogenous variables but one have been removed from a particular equation, and then the substitution of an identity is but one step in this direction, which in no way changes the reduced form. This step is clearly reversible, since the identity is fully specified, and so whether the structural parameters can be evaluated given the reduced form coefficients is not affected by the substitution.

The *rank condition* can also be extended to the case of homogeneous linear restrictions. As before, we seek a non-zero $(G-1) \times (G-1)$ determinant in an array of coefficients which has $G-1$ rows and as many columns as there are restrictions on the equation in question. Previously the elements in a particular column were given as the coefficients in the other equations of the variable that a particular restriction had excluded from the equation in question. Now we obtain these elements by applying the homogeneous linear restriction to the other equations. For example, if the first equation's identifiability is under consideration, and it is specified that y_2 and y_3 appear with the same coefficient, that is, $\beta_{12} - \beta_{13} = 0$, then we form the corresponding column of the array by writing down the difference between the coefficients of y_2 and y_3 in the other equations, that is, $\beta_{22} - \beta_{23}$, $\beta_{32} - \beta_{33}, \ldots, \beta_{G2} - \beta_{G3}$. In effect, we need to check whether other equations satisfy the same restriction: if so, it is likely that the equation in question cannot be distinguished from them, and so is not identified. In general we form the array by applying the left-hand side of each homoegeneous linear restriction to the other equations, and of course this statement covers the previous case of exclusion restrictions: if x_2 is excluded from the first equation, so that the restriction is $\gamma_{12} = 0$, then the elements of the corresponding column of the array are γ_{22}, $\gamma_{32}, \ldots, \gamma_{G2}$. Then the question of whether the array contains a non-zero $(G-1) \times (G-1)$ determinant is tackled as before, and the previous discussion (p. 93) remains relevant. In the above two-equation example, there is one restriction on the second equation, namely that the coefficients of P and E sum to zero, and the rank condition is satisfied if the same restriction applied to the first equation gives a non-zero quantity: since E is excluded from the first equation, the rank condition for identification of the second equation is simply $\alpha_1 \neq 0$.

EXERCISES

4.1 Consider the identification of each equation in the following model:

$$P_t + \beta_{12}W_t \qquad\quad + \gamma_{11}Q_t \qquad\qquad + \gamma_{13}P_{t-1} \qquad\qquad = u_{1t}$$
$$\beta_{21}P_t \quad + W_t + \beta_{23}N_t \qquad\quad + \gamma_{22}S_t \qquad\qquad + \gamma_{24}W_{t-1} = u_{2t}$$
$$\beta_{32}W_t + N_t \qquad\qquad\quad + \gamma_{32}S_t + \gamma_{33}P_{t-1} + \gamma_{34}W_{t-1} = u_{3t}$$

where P_t, W_t and N_t are indices for prices, money wages and trade union membership (endogenous) and Q_t and S_t are indices for productivity and strikes (exogenous).

How are the rank and order conditions affected if it is known *a priori* that

(i) $\gamma_{11} = 0$

(ii) $\beta_{21} = \gamma_{22} = 0$

(iii) $\gamma_{33} = 0$?

Set up the 3×4 matrix relation $\mathbf{B\Pi} + \mathbf{\Gamma} = \mathbf{0}$, choose a just-identified equation, and verify that the relevant row of the matrix relation yields unique values of the β's and γ's given the π's.

4.2 (a) Investigate the identifiability of the equations of the following model of two interrelated markets.

(1) demand for first good:
$$Q_1 + \beta_{11}P_1 + \beta_{13}P_3 + \gamma_{10} + \gamma_{11}Y = u_1$$

(2) supply of first good:
$$Q_1 + \beta_{21}P_1 + \gamma_{20} = u_2$$

(3) demand for second good:
$$Q_2 + \beta_{31}P_1 + \beta_{33}P_3 + \gamma_{30} + \gamma_{31}Y + \gamma_{32}W = u_3$$

(4) supply of second good:

$$Q_2 + \beta_{42}P_2 + \gamma_{40} + \gamma_{42}W = u_4$$

(5) excise tax:

$$P_2 - P_3 + E = 0$$

endogenous variables: Q_1, Q_2, P_1, P_2, P_3;

exogenous variables: Y, W, E.

P_2 is the price of the second good before tax, P_3 the price of the second good after tax.

(b) Consider the following model, equivalent to that given above.

(1) $Q_1 \quad + \beta_{11}P_1 + \beta_{13}P_2 + \gamma_{10} + \gamma_{11}Y \qquad + \beta_{13}E = u_1$

(2) $Q_1 \quad + \beta_{21}P_1 \qquad + \gamma_{20} \qquad = u_2$

(3) $\quad Q_2 + \beta_{31}P_1 + \beta_{33}P_2 + \gamma_{30} + \gamma_{31}Y + \gamma_{32}W + \beta_{33}E = u_3$

(4) $\quad Q_2 \qquad + \beta_{42}P_2 + \gamma_{40} \qquad + \gamma_{42}W \qquad = u_4$

Evaluate any similarities or differences between the identifiability of the parameters of this model and that of part (a).

4.3 (a) Assess the identification of the parameters of the following model:

$$C_t = \alpha_0 + \alpha_1 Y_t + \alpha_2 Y_{t-1} + u_{1t}$$

$$I_t = \beta_0 + \beta_1 Y_t + \beta_2 Y_{t-1} + \beta_3 I_{t-1} + u_{2t}$$

$$Y_t = C_t + I_t + G_t$$

endogenous variables: C_t, I_t, Y_t;

exogenous variable: G_t.

(b) How are your conclusions altered if

the variable G_t has the constant value $\bar{G}$ throughout the sample period, or

the variable G_t is determined by the feedback control rule

$$G_t = \gamma_0 + \gamma_1 Y_{t-1} + \gamma_2 I_{t-1}?$$

(c) What is the effect of the assumption $\beta_2 = -\beta_1$?

V

THE SIMPLE TWO VARIABLE REGRESSION MODEL

In the preceding three chapters we have considered the specification and identification of linear econometric models. In the remaining chapters we consider ways of estimating the parameters of such models and testing various hypotheses about them. The appropriate method of estimation and the properties of the estimators vary according to a number of features of the model being considered:

(i) They depend on whether we are attempting to estimate reduced form or structural equations.

(ii) They depend on whether the predetermined variables in a given equation are all exogenous (the easier case) or include lagged endogenous variables.

(iii) They depend on the assumptions that we make about the error terms in the model, for example, can we assume that successive values of a given error term over time are independent?

We first consider estimation of the parameters of a single reduced form equation. We examine which method of estimation is appropriate under varying circumstances at (ii) and (iii) and consider ways of extending the techniques to cope with various extensions to the basic model. We also consider ways of examining the validity of the assumptions that we make under (iii). In the final chapter we consider ways of estimating structural equations.

5.1 ESTIMATION OF A REDUCED FORM EQUATION

In this chapter we consider a simple relationship involving just two observable variables:

$$Y_t = \alpha + \beta X_t + u_t, \qquad t = 1, \ldots, n$$

where Y_t denotes the tth observation on the dependent variable, X_t the tth observation on the explanatory variable, u_t the corresponding tth value of the disturbance term, and α, β are parameters whose values are unknown and to be estimated. We suppose that X_t is a predetermined variable, so that we are dealing with a reduced form equation. The relationship is not an exact one, but contains an error (or disturbance) term, u_t. The straight line $Y = \alpha + \beta X$ does not tell us the exact value of Y that would result from a given value of X, but rather the value of Y that we should expect *on average*. Economic relationships (other than accounting identities) are not exact and u_t plays an important role in econometrics. We may think of three main reasons for including an error term in our equation:

(i) Other factors:

Most economic behaviour is of a fairly complex nature and involves numerous factors. We cannot expect X to give the full picture. However many of these factors have only very slight effects and we would not wish to include them explicitly in our model. Instead we regard their net effect as the disturbance u_t. (We will see later that there may be serious consequences to omitting specific important factors).

(ii) Human nature:

People are not totally predictable in their behaviour. There is an element of unpredictability in all human behaviour. We might interpret our model as combining a systematic or deterministic component $(\alpha + \beta X_t)$ with a random component (u_t) that represents the unpredictable element in the relationship.

(iii) Errors of measurement:

It may be that a variable Z is exactly related to X:

$$Z = \alpha + \beta X$$

but we observe $Y = Z + u$, where u denotes the measurement error. Thus

$$Y = \alpha + \beta X + u.$$

However this justification is less satisfactory since (as we shall see in section 5.8) similar measurement error in X can cause considerable problems. These three reasons may of course combine.

A given sample of observations $Y_1, \ldots, Y_n$ may then be thought of as being generated by taking a random drawing from the probability distribution of each error term and superimposing them on the line $\alpha + \beta X$ (the systematic component), as illustrated in Figure 5.1. Hence a *full* specification of the relationship requires a set of assumptions about the probability distributions of u_t, $t = 1, \ldots, n$. What these assumptions are crucially affects what estimation method we choose and what conclusions we can draw from the results.

We now look at an intuitively appealing method of estimation known as *Ordinary Least Squares* (OLS), and then consider the properties of the OLS estimates under various assumptions. The parameters to be estimated are α and β. We denote their estimates by $\hat{\alpha}$ and $\hat{\beta}$ respectively, then the line $\hat{Y} = \hat{\alpha} + \hat{\beta} X$ is called the *regression* of Y on X, where $\hat{Y}$ denotes a fitted value of Y, calculated from the equation of

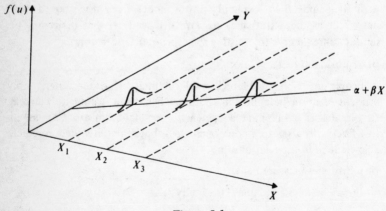

Figure 5.1

the line. In particular, the estimated values of the dependent variable corresponding to the observed values of the explanatory variable or *regressor* are

$$\hat{Y}_t = \hat{\alpha} + \hat{\beta} X_t, \qquad t = 1, \ldots, n.$$

The discrepancies between the observed and estimated values of the dependent variable are the regression *residuals*, denoted e_t, thus

$$e_t = Y_t - \hat{Y}_t, \qquad t = 1, \ldots, n.$$

These can be thought of as the observable counterpart to the unobservable disturbances, u_t. The residuals and the fitted line are illustrated in Figure 5.2.

The *least squares* method of estimation consists of choosing, for a given set of data, those estimates $\hat{\alpha}$, $\hat{\beta}$ which minimise the sum of squared residuals:

$$S = \sum_{t=1}^{n} e_t^{\,2} = \sum_{t=1}^{n} (Y_t - \hat{\alpha} - \hat{\beta} X_t)^2.$$

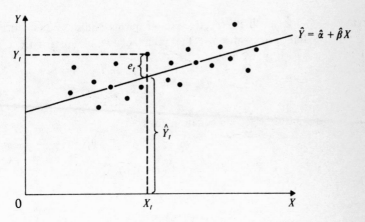

Figure 5.2

To minimise S with respect to $\hat{\alpha}$ and $\hat{\beta}$ we set the first partial derivatives with respect to $\hat{\alpha}$ and $\hat{\beta}$ equal to zero:

$$\frac{\partial S}{\partial \hat{\alpha}} = \sum_{t=1}^{n} 2(Y_t - \hat{\alpha} - \hat{\beta}X_t)(-1) = 0,$$

$$\frac{\partial S}{\partial \hat{\beta}} = \sum_{t=1}^{n} 2(Y_t - \hat{\alpha} - \hat{\beta}X_t)(-X_t) = 0.$$

Rearranging gives what are known as the *least squares normal equations*:

$$\sum_{t=1}^{n} Y_t = n\hat{\alpha} + \hat{\beta} \sum_{t=1}^{n} X_t,$$

$$\sum_{t=1}^{n} Y_t X_t = \hat{\alpha} \sum_{t=1}^{n} X_t + \hat{\beta} \sum_{t=1}^{n} X_t^2.$$

We now solve these equations for $\hat{\alpha}$ and $\hat{\beta}$. Dividing the first by n gives

$$\bar{Y} = \hat{\alpha} + \hat{\beta}\bar{X},$$

where $\bar{Y}$ and $\bar{X}$ are the respective sample means, and so we see that the regression line passes through the point of sample means $(\bar{X}, \bar{Y})$. Rearranging slightly, we have

$$\hat{\alpha} = \bar{Y} - \hat{\beta}\bar{X}.$$

Substitution into the second equation gives

$$\sum_{t=1}^{n} Y_t X_t = \hat{\beta} \sum_{t=1}^{n} X_t^2 + (\bar{Y} - \hat{\beta}\bar{X}) \sum_{t=1}^{n} X_t$$

$$= \hat{\beta} \sum_{t=1}^{n} X_t^2 + n\bar{Y}\bar{X} - n\hat{\beta}\bar{X}^2,$$

and on solving for $\hat{\beta}$ we obtain

$$\hat{\beta} = \frac{\sum\limits_{t=1}^{n} Y_t X_t - n\bar{Y}\,\bar{X}}{\sum\limits_{t=1}^{n} X_t^2 - n\bar{X}^2} = \frac{\sum\limits_{t=1}^{n} (Y_t - \bar{Y})(X_t - \bar{X})}{\sum\limits_{t=1}^{n} (X_t - \bar{X})^2}.$$

Having found $\hat{\beta}$ we can then calculate $\hat{\alpha}$ from

$$\hat{\alpha} = \bar{Y} - \hat{\beta}\bar{X}.$$

(The checking of the second-order conditions for a minimum is left as an exercise for the reader.)

Sums of squares and cross-products around sample means occur fairly often in what follows, and an abbreviated notation is sometimes convenient. We introduce new notation for the sample variances and covariances, denoting them by the letter m with two subscripts. Thus

$$m_{YX} = \frac{1}{n} \sum_{t=1}^{n} (Y_t - \bar{Y})(X_t - \bar{X}), \qquad m_{XX} = \frac{1}{n} \sum_{t=1}^{n} (X_t - \bar{X})^2,$$

and hence

$$\hat{\beta} = \frac{n.m_{YX}}{n.m_{XX}} = \frac{m_{YX}}{m_{XX}}.$$

Note that in calculating a quantity such as m_{YX} only one of the variables needs to be in terms of differences from the mean and not both, that is

$$m_{YX} = \frac{1}{n} \sum_{t=1}^{n} (Y_t - \bar{Y})(X_t - \bar{X})$$

$$= \frac{1}{n} \sum_{t=1}^{n} Y_t(X_t - \bar{X}) - \frac{1}{n}\bar{Y}\sum_{t=1}^{n}(X_t - \bar{X})$$

$$= \frac{1}{n} \sum_{t=1}^{n} Y_t(X_t - \bar{X}),$$

since $\bar{Y}$ is constant as t varies and so can be brought outside the summation, and $(X_t - \bar{X})$ sums to zero by definition of the sample mean $\bar{X}$.

Some further implications of the least squares estimates can be obtained by re-examining the first-order conditions and normal equations. The first gives

$$\sum_{t=1}^{n} (Y_t - \hat{\alpha} - \hat{\beta}X_t) = 0,$$

that is,

$$\sum_{t=1}^{n} e_t = 0,$$

so the residuals sum to zero and have a sample mean, $\bar{e}$, equal to zero. Since $Y_t = \hat{Y}_t + e_t$, it follows that the means of the observed and fitted values of Y are equal:

$$\bar{Y} = \bar{\hat{Y}}.$$

The second of the two first-order conditions gives

$$\sum_{t=1}^{n} (Y_t - \hat{\alpha} - \hat{\beta}X_t)X_t = 0,$$

that is,

$$\sum_{t=1}^{n} e_t X_t = 0,$$

which implies that the covariance between the residuals and the explanatory variable is zero:

$$m_{eX} = \frac{1}{n} \sum_{t=1}^{n} (e_t - \bar{e})(X_t - \bar{X}) = \frac{1}{n} \sum_{t=1}^{n} e_t (X_t - \bar{X})$$

$$= \frac{1}{n} \sum_{t=1}^{n} e_t X_t = 0.$$

Since the deviation of the fitted value from its mean is given as

$$\hat{Y}_t - \bar{Y} = \hat{\alpha} + \hat{\beta}X_t - (\hat{\alpha} + \hat{\beta}\bar{X}) = \hat{\beta}(X_t - \bar{X}), \qquad t = 1, \dots, n,$$

it follows that the covariance between the residuals and the fitted values also is zero:

$$\frac{1}{n} \sum_{t=1}^{n} (e_t - \bar{e})(\hat{Y}_t - \bar{Y}) = \frac{1}{n} \hat{\beta} \sum_{t=1}^{n} (e_t - \bar{e})(X_t - \bar{X}) = 0.$$

Thus OLS estimation splits the dependent variable Y into two components, namely an estimate $\hat{Y} = \hat{\alpha} + \hat{\beta}X$ of the systematic part of Y, and a remainder or residual e, and these two components are uncorrelated.

5.2 PROPERTIES OF LEAST SQUARES ESTIMATES

We have not yet made any assumptions about u_t, and indeed none are needed to obtain the OLS estimates. However the properties of the estimates vary according to the assumptions made. We start by examining a set of assumptions which provide the most desirable properties. They are known as

The Classical Assumptions:

(A1) $E(u_t) = 0$ for all t.

The disturbance term represents the non-systematic part of our equation, but if it has a non-zero mean, this will not be so. In practice, least squares residuals have a sample mean of zero, as we have seen, and any constant effects are automatically ascribed to the intercept term in the regression equation.

(A2) $\text{var}(u_t) = E(u_t^2) = \sigma_u^2$, constant, for all t.

Thus each pair of observations is assumed to be equally reliable. If $\text{var}(u_1) < \text{var}(u_2)$ then the likelihood is that (X_1, Y_1) lies nearer to the line $Y = \alpha + \beta X$ than does (X_2, Y_2), in which case we would want to put more emphasis on (X_1, Y_1) in the estimation procedure. If the constant-variance assumption is satisfied the disturbances are said to be *homoscedastic*, if not, they are said to be *heteroscedastic*.

(A3) $\text{cov}(u_t, u_s) = E(u_t u_s) = 0$ for all t, s with $t \neq s$.

With time series data, this is the assumption that the errors are not *autocorrelated*, using the term introduced in chapter 3, or in general that they correspond to a *random sample*, in the terminology of statistics. This assumption is often not realistic with time series data, and we examine the properties of estimates both with and without it. The term *serial correlation* is often used as an alternative for *autocorrelation*.

(A4) X is *non-stochastic*, that is, contains no random part. This implies that

$$E(u_t X_s) = X_s E(u_t) = 0 \quad \text{for all } t, s.$$

On the other hand endogenous variables, current or lagged, are *stochastic*, being partly determined by the random disturbances in the model. Thus, in the present context of reduced form estimation, this assumption rules out lagged endogenous variables as regressors, and we must examine its impact.

(A5)   The regressor exhibits variation, that is, the values $X_t, t = 1, \ldots, n$ are not all the same. Our model is designed to explain the changes in Y that result from changes in X, but if no changes in X are observed then this effect clearly cannot be evaluated.

We now examine the statistical properties of the OLS estimates in various circumstances, focussing on the regression coefficient $\hat{\beta}$. This is calculated as

$$\hat{\beta} = \frac{\sum_{t=1}^{n} (X_t - \bar{X})(Y_t - \bar{Y})}{\sum_{t=1}^{n} (X_t - \bar{X})^2}$$

or, since it is not necessary to express both X and Y in mean deviation form in the numerator (p. 109), as

$$\hat{\beta} = \frac{\Sigma(X_t - \bar{X})Y_t}{\Sigma(X_t - \bar{X})^2}.$$

We consider the implications for this calculation of the various assumptions about u and X by substituting for Y_t from the regression model

$$Y_t = \alpha + \beta X_t + u_t, \qquad t = 1, \ldots, n,$$

and so obtain

$$\hat{\beta} = \frac{\Sigma(X_t - \bar{X})(\alpha + \beta X_t + u_t)}{\Sigma(X_t - \bar{X})^2}.$$

Separating out the terms involving α and β in the numerator, we first have $\Sigma(X_t - \bar{X})\alpha = \alpha\Sigma(X_t - \bar{X}) = 0$ by definition of the sample mean $\bar{X}$, and then $\Sigma(X_t - \bar{X})\beta X_t = \beta\Sigma(X_t - \bar{X})^2$, giving

$$\hat{\beta} = \beta + \frac{\Sigma(X_t - \bar{X})u_t}{\Sigma(X_t - \bar{X})^2}.$$

For ease of manipulation we define

$$W_t = \frac{X_t - \bar{X}}{\sum_{t=1}^{n}(X_t - \bar{X})^2}, \qquad t = 1, \ldots, n$$

and note for future reference that

$$\sum_{t=1}^{n} W_t = 0, \qquad \sum_{t=1}^{n} W_t^2 = \sum_{t=1}^{n}\left(\frac{X_t - \bar{X}}{\Sigma(X_t - \bar{X})^2}\right)^2 = \frac{1}{\Sigma(X_t - \bar{X})^2}.$$

Then the regression coefficient can be expressed as

$$\hat{\beta} = \beta + \sum_{t=1}^{n} W_t u_t.$$

This is a theoretical exercise, for although we calculate the numerical value of $\hat{\beta}$ from data, on the right-hand side β is, of course, unknown and u_t, $t = 1, \ldots, n$ are unobserved. Nevertheless this expression helps us to study the properties of $\hat{\beta}$ as an estimate of β. Clearly $\hat{\beta}$ will not equal β in general, and the discrepancy

$$\hat{\beta} - \beta = \sum_{t=1}^{n} W_t u_t,$$

known as the *sampling error* of $\hat{\beta}$, depends on the random disturbances. Thus $\hat{\beta}$ is itself a random variable. We can imagine fixing the values $X_1, \ldots, X_n$, observing the Y's corresponding to a particular sample $u_1, \ldots, u_n$ and calculating $\hat{\beta}$, then repeating this for a number of different samples of the u's: the resulting distribution of $\hat{\beta}$-values is called the *sampling distribution* of $\hat{\beta}$.

Unbiasedness

We first consider whether the sampling errors average out to zero, that is, whether the expected value of $\hat{\beta}$ in this sampling distribution is equal to β, $E(\hat{\beta}) = \beta$, so that $\hat{\beta}$ is an *unbiased* estimate of β. We have

$$E(\hat{\beta}) = \beta + E\left(\sum_{t=1}^{n} W_t u_t \right)$$

$$= \beta + \sum_{t=1}^{n} E(W_t u_t),$$

and various possibilities exist. First, if X is non-stochastic, so that W is non-stochastic too, then

$$E(W_t u_t) = W_t E(u_t) = 0$$

by our first assumption, and $\hat{\beta}$ is unbiased. Secondly, if X is stochastic but exogenous, and so independent of u, then an extra step is needed:

$$E(W_t u_t) = E(W_t) E(u_t) = 0,$$

but again $E(\hat{\beta}) = \beta$. Finally, however, if X is a lagged endogenous variable, say $X_t = Y_{t-1}$, then X_t may be independent of current and future disturbances, but not of u_{t-1}, and since W_t depends on all X's, the above factorization does not go through:

$$E(W_t u_t) = E\left(\frac{X_t - \bar{X}}{\Sigma(X_t - \bar{X})^2} \, u_t\right) \neq E(W_t)\,E(u_t).$$

Hence in this case $E(\hat{\beta}) \neq \beta$. Notice that in all these cases assumptions A2 and A3 have played no role. We can summarise as follows:

Is $\hat{\beta}$ an unbiased estimate of β?

X_t ╲ u_t	serially independent	autocorrelated
exogenous	Yes	Yes
lagged endogenous	No	No

Note that $\hat{\beta}$ is also biased if X is a current endogenous variable, that is, if the equation is structural rather than reduced form. This will be considered in chapter 10.

The variance of $\hat{\beta}$

An unbiased estimator which has a large variance around the true parameter value will be of less use than one which has a small variance, since in a given sample of data the one with the smaller variance would be more likely to be near the true parameter value. The variance of $\hat{\beta}$ is given by

$$\text{var}\,(\hat{\beta}) = E\{\hat{\beta} - E(\hat{\beta})\}^2$$
$$= E(\hat{\beta} - \beta)^2$$

if $\hat{\beta}$ is unbiased. Substituting for $\hat{\beta} - \beta$ we have

$$\text{var}(\hat{\beta}) = E\left(\sum_{t=1}^{n} W_t u_t\right)^2.$$

Squaring this summation gives squared terms of the form $(W_t u_t)^2$, and cross-product terms $(W_t u_t)(W_s u_s)$, $t \neq s$. In total we have

$$\text{var}(\hat{\beta}) = \sum_{t=1}^{n} E(W_t u_t)^2 + \sum\sum_{t \neq s} E(W_t W_s u_t u_s)$$

$$= \sum_{t=1}^{n} W_t^2 E(u_t^2) + \sum\sum_{t \neq s} W_t W_s E(u_t u_s)$$

if X and hence W is non-stochastic. If assumption A3 (non-autocorrelated errors) holds, then $E(u_t u_s) = 0$ for $t \neq s$, and if assumption A2 (homoscedasticity) holds, then $E(u_t^2) = \sigma_u^2$ for all t, whereupon

$$\text{var}(\hat{\beta}) = \sigma_u^2 \sum_{t=1}^{n} W_t^2 = \frac{\sigma_u^2}{\sum_{t=1}^{n} (X_t - \bar{X})^2}.$$

Notice firstly that the larger is σ_u^2 the larger is var $(\hat{\beta})$, that is, the more variation there is around the regression line, the more variable will be our estimate of its slope. Notice also that as the sample size n increases, the number of terms in the denominator, which are all positive, increases and hence var $(\hat{\beta})$ decreases, confirming the usual intuition that a larger sample results in more accurate estimates, other things being equal.

It can be shown that this variance is the smallest that can be attained by any linear unbiased estimator under these assumptions. For this reason, the OLS estimator is often called the *best linear unbiased estimator* (BLUE). If either assumption A2 or A3 does not hold, the above derivation breaks down. And if X is a lagged endogenous variable then $\hat{\beta}$ is not unbiased, as we have seen. To summarise:

$$Does \; var \, (\hat{\beta}) = \frac{\sigma_u{}^2}{\Sigma (X_t - \bar{X})^2} \; and \; is \; the \; OLS \; \hat{\beta} \; the \; BLUE?$$

X_t \ u_t	serially independent	autocorrelated
exogenous	Yes	No
lagged endogenous	No	No

Consistency

What can we do if we cannot obtain an unbiased estimator? We now look at an asymptotic property, that is a property that holds in the limiting case as the sample size, n, tends to infinity. If we cannot obtain finite sample results, then the limiting case is the best we can do. This is the situation for example when X is a lagged endogenous variable.

The asymptotic property we consider here is that of consistency. $\hat{\beta}$ is a *consistent* estimator of β if, as $n \to \infty$, the sampling distribution of $\hat{\beta}$ concentrates around the true value, β (and tends towards a degenerate distribution at β). In that case we say that the *probability limit* of $\hat{\beta}$ is β and write

$$\plim_{n \to \infty} \hat{\beta} = \beta.$$

A sufficient condition for consistency is that the bias and variance both tend to zero, that is,

$$\lim_{n \to \infty} E(\hat{\beta}) = \beta \quad and \quad \lim_{n \to \infty} var \, (\hat{\beta}) = 0.$$

This is illustrated in Figure 5.3, where the sampling distributions of $\hat{\beta}$ for different sample sizes are sketched, these distributions becoming more concentrated around the true value β at larger sample sizes.

In the simplest case (X exogenous and the u's serially independent) $\hat{\beta}$ is consistent since $E(\hat{\beta}) = \beta$ for all n, and

$$\text{var}\,(\hat{\beta}) = \frac{\sigma_u{}^2}{\displaystyle\sum_{t=1}^{n} (X_t - \bar{X})^2} \to 0 \qquad \text{as} \qquad n \to \infty,$$

the denominator increasing without limit as the number of terms, n, goes to infinity.

Probability limits have certain useful properties, not satisfied by the algebra of expectations, which enable us to prove consistency in certain situations where unbiasedness does not hold. In particular, if θ is some continuous function, and Q a random variable, then $\text{plim}\,\{\theta(Q)\} = \theta\,\{\text{plim}\,(Q)\}$. More generally, the probability limit of a function of several random variables is equal to the function evaluated at the probability limits of the random variables. Two specific applications of this result that are useful to us are

(i) $\text{plim}\,(Q_1 Q_2) = (\text{plim}\,Q_1)(\text{plim}\,Q_2)$

(ii) $\text{plim}\,(Q_1/Q_2) = \text{plim}\,Q_1/\text{plim}\,Q_2,$

where Q_1 and Q_2 are random variables.

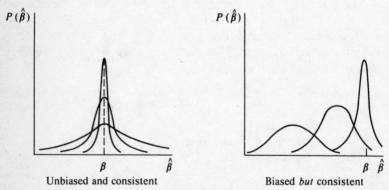

Figure 5.3

This last result allows us to say something about the lagged endogenous variable case, where we are not able to prove unbiasedness. We have

$$\hat{\beta} = \beta + \frac{\Sigma(X_t - \bar{X})u_t}{\Sigma(X_t - \bar{X})^2},$$

and taking probability limits gives

$$\text{plim}\,\hat{\beta} = \beta + \text{plim}\,\frac{\dfrac{1}{n}\Sigma(X_t - \bar{X})u_t}{\dfrac{1}{n}\Sigma(X_t - \bar{X})^2}$$

$$= \beta + \frac{\text{plim}\,\dfrac{1}{n}\Sigma(X_t - \bar{X})u_t}{\text{plim}\,\dfrac{1}{n}\Sigma(X_t - \bar{X})^2},$$

using (ii) above. We divide numerator and denominator by n to convert them to sample moments so that, in particular, the denominator has a finite probability limit, equal to the variance of X. The key element in then going on to show that the numerator has a probability limit of zero is the assumption that $E(X_t u_t) = 0$. If $X_t = Y_{t-1}$ and u_t is non-autocorrelated this is true, but if $X_t = Y_{t-1}$ and u_t is autocorrelated it is not. Thus in the case of a lagged endogenous regressor and non-autocorrelated errors, the bias in $\hat{\beta}$ diminishes when we have a reasonably large sample of observations. We have the following results:

Is $\hat{\beta}$ a consistent estimator of $\hat{\beta}$? i.e. does $\text{plim}\,\hat{\beta} = \beta$?

X_t \ u_t	serially independent	autocorrelated
exogenous	Yes	Yes
lagged endogenous	Yes	No

5.3 TESTING THE SIGNIFICANCE OF THE COEFFICIENTS

One of our prime objectives is to test whether X has a significant effect on Y. Since the magnitude of any effect of X on Y is unknown, we pose the question the opposite way round, and ask whether the data provide evidence against the view that X has no effect on Y. This last view is formalised as the null hypothesis, denoted H_0, and since X has no effect on Y if the value of the regression coefficient β is zero, we write

$$H_0 : \beta = 0.$$

Our test is based on the estimated coefficient $\hat{\beta}$, and in order to make statements about its statistical distribution we need an assumption about the distribution of the random disturbances. We assume that the disturbances are normally distributed and write this, also assuming homoscedasticity, as

$$u_t \sim N(0, \sigma_u^2), \qquad t = 1, \ldots, n.$$

Since the sampling error of $\hat{\beta}$, namely

$$\hat{\beta} - \beta = \sum_{t=1}^{n} W_t u_t,$$

is a linear combination of normally distributed random variables, it follows that $\hat{\beta}$ is itself normally distributed. If X is exogenous and the disturbances are non-autocorrelated, so that the previous results about the mean and variance of $\hat{\beta}$ apply, we have

$$\hat{\beta} - \beta \sim N\left(0, \frac{\sigma_u^2}{\Sigma(X_t - \bar{X})^2}\right).$$

Thus a normal distribution with this variance describes the variation of $\hat{\beta}$, in repeated samples of size n, around the true value β. On dividing by the standard deviation of $\hat{\beta}$, we obtain a quantity that has the standard normal distribution, which is widely tabulated:

$$\frac{\hat{\beta} - \beta}{\sqrt{\dfrac{\sigma_u^2}{\Sigma(X_t - \bar{X})^2}}} \sim N(0, 1).$$

So if we knew σ_u^2 we could test $H_0 : \beta = 0$ using the standard normal distribution. In general of course we do not and so must replace it by an unbiased estimate and use the t-distribution.

It can be shown that an unbiased estimate of σ_u^2 is provided by the residual sum of squares divided by the number of degrees of freedom (in this case $n - 2$). The estimate is

$$\hat{\sigma}_u^2 = \frac{\displaystyle\sum_{t=1}^{n} e_t^2}{n - 2},$$

and its square root, $\hat{\sigma}_u$, is known as the *standard error of the equation.* It can be shown that

$$E(\hat{\sigma}_u^2) = \sigma_u^2,$$

and it follows that

$$\frac{\hat{\sigma}_u^2}{\Sigma(X_t - \bar{X})^2}$$

is an unbiased estimator of $\mathrm{var}(\hat{\beta})$. The resulting estimate of the standard deviation of the distribution of $\hat{\beta}$ is known as the *standard error of $\hat{\beta}$:*

$$\mathrm{SE}(\hat{\beta}) = \sqrt{\frac{\hat{\sigma}_u^2}{\Sigma(X_t - \bar{X})^2}} = \sqrt{\frac{\Sigma e_t^2}{(n - 2)\,\Sigma(X_t - \bar{X})^2}}.$$

Under the above assumptions the sampling error $\hat{\beta} - \beta$ divided by the standard error has a t-distribution with $n - 2$ degrees of freedom, which we write

$$\frac{\hat{\beta} - \beta}{SE(\hat{\beta})} \sim t_{n-2}.$$

and this quantity can be used for testing hypotheses about β. If the null hypothesis $\beta = 0$ is true, then

$$\frac{\hat{\beta}}{SE(\hat{\beta})} \sim t_{n-2},$$

and this quantity is known as the *t-ratio* of $\hat{\beta}$.

Thus to test the hypothesis we calculate this ratio and compare it with the tabulated t-distribution with $n - 2$ degrees of freedom. If the result is small we say that the difference from zero probably arose due to sampling variability alone, and accept the null hypothesis $\beta = 0$.

If the calculated t-ratio is larger in aboslute value than the tabulated critical value, we are unable to accept the null hypothesis. In this case we say that $\hat{\beta}$ is significantly different from zero (and that X has a significant effect on Y).

We can also use this procedure to test the hypothesis that β is equal to some other specified value. For example we might want to test the hypothesis $H_0 : \beta = 1$ (e.g. if β were an elasticity). In this case we would substitute $\beta = 1$ in the above expression to give as our test statistic

$$\frac{\hat{\beta} - 1}{SE(\hat{\beta})}.$$

As $n \to \infty$ the t-distribution approaches the normal distribution, and so the critical value for testing at the 5% significance level approaches that of the normal distribution, namely 1.96. If $n > 25$ then the critical value is less than 2.06. This has led to a simple rule of thumb being used to test $\beta = 0$: a coefficient is said to be significant if its absolute value is more than twice its standard error.

In reporting empirical work the usual practice is to present either the standard error or the t-ratio or its absolute value in parentheses beneath the estimated coefficient. It is important to indicate which is being presented.

In devising this test we have made use of assumptions A2, A3 and A4. So what happens to the test if we have either autocorrelated errors or X is a lagged dependent variable or both?

In the presence of autocorrelation the expression derived for SE$(\hat{\beta})$ is no longer correct, and so the test statistic no longer has a t-distribution. Thus the testing procedure breaks down.

If X is a lagged endogenous variable then strictly the test procedure is only valid asymptotically. For samples of reasonable size the test statistic has a distribution that is approximately normal (and therefore t) but with smallish samples the test can be misleading.

Is the test procedure outlined above valid?

X_t \ u_t	serially independent	autocorrelated
exogenous	Yes	No
lagged endogenous	Only asymptotically	No

5.4 GOODNESS OF FIT

The next question we examine is how much of the variation in Y is explained by the fitted line $\hat{\alpha} + \hat{\beta}X$. We seek a measure of the explanatory power of the equation. In section 5.1 we showed that the observed value Y_t can be split into two uncorrelated parts: the fitted value $\hat{Y}_t = \hat{\alpha} + \hat{\beta}X_t$ and the residual e_t,

$$Y_t = \hat{Y}_t + e_t, \qquad t = 1, \ldots, n.$$

Since the residuals have zero mean ($\bar{e} = 0$), the means of the observed and fitted values are equal, so the equation

$$(Y_t - \bar{Y}) = (\hat{Y}_t - \bar{Y}) + e_t, \qquad t = 1, \ldots, n$$

expresses the same split in terms of deviations from means. Squaring both sides of this equation and summing over t gives

$$\sum_{t=1}^{n} (Y_t - \bar{Y})^2 = \sum_{t=1}^{n} (\hat{Y}_t - \bar{Y})^2 + \sum_{t=1}^{n} e_t^2,$$

the cross-products $(\hat{Y}_t - \bar{Y}) e_t$ summing to zero since, as shown in section 5.1, the covariance between residuals and fitted values is zero. This last equation gives a corresponding partition of the sum of squares of mean deviations, which can be variously expressed in words as

total variation in Y = explained variation + unexplained variation

or as

original sum of squares = sum of squares due to regression

+ residual sum of squares.

Similarly, dividing by n across the equation gives the corresponding partition of the variance of the dependent variable.

A natural measure of the goodness of fit of a regression equation is the proportion of the total variation in Y that is explained by the regression. This is denoted R^2 and called the *coefficient of determination* or *multiple correlation coefficient*:

$$R^2 = \frac{\text{explained variation}}{\text{total variation}} = 1 - \frac{\text{unexplained variation}}{\text{total variation}}$$

$$= 1 - \frac{\Sigma e_t^2}{\Sigma (Y_t - \bar{Y})^2}.$$

This measure has several noteworthy features. Firstly it can be shown that it is the square of the simple correlation between Y and $\hat{Y}$, a result which also holds true in the multiple regression case. Secondly $0 \leqslant R^2 \leqslant 1$, with $R^2 = 1$ only if all the data points lie on the regression line and $R^2 = 0$ indicating that X and Y are uncorrelated. Thirdly, in the two-variable case only, $R^2 = r_{YX}^2$ and R^2 does not give us any additional information to the simple correlation coefficient: this will not be the case for multiple regression. Finally if there were no constant term included in the regression equation it would no longer necessarily be true that $\bar{e} = 0$, and therefore no longer necessarily true that $\bar{Y} = \hat{Y}$ and the above partition of the sum of squares of mean deviations would not hold. In this case the meaning of R^2 is not clear, and depending on which of the above expressions is used for its computation, it is possible for its value to be negative or to exceed 1. So R^2 should not be used in the absence of a constant term.

In the general case we have $\hat{Y}_t - \bar{Y} = \hat{\beta}(X_t - \bar{X})$ and so the explained sum of squares can be calculated from either of the following expressions:

$$\sum_{t=1}^{n} (\hat{Y}_t - \bar{Y})^2 = \hat{\beta}^2 \sum_{t=1}^{n} (X_t - \bar{X})^2 = \hat{\beta} \sum_{t=1}^{n} (X_t - \bar{X})(Y_t - \bar{Y}).$$

The two expressions on the right involve $\hat{\beta}$ and the quantities calculated on the way to the calculation of $\hat{\beta}$, and so the explained sum of squares is easily obtained, in particular without calculating the n $\hat{Y}$-values. If the original sum of squares has been computed the residual sum of squares can then be obtained by subtraction, again without calculating each individual residual. However the calculation of the individual $\hat{Y}$ and e values is to be recommended on other grounds, for they can provide valuable information about the adequacy of the regression specification, and an examination of their behaviour across the sample may suggest ways in which the model can be improved.

5.5 PREDICTION

One of the important roles of econometrics is that of predicting the effect on one variable of certain changes in others. For example, suppose we wanted to examine the effect of various possible tax cuts on the level of consumers' expenditure. If we knew by how much each of the alternative tax cuts would increase disposable income, then we could use an estimated consumption function to predict the effects of the tax cuts on consumption.

Consider our simple two variable equation again

$$Y_t = \alpha + \beta X_t + u_t, \qquad t = 1, \ldots, n.$$

Assume that we know the value of X in some forecast period f, and denote it by X_f. (This could be an actual or hypothetical value). If we assume that the structure of the equation does not change, then the value of Y in this period f (denoted Y_f) will be given by

$$Y_f = \alpha + \beta X_f + u_f.$$

When we use such a relationship to predict Y_f there are *two* sources of imprecision in our predictions:

(i) Firstly we do not know α and β. Thus we have to use our estimates of them in order to estimate the first component of Y_f above. This first component is, of course, the mean of Y corresponding to X_f: $E(Y_f | X_f) = \alpha + \beta X_f$.

(ii) In addition u_f is an unobservable random variable. Thus even if we knew α and β and so could calculate $E(Y_f | X_f)$, we would still be unable to predict Y_f perfectly because of u_f.

We first consider an estimate of $E(Y_f | X_f)$. This will then be used to predict Y_f itself and we will set up a prediction interval for Y_f. Since $E(Y_f | X_f) = \alpha + \beta X_f$, a natural estimator for it is given by

$$\hat{Y}_f = \hat{\alpha} + \hat{\beta} X_f.$$

We can show that this is an unbiased estimator of $E(Y_f | X_f)$, and that among linear unbiased estimators it is best (i.e. has minimum variance). This follows from the fact that $\hat{\alpha}$ and $\hat{\beta}$ have these properties. If we assume that X is non-stochastic, then the variance of $\hat{Y}_f$ is given by

$$\text{var}(\hat{Y}_f) = \text{var}(\hat{\alpha}) + X_f^2 \, \text{var}(\hat{\beta}) + 2X_f \, \text{cov}(\hat{\alpha}, \hat{\beta}).$$

We can obtain expressions for $\text{var}(\hat{\alpha})$, $\text{var}(\hat{\beta})$ and $\text{cov}(\hat{\alpha}, \hat{\beta})$ as before and substitute to give

$$\text{var}(\hat{Y}_f) = \sigma_u^2 \left[\frac{1}{n} + \frac{(X_f - \bar{X})^2}{\displaystyle\sum_{t=1}^{n} (X_t - \bar{X})^2} \right].$$

Notice that $\text{var}(\hat{Y}_f)$ decreases as:

(i) $(X_f - \bar{X})^2$ decreases, i.e. the nearer X_f is to the sample mean of X.

(ii) n increases, i.e. the larger the sample size.

(iii) $\displaystyle\sum_{t=1}^{n} (X_t - \bar{X})^2$ increases,

i.e. the larger the variation within the sample of X's over which the equation is estimated.

All these seem intuitively reasonable.

We now take this estimator of $E(Y_f | X_f)$ as our predictor of Y_f. This seems a natural thing to do: since $E(u_f) = 0$ we predict the level of Y_f simply by estimating its mean.

The error involved in this prediction is given by $e_f = Y_f - \hat{Y}_f$, and is called the *prediction error* (or *forecast error*). We can easily see that

$$
\begin{aligned}
E(e_f) &= E(Y_f) - E(\hat{Y}_f) \\
&= E(\alpha + \beta X_f + u_f) - E(\hat{\alpha} + \hat{\beta} X_f) \\
&= (\alpha + \beta X_f) - (\alpha + \beta X_f) \\
&= 0
\end{aligned}
$$

and that the variance of the forecast error is given by

$$\text{var}(e_f) = \text{var}(Y_f - \hat{Y}_f)$$
$$= \text{var}(Y_f) + \text{var}(\hat{Y}_f) - 2\,\text{cov}(Y_f, \hat{Y}_f).$$

As far as their random components are concerned, Y_f depends on u_f, while $\hat{Y}_f$ depends on $u_1, \ldots, u_n$ through $\hat{\alpha}$ and $\hat{\beta}$. So if the u's are serially independent, then Y_f is independent of $\hat{Y}_f$. Thus $\text{cov}(Y_f, \hat{Y}_f) = 0$ and hence

$$\text{var}(e_f) = \text{var}(Y_f) + \text{var}(\hat{Y}_f).$$

Notice that $\text{var}(Y_f) = \text{var}(u_f)$ if X is non-stochastic, and recall that $\text{var}(\hat{Y}_f) = \text{var}(\hat{\alpha}) + X_f^2\,\text{var}(\hat{\beta}) + 2X_f\,\text{cov}(\hat{\alpha}, \hat{\beta})$ so that

$$\text{var}(e_f) = \text{var}(u_f) + [\text{var}(\hat{\alpha}) + X_f^2\,\text{var}(\hat{\beta}) + 2X_f\,\text{cov}(\hat{\alpha}, \hat{\beta})]$$

$$= \text{imprecision due to } u_f$$

$$+ \text{imprecision due to lack of knowledge of } \alpha \text{ and } \beta.$$

Returning to our above expression for $\text{var}(e_f)$ and substituting in the earlier expression for $\text{var}(\hat{Y}_f)$ gives

$$\sigma_e^2 = \sigma_u^2 + \sigma_u^2 \left[\frac{1}{n} + \frac{(X_f - \bar{X})^2}{\sum\limits_{t=1}^{n}(X_t - \bar{X})^2} \right]$$

$$= \sigma_u^2 \left[1 + \frac{1}{n} + \frac{(X_f - \bar{X})^2}{\sum\limits_{t=1}^{n}(X_t - \bar{X})^2} \right]$$

Thus an unbiased estimator of $\text{var}(e_f)$ is given by

$$\hat{\sigma}_e^2 = \hat{\sigma}_u^2 \left[1 + \frac{1}{n} + \frac{(X_f - \bar{X})^2}{\sum\limits_{t=1}^{n}(X_t - \bar{X})^2} \right]$$

Note that as $n \to \infty$, $\hat{\sigma}_e^2 \to \hat{\sigma}_u^2$. Thus when using large samples, $\hat{\sigma}_u$ (the standard error of the equation) could be used as an approximation to $\hat{\sigma}_e$.

We now wish to attach a measure of accuracy to this prediction of Y_f. To do this we again assume a particular probability distribution for the random disturbances, namely the normal distribution. Then since u_f is normally distributed so is Y_f, and since $u_1, \ldots, u_n$ are normally distributed so are $\hat{\alpha}$ and $\hat{\beta}$ and hence $\hat{Y}_f$. Thus the prediction error $e_f = Y_f - \hat{Y}_f$ is a normally distributed random variable with mean zero and variance σ_e^2 as already calculated, and so e_f/σ_e has a standard normal distribution. However σ_e^2 depends on the unknown σ_u^2, and for practical implementation the above estimate must be substituted, which gives a t-distributed random variable:

$$\frac{e_f}{\hat{\sigma}_e} = \frac{Y_f - \hat{Y}_f}{\hat{\sigma}_e} \sim t_{n-2}.$$

If t^* is the critical value of the t-distribution with $n-2$ degrees of freedom, such that Prob $(t > t^*) = 0.025$, then

$$\text{Prob}\left(-t^* < \frac{Y_f - \hat{Y}_f}{\hat{\sigma}_e} < t^*\right) = 0.95,$$

and a 95% *prediction interval* or *forecast interval* for Y_f is given by

$$\hat{Y}_f \pm t^* \hat{\sigma}_e.$$

(Again for large n we can take $t^* \simeq 2$.) Such an interval is illustrated in Figure 5.4. The confidence bounds are nearest together at $\bar{X}$. The forecast interval gets larger the further is X_f from $\bar{X}$.

5.6 AN EMPIRICAL ILLUSTRATION

In this section we consider an empirical illustration of the concepts and techniques introduced in the preceding sections. We employ

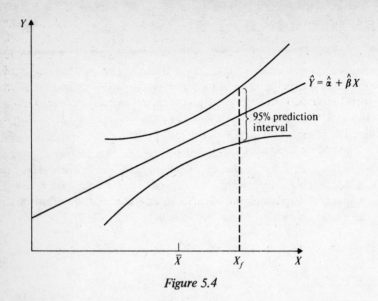

Figure 5.4

quarterly data to estimate a simple consumption function for the U.K. economy. The two variables used are

$$C = \text{Real consumers' expenditure}$$

$$DI = \text{Real personal disposable income}$$

(both in £million at 1975 prices) and the sample contains 72 observations for the period 1960 quarter 1 to 1977 quarter 4.

The fitted equation is given by

$$C = 2571 + 0.7331\, DI$$
$$(361)\quad (0.0228)$$

where the numbers in parentheses beneath the estimated coefficients are the corresponding standard errors (see p. 121). The t-ratios are given by division of the coefficient estimates by their respective standard errors:

Constant	7.12
Coefficient on DI	32.11

Both are considerably greater than 2.0, the 5% critical point from the *t*-distribution with 70 degrees of freedom. Hence we judge both parameters to be significantly different from zero. The estimated marginal propensity to consume is 0.7331 so that the estimated effect of a £10 million rise in real personal disposable income (at 1975 prices) is an increase of £7.331 million in real consumers' expenditure (also at 1975 prices). The estimated m.p.c. gives the slope of the fitted line. The intercept on the *C*-axis is £2571 million.

The various sums of squares are as follows:

$$\text{Residual sum of squares} = 128.006 \times 10^5$$

$$\text{Explained sum of squares} = 1884.667 \times 10^5$$

$$\text{Total sum of squares} = 2012.673 \times 10^5$$

Hence the coefficient of determination (see p. 124) is given by

$$R^2 = \frac{1884.667}{2012.673} = 0.9364$$

so that 93.64% of the variation in real consumers' expenditure is explained by this equation. The standard error of the equation (see p. 121), already used to calculate the standard errors of the coefficients, is given by

$$\hat{\sigma}_u = \sqrt{\frac{128.006 \times 10^5}{70}} = 427.628$$

Finally we consider using this equation to predict real consumers' expenditure. Point predictions are obtained simply by substitution of appropriate values for *DI* into the fitted equation given above. The results for the six quarters immediately following the sample period are given in the third column of the table below. The estimated variances and covariances of the coefficient estimates are as follows:

$$\text{Estimated variance of } \hat{\alpha} = 130423$$

$$\text{Estimated variance of } \hat{\beta} = 5.2135 \times 10^{-4}$$

$$\text{Estimated covariance of } \hat{\alpha} \text{ and } \hat{\beta} = -8.1653$$

Predictions of real consumers' expenditure for 1978.1 to 1979.2

Period	Real Income DI (£m.)	Point Prediction, $\hat{C}$	$\hat{\sigma}_e$	95% Confidence Interval	Actual Value of C	Difference $C-\hat{C}$
1978.1	18,650	16,243	436.0	15,371; 17,115	15,772	−471
1978.2	19,378	16,777	438.9	15,899; 17,655	16,106	−671
1978.3	20,174	17,360	442.7	16,474; 18,245	16,998	−362
1978.4	20,480	17,585	444.4	16,696; 18,474	17,852	+267
1979.1	20,062	17,278	442.2	16,394; 18,162	16,393	−885
1979.2	20,701	17,747	445.7	16,856; 18,638	17,309	−438

(Note that the square roots of the estimated variances give the standard errors already presented above). Given these and the standard error of the equation we can calculate estimates of the variance of the prediction error (see p. 128) and hence values of $\hat{\sigma}_e$. These are presented in the fourth column of the table facing. Then given a value of t^* of 2.0 we can construct prediction intervals (see p. 129). These are presented in the fifth column of the table. The final two columns give the actual value of real consumers' expenditure in each quarter for comparison and the difference of our point prediction from it.

5.7 MAXIMUM LIKELIHOOD ESTIMATION

We now turn our attention to the consideration of an alternative approach to estimation known as the method of *Maximum Likelihood*. The approach is based on an idea with considerable intuitive appeal: if we are faced with several possible values for a parameter, we choose that value under which the model would have been most likely to generate the observed sample. Such a criterion obviously requires us to be able to state the *probability* of the observed sample being generated by the model given a certain parameter value. Hence, unlike the least squares technique, this approach requires us to specify (i.e. assume) a certain probability distribution for the population from which the sample is drawn. Whilst the approach is obviously applicable to a wide range of situations, we will restrict our attention here to the estimation of the single reduced form equation with which we have been concerned in this chapter. We will assume, as was done to construct significance tests in section 5.3, that the stochastic error terms are independent drawings from identical normal distributions:

$$u_t \sim N(0, \sigma_u^2) \qquad \text{for all } t.$$

If the X_t are non-stochastic, then Y_t also will be normally distributed. Its mean will be given by

$$E(Y_t) = E(\alpha + \beta X_t + u_t) = \alpha + \beta X_t + E(u_t) = \alpha + \beta X_t.$$

Hence

$$Y_t - E(Y_t) = (\alpha + \beta X_t + u_t) - (\alpha + \beta X_t) = u_t$$

and therefore its variance is given by

$$\text{var}(Y_t) = E(Y_t - E(Y_t))^2 = E(u_t^2) = \sigma_u^2.$$

Thus

$$Y_t \sim N(\alpha + \beta X_t, \sigma_u^2)$$

and the probability density function of Y_t is given by

$$p(Y_t) = \frac{1}{\sqrt{(2\pi\sigma_u^2)}} \exp\left\{-\frac{1}{2\sigma_u^2}(Y_t - \alpha - \beta X_t)^2\right\}$$

Under the assumption of independence, the joint probability density of $Y_1, Y_2, \ldots, Y_n$ is given by

$$p(Y_1, Y_2, \ldots, Y_n) = \prod_{t=1}^{n} p(Y_t)$$

$$= \frac{1}{(2\pi\sigma_u^2)^{n/2}} \exp\left\{-\frac{1}{2\sigma_u^2}\sum_{t=1}^{n}(Y_t - \alpha - \beta X_t)^2\right\}.$$

This is clearly a function of the unknown parameters α, β, σ_u^2 as well as of $Y_1, Y_2, \ldots, Y_n$. As a function of the latter it is the joint probability density function, whilst as a function of the former it is called the *likelihood function* for α, β, and σ_u^2 and written

$$L(\alpha, \beta, \sigma_u^2) = \frac{1}{(2\pi\sigma_u^2)^{n/2}} \exp\left\{-\frac{1}{2\sigma_u^2}\sum_{t=1}^{n}(Y_t - \alpha - \beta X_t)^2\right\}.$$

The method of *maximum likelihood*, as the name suggests, consists of choosing those values of α, β and σ_u^2 that maximise $L(\alpha, \beta, \sigma_u^2)$, the likelihood of observing the sample of Y's given the parameter values. A simplification that is often useful is to consider $\log L$ instead of L. Since log is a monotonic function, $\log L$ will attain its maximum value at the same point as L, and consideration of $\log L$ is more convenient in cases like the present one because it removes the exponential term.

$$\log L = -\frac{n}{2} \log 2\pi - \frac{n}{2} \log \sigma_u^2 - \frac{1}{2\sigma_u^2} \sum_{t=1}^{n} (Y_t - \alpha - \beta X_t)^2$$

Partial differentiation with respect to α, β and σ_u^2 gives

$$\frac{\partial \log L}{\partial \alpha} = \frac{1}{\sigma_u^2} \sum_{t=1}^{n} (Y_t - \alpha - \beta X_t)$$

$$\frac{\partial \log L}{\partial \beta} = \frac{1}{\sigma_u^2} \sum_{t=1}^{n} X_t(Y_t - \alpha - \beta X_t)$$

$$\frac{\partial \log L}{\partial \sigma^2} = -\frac{n}{2\sigma_u^2} + \frac{1}{2\sigma_u^4} \sum_{t=1}^{n} (Y_t - \alpha - \beta X_t)^2$$

The maximum likelihood estimates, which we will denote by $\tilde{\alpha}$, $\tilde{\beta}$ and $\tilde{\sigma}_u^2$, are obtained by setting these equal to zero and solving. The first two equations simplify to

$$\Sigma Y_t = n\tilde{\alpha} + \tilde{\beta}\Sigma X_t$$

$$\Sigma X_t Y_t = \tilde{\alpha}\Sigma X_t + \tilde{\beta}\Sigma X_t^2.$$

However these are the least squares normal equations seen earlier. Hence $\tilde{\alpha}$ and $\tilde{\beta}$ will be identical to the least squares estimates. The third equation then gives the maximum likelihood estimate of the error variance as

$$\tilde{\sigma}_u{}^2 = \frac{1}{n} \sum_{t=1}^n (Y_t - \tilde{\alpha} - \tilde{\beta}X_t)^2 = \frac{1}{n}\Sigma e_t{}^2$$

This is different from the unbiased estimate of $\sigma_u{}^2$ seen in section 5.2 and will be biased downwards in small samples:

$$E(\tilde{\sigma}_u{}^2) = \frac{n-2}{n}\,\sigma_u{}^2 = \sigma_u{}^2 - \frac{2}{n}\,\sigma_u{}^2 \quad .$$

However it does provide a consistent estimate of $\sigma_u{}^2$. This is in fact a general property of maximum likelihood estimates: under certain fairly general conditions maximum likelihood estimates are consistent. They are also asymptotically efficient.

5.8 ERRORS IN VARIABLES

In this section we consider the consequences of the fact that most economic variables are measured with less than perfect accuracy. This may be the result of errors by the individuals filling in the forms that go to make up the published aggregate variables. Or it may be the result of our use of a proxy to a theoretical variable which is unobservable. We examine only the simple two-variable case here (the results generalise to the multi-variable case in a straightforward way) and consider separately the cases of measurement error in the explanatory and the dependent variable.

(1) *Measurement error in an explanatory variable*

Suppose that the "true" relationship between Y and X is given by the equation

$$Y_t = \alpha + \beta X_t + u_t.$$

However our observations on X contain errors, so that we observe X_t^* instead of X_t. Suppose that these errors are additive and random:

$$X_t^* = X_t + \omega_t$$

where ω_t represents the error in measuring the tth value of X. In addition suppose that ω_t satisfies the classical assumptions and is independent of both u_t and X_t. The above equation can be written as

$$Y_t = \alpha + \beta(X_t^* - \omega_t) + u_t.$$

Hence the equation we estimate will be given by

$$Y_t = \alpha + \beta X_t^* + u_t^*$$

where

$$u_t^* = u_t - \beta\omega_t.$$

However the error term in this equation is not independent of the explanatory variable:

$$E(X_t^* u_t^*) = E(X_t + \omega_t)(u_t - \beta\omega_t)$$
$$= E(X_t u_t) + E(\omega_t u_t) - \beta E(X_t \omega_t) - \beta E(\omega_t^2).$$

Each of these terms is zero under the stated assumptions, except the last. Hence

$$E(X_t^* u_t^*) = -\beta\sigma_\omega^2$$

which is non-zero. Therefore the OLS estimator of β from the observed equation will be both biased and inconsistent.

The method of instrumental variables, discussed in chapter 10, can provide consistent estimates in this situation. In this section we look instead at a way of using OLS to provide estimated (asymptotic) bounds for the true β. We will assume for ease of manipulation that $\beta > 0$. If in fact β is negative the direction of the bounds is reversed.

We consider first the probability limit of $\hat{\beta}$ from the estimation of the above equation. We have

$$\hat{\beta} - \beta = \frac{\Sigma(X_t^* - \bar{X})u_t^*}{\Sigma(X_t^* - \bar{X})^2} .$$

Substituting $X_t^* = X_t + \omega_t$ and $u_t^* = u_t - \beta\omega_t$ gives

$$\hat{\beta} - \beta = \frac{\Sigma(X_t - \bar{X})u_t + \Sigma\omega_t u_t - \beta\Sigma(X_t - \bar{X})\omega_t - \beta\Sigma\omega_t^2}{\Sigma(X_t - \bar{X})^2 + 2\Sigma(X_t - \bar{X})\omega_t + \Sigma\omega_t^2} .$$

Dividing numerator and denominator by n and taking probability limits gives

$$\text{plim } \hat{\beta} = \beta - \frac{\beta\sigma_\omega^2}{\sigma_X^2 + \sigma_\omega^2}$$

$$= \frac{\beta}{1 + \sigma_\omega^2/\sigma_X^2}$$

$$< \beta \qquad \text{if } \beta \text{ is positive.}$$

Hence in large samples the OLS estimate $\hat{\beta}$ provides an underestimate of β if β is positive. Consider next the OLS regression of X^* on Y. Let $\hat{\gamma}$ be the estimated slope coefficient from this regression. Then

$$\hat{\gamma} = \frac{\Sigma(Y_t - \bar{Y})X_t^*}{\Sigma(Y_t - \bar{Y})^2}$$

Substituting $(Y_t - \bar{Y}) = \beta(X_t - \bar{X}) + (u_t - \bar{u})$ and $X_t^* = X_t + \omega_t$ gives

$$\hat{\gamma} = \frac{\beta\Sigma(X_t - \bar{X})X_t + \Sigma X_t(u_t - \bar{u}) + \beta\Sigma(X_t - \bar{X})\omega_t + \Sigma(u_t - \bar{u})\omega_t}{\beta^2\Sigma(X_t - \bar{X})^2 + 2\beta\Sigma(X_t - \bar{X})(u_t - \bar{u}) + \Sigma(u_t - \bar{u})^2} .$$

Dividing numerator and denominator by n and taking probability limits gives

$$\text{plim } \hat{\gamma} = \frac{\beta \sigma_X{}^2}{\beta^2 \sigma_X{}^2 + \sigma_u{}^2}$$

Taking the reciprocal of this coefficient as an estimate of the effect of X on Y, we have

$$\text{plim } \frac{1}{\hat{\gamma}} = \beta \left(1 + \frac{\sigma_u{}^2}{\beta^2 \sigma_X{}^2} \right)$$

$$> \beta \qquad \text{if } \beta \text{ is positive.}$$

Hence in large samples $1/\hat{\gamma}$ provides an overestimate of β if β is positive.

If β is negative the direction of both these inequalities is reversed. Irrespective of the sign of β, however, $\hat{\beta}$ and $1/\hat{\gamma}$ provide an under-estimate and an overestimate of the true β. If they are fairly close together, they provide us with some information on the magnitude of β. If they differ considerably they will not be very helpful.

(2) *Measurement error in the dependent variable*

Again suppose that the "true" relationship between Y and X is given by the equation

$$Y_t = \alpha + \beta X_t + u_t$$

and now suppose that our observations on Y contain errors, so that we observe Y_t^* instead of Y_t. Suppose that these errors are, once again, additive and random:

$$Y_t^* = Y_t + v_t$$

where v_t represents the error in measuring the tth value of Y. In addition suppose that v_t satisfies the classical assumptions and is independent of both u_t and X_t. The above equation can be written as

$$Y_t^* - v_t = \alpha + \beta X_t + u_t$$

and hence the equation we estimate is given by

$$Y_t^* = \alpha + \beta X_t + u_t^*$$

where now

$$u_t^* = u_t + v_t.$$

In this case u_t^* satisfies the same assumption as u_t including being independent of X. Thus the OLS estimate of β is unbiased and consistent. Also the usual t-tests, etc will be valid.

However there is the possibility of another problem as a result of the measurement error in Y. If the methods used to measure economic variables have improved over time, then var (v_t) may have declined over time. Since

$$\text{var}(u_t^*) = \text{var}(u_t) + \text{var}(v_t)$$

it follows that var(u_t^*) may have fallen over time and there is thus a possibility of heteroscedasticity in the equation.

EXERCISES

5.1 The table contains 20 quarterly observations on C = real consumers' expenditure and DI = real personal disposable income (both in £million at 1975 prices) for the period 1972 to 1976 (part of the data used in the empirical illustration of section 5.6).

(a) Estimate the coefficients in the equation

$$C_t = \alpha + \beta DI_t + u_t.$$

(b) Construct a 95% confidence interval for the m.p.c.

(c) Test the hypothesis that the m.p.c. is unity.

(d) Calculate R^2.

(e) Construct a 95% prediction interval for C given the value of DI in the first quarter of 1977 is £17803 m.

Period	C_t	DI_t	Period	C_t	DI_t
1972.1	14528	16424	1975.1	15263	18734
1972.2	15519	17675	1975.2	15659	18447
1972.3	15865	17506	1975.3	15781	18650
1972.4	16850	18476	1975.4	16489	18530
1973.1	15752	17913	1976.1	15026	18257
1973.2	16037	18587	1976.2	15506	18290
1973.3	16552	18826	1976.3	15917	19113
1973.4	17156	19036	1976.4	16871	18524
1974.1	15156	18253			
1974.2	15612	17878			
1974.3	16249	19128			
1974.4	17053	19622			

5.2 The following sums were obtained from 16 pairs of observations on Y and X:

$$\Sigma Y^2 = 526 \qquad \Sigma X^2 = 657 \qquad \Sigma XY = 492$$

$$\Sigma Y = 64 \qquad \Sigma X = 96$$

Estimate the regression of Y on X and test the hypothesis that the slope coefficient is 1.0.

5.3   Estimate the coefficients in the equation

$$\log C_t = \alpha + \beta \log DI_t + u_{2t}$$

using the data of exercise 5.1. Compare the results with those in exercise 5.1 and discuss.

Find the estimated value of the m.p.c. in the first quarters of 1973 and 1976.

Find the average of the estimated m.p.c. for each of the four quarters of the year.

5.4   Show that

$$\hat{\beta} = r \cdot \frac{S_Y}{S_X}$$

where r is the coefficient of correlation between X and Y and S_X, S_Y are the sample standard deviations of X and Y respectively.

5.5   Show that the stationary point found when minimising the residual sum of squares on p. 108 is indeed a minimum.

5.6   Show that

$$\text{var}(\hat{\alpha}) = \frac{\sigma_u^2 \sum_{t=1}^{n} X_t^2}{n \sum_{t=1}^{n} (X_t - \bar{X})^2}$$

and

$$\text{cov}(\hat{\alpha}, \hat{\beta}) = \frac{-\sigma_u^2 \bar{X}}{\sum_{t=1}^{n} (X_t - \bar{X})^2}.$$

5.7 We can see from exercise 5.6 that $\text{cov}(\hat{\alpha}, \hat{\beta}) = 0$ if the sample mean of X is zero. Given an intuitive explanation of why this should be so.

5.8 Let $\hat{\beta}$ be the slope coefficient from the regression of Y on X and let $\hat{\gamma}$ be the slope coefficient from the regression of X on Y. Show that $\hat{\beta} = 1/\hat{\gamma}$ if and only if $R^2 = 1$.

5.9 Given the expression for $\text{var}(\hat{\beta})$ derived on p. 116 and the expressions in exercise 5.6 for $\text{var}(\hat{\alpha})$ and $\text{cov}(\hat{\alpha}, \hat{\beta})$, derive the expression for $\text{var}(\hat{Y}_f)$ stated on p. 127.

5.10 Show that

$$\hat{\sigma}_u^2 = \frac{\Sigma e_t^2}{n - 2}$$

is an unbiased estimate of σ_u^2.

VI

MULTIPLE REGRESSION ANALYSIS

6.1. ESTIMATION OF A REDUCED FORM EQUATION

We now extend the analysis to consider a regression equation with more than one explanatory variable, but retain the reduced form assumption, so that the dependent variable is the only current endogenous variable in the equation. In a natural extension of the notation of chapter 5 we write our equation as

$$Y_t = \beta_1 + \beta_2 X_{2t} + \beta_3 X_{3t} + \ldots + \beta_k X_{kt} + u_t, \qquad t = 1, 2, \ldots, n.$$

This can also be written

$$Y_t = \sum_{i=1}^{k} \beta_i X_{it} + u_t, \qquad t = 1, 2, \ldots, n$$

where $X_{1t} = 1$ for all t so that β_1 is the constant term. This formulation is of course more general since it also covers the case where a constant term is not included and X_1 is a genuine variable. We can write the equation for all n observations in matrix notation as

$$
\begin{bmatrix} Y_1 \\ Y_2 \\ \cdot \\ \cdot \\ \cdot \\ Y_n \end{bmatrix}
=
\begin{bmatrix}
X_{11} & X_{21} & \cdot & \cdot & \cdot & X_{k1} \\
X_{12} & X_{22} & \cdot & \cdot & \cdot & X_{k2} \\
\cdot & \cdot & & & \cdot & \\
\cdot & \cdot & & & \cdot & \\
\cdot & \cdot & & & \cdot & \\
X_{1n} & X_{2n} & \cdot & \cdot & \cdot & X_{kn}
\end{bmatrix}
\begin{bmatrix} \beta_1 \\ \beta_2 \\ \cdot \\ \cdot \\ \cdot \\ \beta_k \end{bmatrix}
+
\begin{bmatrix} u_1 \\ u_2 \\ \cdot \\ \cdot \\ \cdot \\ u_n \end{bmatrix}
$$

which we denote by

$$\mathbf{y} = \mathbf{X}\beta + \mathbf{u}.$$

($\mathbf{y}$ and $\mathbf{u}$ are $n \times 1$ column vectors, $\mathbf{X}$ is a $n \times k$ matrix and β is a $k \times 1$ column vector of coefficients).

This is the conventional formulation in econometrics. Notice that the notation is at variance with the usual matrix algebra notation, where the first subscript denotes the row and the second denotes the column. Here X_{it} (the tth observation on the ith variable) is the element in the ith column and tth row of the matrix $\mathbf{X}$.

In a natural extension of our previous notation, $\hat{\beta}$ is the $k \times 1$ column vector of estimated coefficients, $\hat{\beta}_i$ being the estimate of β_i ($i = 1, 2, \ldots, k$), and $\mathbf{e}$ is the $n \times 1$ column vector of residuals

$$\mathbf{e} = \mathbf{y} - \mathbf{X}\hat{\beta}$$

$$= \mathbf{y} - \hat{\mathbf{y}}$$

where $\hat{\mathbf{y}}$ is the $n \times 1$ column vector of fitted Y-values. It is assumed that $n > k$.

The least squares estimates of the k elements of $\hat{\beta}$ are obtained, as before, by minimising the residual sum of squares:

$$S = \sum_{t=1}^{n} e_t^2 = \mathbf{e}'\mathbf{e}$$

$$= (\mathbf{y} - \mathbf{X}\hat{\beta})'(\mathbf{y} - \mathbf{X}\hat{\beta})$$

$$= \mathbf{y}'\mathbf{y} - \hat{\beta}'\mathbf{X}'\mathbf{y} - \mathbf{y}'\mathbf{X}\hat{\beta} + \hat{\beta}'\mathbf{X}'\mathbf{X}\hat{\beta}$$

$$= \mathbf{y}'\mathbf{y} - 2\hat{\beta}'\mathbf{X}'\mathbf{y} + \hat{\beta}'\mathbf{X}'\mathbf{X}\hat{\beta}.$$

Differentiating with respect to $\hat{\beta}$ gives

$$\frac{\partial}{\partial \hat{\beta}}(\mathbf{e}'\mathbf{e}) = -2\mathbf{X}'\mathbf{y} + 2\mathbf{X}'\mathbf{X}\hat{\beta}$$

and equating this to zero gives the *normal equations*

$$\mathbf{X}'\mathbf{X}\hat{\beta} = \mathbf{X}'\mathbf{y}.$$

The multivariate extension of assumption A5 is:

(A5) **X** has rank $k < n$ (i.e. the columns of X are linearly independent.)

Under this assumption **X'X** is invertible and so

$$\hat{\beta} = (\mathbf{X'X})^{-1}\mathbf{X'y}.$$

Note that the normal equations can be written

$$\Sigma X_{1t}Y_t = \hat{\beta}_1 \Sigma X_{1t}^2 + \hat{\beta}_2 \Sigma X_{1t}X_{2t} + \ldots + \hat{\beta}_k \Sigma X_{1t}X_{kt}$$

.
.
.

$$\Sigma X_{kt}Y_t = \hat{\beta}_1 \Sigma X_{kt}X_{1t} + \hat{\beta}_2 \Sigma X_{kt}X_{2t} + \ldots + \hat{\beta}_k \Sigma X_{kt}^2$$

which we can see to be a generalisation of the two-variable case considered in chapter 5. Note further that these are equivalent to writing

$$\left. \begin{array}{c} \Sigma X_{1t}e_t = 0 \\ \cdot \\ \cdot \\ \cdot \\ \Sigma X_{kt}e_t = 0 \end{array} \right\} \quad \text{or} \quad \mathbf{X'e} = \mathbf{0}.$$

Only if a constant term is included so that $X_{1t} = 1$ for all t, does the first normal equation give $\Sigma e_t = 0$.

Also, in the presence of a constant term the first normal equation on division through by n can be written as

$$\bar{Y} = \hat{\beta}_1 + \hat{\beta}_2 \bar{X}_2 + \ldots + \hat{\beta}_k \bar{X}_k.$$

If we use this equation to substitute for $\hat{\beta}_1$ in the other normal equations (in the same way as we did in the two-dimensional case on p. 108) then on division of each through by n we can write them (using the notation for sample moments introduced on p. 109) as

$$m_{YX_2} = \hat{\beta}_2 m_{X_2 X_2} + \ldots + \hat{\beta}_k m_{X_k X_2}$$

$$\cdot$$
$$\cdot$$
$$\cdot$$

$$m_{YX_k} = \hat{\beta}_2 m_{X_2 X_k} + \ldots + \hat{\beta}_k m_{X_k X_k}$$

These $k - 1$ equations in $k - 1$ unknowns can be solved for $\hat{\beta}_2, \ldots, \hat{\beta}_k$ which can then be substituted into the first normal equation as written above to give $\hat{\beta}_1$. This can be a convenient alternative way of writing the normal equations.

6.2 PROPERTIES AND SIGNIFICANCE TESTS

In this section we consider the extension to the multiple regression case of sections 5.2 to 5.4. The unbiasedness and consistency properties of $\hat{\beta}$ carry over from the two-variable case (section 5.2). As an illustration of the method of proof, we show unbiasedness in the case where all the columns of $\mathbf{X}$ are exogenous.

$$\begin{aligned}
\hat{\beta} = (\mathbf{X}'\mathbf{X})^{-1}\mathbf{X}'\mathbf{y} &= (\mathbf{X}'\mathbf{X})^{-1}\mathbf{X}'(\mathbf{X}\beta + \mathbf{u}) \\
&= (\mathbf{X}'\mathbf{X})^{-1}\mathbf{X}'\mathbf{X}\beta + (\mathbf{X}'\mathbf{X})^{-1}\mathbf{X}'\mathbf{u} \\
&= \beta + (\mathbf{X}'\mathbf{X})^{-1}\mathbf{X}'\mathbf{u}.
\end{aligned}$$

Thus

$$\begin{aligned}
E(\hat{\beta}) &= \beta + E[(\mathbf{X}'\mathbf{X})^{-1}\mathbf{X}'\mathbf{u}] \\
&= \beta + E[(\mathbf{X}'\mathbf{X})^{-1}\mathbf{X}']E(\mathbf{u}) \quad &\text{(By independence (A4))} \\
&= \beta \quad &\text{(By A1: } E(\mathbf{u}) = \mathbf{0}\text{).}
\end{aligned}$$

An unbiased estimate of $\sigma_u{}^2$, the variance of the error term, is given by dividing the residual sum of squares by the degrees of freedom remaining after estimation (the sample size, n, minus the number of estimated coefficients, k).

$$\hat{\sigma}_u{}^2 = \frac{\Sigma e_t{}^2}{n-k} = \frac{\mathbf{e'e}}{n-k}$$

$$E(\hat{\sigma}_u{}^2) = \sigma_u{}^2$$

The partition of the original sum of squares goes through as before:

$$\mathbf{y'y} = \mathbf{\hat{y}'\hat{y}} + \mathbf{e'e}$$

since $\mathbf{X'e} = 0$ implies $\mathbf{\hat{y}'e} = \hat{\beta}'\mathbf{X'e} = 0$. It is still true that $\bar{Y} = \bar{\hat{Y}}$ providing a constant term is included. Thus

$$\mathbf{y'y} - n\bar{Y}^2 = \mathbf{\hat{y}'\hat{y}} - n\bar{Y}^2 + \mathbf{e'e}$$

or

$$\Sigma(Y_t - \bar{Y})^2 = \Sigma(\hat{Y}_t - \bar{Y})^2 + \Sigma e_t{}^2$$

and as before we define

$$R^2 = \frac{\Sigma(\hat{Y}_t - \bar{Y})^2}{\Sigma(Y_t - \bar{Y})^2} = 1 - \frac{\Sigma e_t{}^2}{\Sigma(Y_t - \bar{Y})^2}$$

the *coefficient of determination*.

Notice that in the absence of a constant term, $\bar{Y} = \bar{\hat{Y}} + \bar{e} \neq \bar{\hat{Y}}$, so that the above partition is no longer valid and R^2 as usually calculated should not be used in this case as a measure of goodness of fit.

R^2 has a property that is sometimes considered rather undesirable. Addition of an extra explanatory variable, however useless, to the equation will never reduce R^2. At worst it will leave it the same. It is sometimes thought that inclusion of variables that explain very little should be penalised. An alternative measure which is sometimes reported in empirical work is $\bar{R}^2$, or R^2 *corrected for degrees of freedom*. This is defined by taking unbiased estimates of the error variance and the total variance:

$$\bar{R}^2 = 1 - \frac{\dfrac{1}{n-k}\Sigma e_t{}^2}{\dfrac{1}{n-1}\Sigma(Y_t - \bar{Y})^2}$$

$$= 1 - \frac{n-1}{n-k}(1 - R^2)$$

$\bar{R}^2$ increases or decreases when an extra variable is added according to whether the new variable's t-ratio is greater than or less than 1, which seems rather a low target.

In a natural extension of the simple two-variable case, we are interested in testing whether a single coefficient is significantly different from zero. In section 5.2 an expression was derived for the variance of a simple regression coefficient. This concept generalises to the *variance-covariance matrix* of the vector $\hat{\beta}$, defined as the $k \times k$ matrix $E[(\hat{\beta} - \beta)(\hat{\beta} - \beta)']$. This matrix is symmetric and contains the variances of the $\hat{\beta}_i$ on the main diagonal and covariances everywhere else:

$$E[(\hat{\beta} - \beta)(\hat{\beta} - \beta)']$$

$$= \begin{bmatrix} E(\hat{\beta}_1 - \beta_1)^2 & E(\hat{\beta}_1 - \beta_1)(\hat{\beta}_2 - \beta_2) & \cdots & E(\hat{\beta}_1 - \beta_1)(\hat{\beta}_k - \beta_k) \\ E(\hat{\beta}_2 - \beta_2)(\hat{\beta}_1 - \beta_1) & E(\hat{\beta}_2 - \beta_2)^2 & & \cdot \\ \cdot & & & \cdot \\ \cdot & & & \cdot \\ E(\hat{\beta}_k - \beta_k)(\hat{\beta}_1 - \beta_1) & \cdots & & E(\hat{\beta}_k - \beta_k)^2 \end{bmatrix}$$

$$= \begin{bmatrix} \text{var}(\hat{\beta}_1) & \text{cov}(\hat{\beta}_1, \hat{\beta}_2) & \cdots & \text{cov}(\hat{\beta}_1, \hat{\beta}_k) \\ \text{cov}(\hat{\beta}_1, \hat{\beta}_2) & \text{var}(\hat{\beta}_2) & \cdots & \text{cov}(\hat{\beta}_2, \hat{\beta}_k) \\ \cdot & & & \cdot \\ \cdot & & & \cdot \\ \text{cov}(\hat{\beta}_1, \hat{\beta}_k) & \text{cov}(\hat{\beta}_2, \hat{\beta}_k) & \cdots & \text{var}(\hat{\beta}_k) \end{bmatrix}$$

When testing a single coefficient we are interested in the elements on the main diagonal; but in some other situations the covariances are of interest too.

When deriving an expression for the variance in section 5.2 we needed to assume serial independence of the error terms. This is also required here. It can be conveniently expressed in terms of the *variance-covariance matrix* of the u's:

$$E(\mathbf{u}\mathbf{u}') = \begin{bmatrix} E(u_1{}^2) & E(u_1u_2) & . & . & . & E(u_1u_n) \\ E(u_2u_1) & E(u_2{}^2) & . & . & . & E(u_2u_n) \\ . & & & . & & \\ . & & & & . & \\ . & & & & & . \\ E(u_nu_1) & E(u_nu_2) & . & . & . & E(u_n{}^2) \end{bmatrix}$$

The serial independence assumption implies that all the off-diagonal elements are zero. The homoscedasticity (constant variance) assumption implies that the diagonal elements are all $\sigma_u{}^2$. Hence assumptions A2 and A3 of section 5.2 can be combined as:

$$E(\mathbf{u}\mathbf{u}') = \sigma_u{}^2 \mathbf{I}$$

where $\mathbf{I}$ is the $n \times n$ identity matrix.

We saw on p. 147 that by substitution

$$\hat{\beta} - \beta = (\mathbf{X}'\mathbf{X})^{-1}\mathbf{X}'\mathbf{u}.$$

Thus

$$E[(\hat{\beta} - \beta)(\hat{\beta} - \beta)'] = E\{[(\mathbf{X}'\mathbf{X})^{-1}\mathbf{X}'\mathbf{u}] \, [\mathbf{u}'\mathbf{X}(\mathbf{X}'\mathbf{X})^{-1}]\}$$

$$= (\mathbf{X}'\mathbf{X})^{-1}\mathbf{X}'E(\mathbf{u}\mathbf{u}')\mathbf{X}(\mathbf{X}'\mathbf{X})^{-1}$$

$$\text{if } \mathbf{X} \text{ non-stochastic}$$

$$= (\mathbf{X}'\mathbf{X})^{-1}\mathbf{X}'[\sigma_u{}^2\mathbf{I}]\mathbf{X}(\mathbf{X}'\mathbf{X})^{-1}$$

$$= \sigma_u{}^2(\mathbf{X}'\mathbf{X})^{-1}\mathbf{X}'\mathbf{X}(\mathbf{X}'\mathbf{X})^{-1}$$

$$= \sigma_u{}^2(\mathbf{X}'\mathbf{X})^{-1}$$

The variances of the regression coefficients are given by the diagonal elements of this matrix.

Under the classical assumptions (A1–A5) these variances are the *smallest* of any linear unbiased estimator. Thus the OLS estimates are *best* linear unbiased estimates. The variances are estimated by replacing the unknown σ_u^2 by the estimate $\hat{\sigma}_u^2 = \mathbf{e}'\mathbf{e}/(n-k)$. The *standard error* of $\hat{\beta}_i$ (which recall is the estimate of the standard deviation) is given by:

$$SE(\hat{\beta}_i) = \hat{\sigma}_u \sqrt{\{i\text{th diagonal element of } (\mathbf{X}'\mathbf{X})^{-1}\}}$$

We can proceed from this formula to t-ratios and tests of hypotheses just as in section 5.3. If we want to test the null hypothesis $H_0 : \beta_i = 0$, then we calculate the t-ratio, $\hat{\beta}_i/SE(\hat{\beta}_i)$ and compare it with the tabulated percentage points of the t-distribution with $(n-k)$ degrees of freedom. As in section 5.3 this procedure is only valid if the errors are serially independent. If the errors are autocorrelated, then $E(u_t u_s) \neq 0$ for some $t \neq s$ and so $E(\mathbf{u}\mathbf{u}')$ is no longer diagonal. Hence we must replace the assumption $E(\mathbf{u}\mathbf{u}') = \sigma_u^2 \mathbf{I}$ by the more general $n \times n$ matrix: $E(\mathbf{u}\mathbf{u}') = \mathbf{V}$. Then $E[\hat{\beta} - \beta)(\hat{\beta} - \beta)'] = (\mathbf{X}'\mathbf{X})^{-1}\mathbf{X}'\mathbf{V}\mathbf{X}(\mathbf{X}'\mathbf{X})^{-1}$. These variances are no longer the smallest possible – so the OLS estimates are *no longer BLUE*. Calculating standard errors by the previous formula will give *biased* answers since they are based on the *wrong* covariance matrix. The table for validity of our testing procedure is identical to that for the two-variable case given in section 5.3. This is a problem to which we will return when considering autocorrelation in chapter 8.

6.3 MULTICOLLINEARITY

Recall that assumption A5 now requires that $\mathbf{X}$ be of rank k. This will be violated if any two columns of $\mathbf{X}$ are linearly dependent. For example, suppose that we are trying to estimate the equation

$$Y_t = \beta_1 + \beta_2 X_{2t} + \beta_3 X_{3t} + u_t, \qquad t = 1, \ldots, n$$

but that $X_{3t} = \lambda X_{2t}$. In this case every movement in X_2 will be matched by a movement in X_3 and we will not be able to separate the influence of X_2 on Y from that of X_3. By substitution

$$Y_t = \beta_1 + (\beta_2 + \lambda\beta_3)X_{2t} + u_t.$$

Thus we can estimate $(\beta_2 + \lambda\beta_3)$ but cannot separate it to give estimates of β_2 and β_3. In a more general context, if rank $(\mathbf{X}) < k$, then $\mathbf{X'X}$ will not be invertible. Thus $\hat{\beta} = (\mathbf{X'X})^{-1}\mathbf{X'y}$ will not be calculable. Such a situation is called *perfect multicollinearity*. It usually arises from a misformulation of the regression equation. (X_2 and X_3 should not have *both* been in the equation in the first place).

However the problem of multicollinearity comes in all degrees. Usually it is ("*less-than-perfect*") *multicollinearity* that we experience. The simplest case in which this arises is when two of the explanatory variables are highly, but *not* perfectly, correlated. The effect is to make it difficult to separate their influences with any degree of accuracy. Two columns of $\mathbf{X}$ being highly (but not perfectly) correlated implies that the determinant of $\mathbf{X'X}$ will be close to (but not equal to) zero. Thus the elements of $(\mathbf{X'X})^{-1}$ will be very large, since $(\mathbf{X'X})^{-1} = (1/\det(\mathbf{X'X})).\mathrm{Adj}(\mathbf{X'X})$. The consequence of this is that the variances of the $\hat{\beta}_i$ will be large, since $\mathrm{SE}(\hat{\beta}_i) = \hat{\sigma}_u\sqrt{}$ {ith diagonal element of $(\mathbf{X'X})^{-1}$}, and thus the $\hat{\beta}_i$ will not be very accurately determined. The observed t-ratios will be low. Thus the classic symptoms of multicollinearity are "a highish R^2 together with insignificant coefficients". This means that one or more of the explanatory variables has a systematic influence on the dependent variable (as indicated by the high R^2) but that we cannot tell which ones. If we find that inclusion of either one of a pair of variables in our equation without the other results in it being significant, but that when both are included they are both insignificant, this also is evidence of multicollinearity. It should be noted however that we cannot always detect multicollinearity merely by looking at the simple correlation coefficients. Suppose, for example, that we wish to estimate the equation

$$Y_t = \beta_1 + \beta_2 X_{2t} + \beta_3 X_{3t} + \beta_4 X_{4t} + u_t.$$

If it was the case that $X_{4t} = X_{3t} + X_{2t}$ for all t, we would have a situation of perfect multicollinearity. However the simple correlation coefficients between any pair of X's may be quite low.

It should be noted that correlation between the explanatory variables is the norm and is not of itself a problem. In its absence $\mathbf{X'X}$ is diagonal and all the coefficient estimates in the multiple regression case reduce to the corresponding simple regression estimates. The problem is one of degree — whether the correlation is so high as to prevent separation of different effects.

If the multicollinearity is severe the most commonly suggested solution is to get more data. Multicollinearity (in its less-than-perfect form) is mainly a problem of weak data. Generation of a completely new data set is generally not possible in economics as it might be in an experimental science. However if we can increase the number of observations in the data set, the estimated variances of the $\hat{\beta}_i$ should decrease, giving our estimators greater precision. This might be done by extending the time period covered. If annual data were used initially we might try to obtain quarterly data. Finally we might try to combine time series and cross section data. It may be, however, that none of these are possible.

Another possible approach is to attempt to remove the multicollinearity by dropping one of the problem variables. However this may cause more severe problems than it solves. As we shall see in section 6.6, omission of a relevant variable biases the estimated coefficient on any variable that is correlated with it. So this is not a good idea unless economic theory suggests that the variable is not a relevant one (in which case it should not have been there in the first place).

The final possibility to be discussed here is to introduce additional information into the model. The problem of multicollinearity makes it difficult to separate the effects of the different variables. We might try to get some extra information to aid in this separation. This would most likely be either an extraneous estimate of one or more of the parameters from some other source or the imposition of *a priori* restrictions on some of the parameters as indicated by economic theory.

The extraneous estimate approach was used in some of the early attempts to estimate demand functions. The problem was that the time-series data on income and price were highly correlated. This made accurate estimation of the income and price elasticities difficult. The method adopted was to estimate the income elasticity from cross-section expenditure survey data (on the assumption that prices are fairly constant across households at a point in time) and then impose this "extraneous" estimate on the time series equation. To illustrate, suppose the equation to be estimated is

$$\log Q_t = \beta_1 + \beta_2 \log P_t + \beta_3 \log Y_t + u_t$$

Then the method is to get an estimate $\tilde{\beta}_3$ of the income elasticity from the cross-section analysis and impose it on the equation. So we would then estimate

$$(\log Q_t - \tilde{\beta}_3 \log Y_t) = \beta_1 + \beta_2 \log P_t + u_t^*$$

i.e. we would regress $(\log Q_t - \tilde{\beta}_3 \log Y_t)$ on $\log P_t$. The main problem with this method is that the cross-section income elasticity and the time-series income elasticity may not be equal. They measure different things. Finally, it is sometimes forgotten that $\tilde{\beta}_3$ is an estimator and therefore a random variable with its own probability distribution. This requires in particular a modification in the calculation of the standard error of $\hat{\beta}_2$: the usual calculation assumes that $\tilde{\beta}_3$ is a known constant, but if it is a random variable then this calculation underestimates the true standard error of $\hat{\beta}_2$.

The *a priori* restrictions approach might be used by imposing constant returns to scale on a Cobb-Douglas production function or imposing a unit long-run price-level elasticity on a demand for money equation. However this may not be a very desirable solution since in general we will want to test economic theory's *a priori* predictions rather than simply impose them on data for which they may not be true.

6.4. PREDICTION

The extension of the two-variable case dealt with in section 5.5 is fairly straightforward.

Suppose we specify an equation of the form

$$Y_t = \beta_1 + \beta_2 X_{2t} + \ldots + \beta_k X_{kt} + u_t$$

and want to use it to predict the value of Y at some future or hypothetical point.

As before we can show that

$$\hat{Y}_f = \hat{\beta}_1 + \hat{\beta}_2 X_{2f} + \ldots + \hat{\beta}_k X_{kf}$$

is an unbiased predictor of Y_f, and that its variance is given by:

$$\text{var}(\hat{Y}_f) = \sum_{j=1}^{k} \sum_{i=1}^{k} X_{if} \, \text{cov}(\hat{\beta}_i, \hat{\beta}_j) \, X_{jf}$$

where $X_{1f} = 1$ and recall that $\text{cov}(\hat{\beta}_i, \hat{\beta}_i) = \text{var}(\hat{\beta}_i)$.

In matrix notation, let $\mathbf{x}_f$ be the $k \times 1$ vector of future or hypothesised values of the X's. Then

$$\hat{Y}_f = \mathbf{x}'_f \hat{\beta}.$$

The mean and variance of $\hat{Y}_f$ are given by

$$E(\hat{Y}_f) = \mathbf{x}'_f \beta = E(Y_f)$$

and

$$\begin{aligned} \text{var}(\hat{Y}_f) &= E[(\mathbf{x}'_f\hat{\beta} - \mathbf{x}'_f\beta)(\mathbf{x}'_f\hat{\beta} - \mathbf{x}'_f\beta)'] \\ &= \mathbf{x}'_f [V(\hat{\beta})] \mathbf{x}_f \\ &= \sigma_u^2 \mathbf{x}'_f (\mathbf{X'X})^{-1} \mathbf{x}_f \end{aligned}$$

Recall from section 5.5 that the variance of the prediction error is given by

$$\text{var}(e_f) = \sigma_u^2 + \text{var}(\hat{Y}_f)$$

Hence

$$\text{var}\,(e_f) = \sigma_u{}^2(1 + \mathbf{x}'_f(\mathbf{X}'\mathbf{X})^{-1}\mathbf{x}_f)$$

The prediction interval is then constructed as in section 5.5:

$$(\hat{Y}_f \pm t^*\hat{\sigma}_e)$$

where $\text{Prob}(t_{n-k} > t^*) = 0.025$ and

$$\hat{\sigma}_e = \hat{\sigma}_u\sqrt{(1 + \mathbf{x}'_f(\mathbf{X}'\mathbf{X})^{-1}\mathbf{x}_f)}$$

Given the details printed out by most computer regression packages, we would take the following steps to construct a prediction interval for Y_f:

(1) Obtain estimates of the parameters: $\hat{\beta}_1, \ldots, \hat{\beta}_k$

(2) Use these to predict Y by substitution of the future values of the explanatory variables in the fitted equation

$$\hat{Y}_f = \hat{\beta}_1 + \hat{\beta}_2\mathbf{X}_{2f} + \ldots + \hat{\beta}_k\mathbf{X}_{kf}$$

(3) Calculate

$$\hat{\sigma}_u{}^2 = \frac{1}{n-k}\sum_{t=1}^{n} e_t{}^2$$

(4) Calculate the variance-covariance matrix of the coefficients to give

$$\text{cov}\,(\hat{\beta}_i, \hat{\beta}_j) \quad \text{for all } i, j.$$

(This is generally printed out by the regression package).

(5) Calculate

$$c^2 = \sum_{j=1}^{k}\sum_{i=1}^{k} X_{if}\,\text{cov}\,(\hat{\beta}_i, \hat{\beta}_j)\,X_{jf}$$

(this consists of multiplying the (i, j)th element of the variance-covariance matrix by $X_{if}X_{if}$ and then summing over all the elements).

(6) Look up the appropriate t^* from the tables, with $n - k$ degrees of freedom, such that $\text{Prob}(t_{n-k} > t^*) = 0.025$.

(7) Set up the forecast interval for Y_f:

$$\hat{Y}_f \pm t^* \sqrt{\hat{\sigma}_u^{\,2} + c^2}$$

6.5 PARTITIONED REGRESSION

This section looks at the consequences of removing the influence of some variable, or set of variables, from all the variables in an equation prior to its estimation. The most common illustration of this is probably the practice of "detrending" a series. We will demonstrate in this section that detrending all the variables in an equation (by a certain method) prior to its estimation is equivalent to including a linear time trend in a regression using the original data.

We examine this phenomenon in the general case and will return to the special case of detrending at the end of the section. We will compare the result of estimating the equation

$$y = X\beta + Z\gamma + u$$

with the result of regressing y with the influence of Z removed on X with the influence of Z removed. We remove the influence of Z from y by regressing y on Z and taking the residuals as the "adjusted" version of y, say y^*. Then

$$y^* = y - Z\{(Z'Z)^{-1}Z'y\}$$
$$= \{I - Z(Z'Z)^{-1}Z'\}\, y$$
$$= My$$

where M is the $n \times n$ matrix given by $M = I - Z(Z'Z)^{-1}Z'$. Similarly if x is a typical column of X (i.e. one of the explanatory variables) and x* is its "adjusted" version, then

$$x^* = Mx.$$

Forming these column vectors up in the correct order gives X^*, the "adjusted" version of X, as

$$X^* = MX.$$

Consider now the regression of y^* on X^*, i.e. the estimation of the equation

$$y^* = X^*\theta + u^*.$$

The OLS estimate of θ will be given by

$$\hat{\theta} = (X^{*'}X^*)^{-1}X^{*'}y^*$$
$$= (X'M'MX)^{-1}X'M'M y$$

Closer examination of the matrix M reveals some interesting properties that can be used to simplify this expression.

(i) $M' = M$

(ii) $MZ = \{I - Z(Z'Z)^{-1}Z'\}Z = Z - Z(Z'Z)^{-1}Z'Z = Z - Z = 0$,

the zero matrix. (M and Z are said to be *orthogonal* to one another).

(iii) $M'M = MM = M\{I - Z(Z'Z)^{-1}Z'\} = M - MZ(Z'Z)^{-1}Z' = M - 0 = M$

(A matrix with this property is called *idempotent*).

Given these properties of the matrix M, the OLS estimate of θ will be given by

$$\hat{\theta} = (X'MX)^{-1}X'My.$$

We now turn our attention to the direct estimation of the equation

$$y = X\beta + Z\gamma + u.$$

This is a multiple regression equation identical to that discussed earlier in the chapter except that the right-hand-side matrix of observations has been partitioned into two sub-matrices X and Z. The equation could be equivalently written as:

$$y = (X : Z) \binom{\beta}{\gamma} + u.$$

The normal equations for the least squares estimates are given by

$$(X : Z)'y = (X : Z)'(X : Z) \binom{\hat{\beta}}{\hat{\gamma}}.$$

Multiplication out of the partitioned matrices gives

$$\begin{cases} X'y = X'X\hat{\beta} + X'Z\hat{\gamma} \\ Z'y = Z'X\hat{\beta} + Z'Z\hat{\gamma}, \end{cases}$$

the normal equations written in two blocks. Solution of these will give the OLS estimates of β and γ. The second block gives

$$\hat{\gamma} = (Z'Z)^{-1}Z'(y - X\hat{\beta}).$$

Substitution for $\hat{\gamma}$ in the first block gives

$$X'y = X'X\hat{\beta} + X'Z(Z'Z)^{-1}Z'(y - X\hat{\beta}).$$

Thus

$$X'y - X'Z(Z'Z)^{-1}Zy = X'X\hat{\beta} - X'Z(Z'Z)^{-1}Z'X\hat{\beta}$$

and so

$$X'My = X'MX\hat{\beta}$$

giving

$$\hat{\beta} = (\mathbf{X'MX})^{-1}\mathbf{X'My}$$
$$= \hat{\boldsymbol{\theta}}.$$

Thus if we remove the influence of $\mathbf{Z}$ from $\mathbf{y}$ and $\mathbf{X}$ by regressing $\mathbf{y}$ and each column of $\mathbf{X}$ on $\mathbf{Z}$ and taking the residuals, and then regress the "adjusted" version of $\mathbf{y}$ on the "adjusted" version of $\mathbf{X}$ we get the same coefficients on the X-variables as from a regression of $\mathbf{y}$ on both $\mathbf{X}$ and $\mathbf{Z}$. Note in passing that the "adjustment" of y is in fact superfluous. A regression of $\mathbf{y}$ on $\mathbf{X^*}$ gives

$$(\mathbf{X^{*'}X^*})^{-1}\mathbf{X^{*'}y} = (\mathbf{X'M'Mx})^{-1}\mathbf{X'M'y}$$
$$= (\mathbf{X'Mx})^{-1}\mathbf{X'My}$$
$$= \hat{\boldsymbol{\theta}}.$$

So that regression of either $\mathbf{y}$ or $\mathbf{y^*}$ on $\mathbf{X^*}$ gives the same results.

As mentioned at the start of this section a useful illustration of this result is given by the practice of "detrending" a series. In this context the above finding can be stated as follows. If we "detrend" a variable by regressing it on a linear time trend and take the residuals from this regression as the "detrended" series, the following give the same coefficients on the X-variables:

(i) Regress "detrended" $\mathbf{y}$ on "detrended" $\mathbf{X}$.

(ii) Regress $\mathbf{y}$ on "detrended" $\mathbf{X}$.

(iii) Regress $\mathbf{y}$ on $\mathbf{X}$ and a linear time trend.

We can illustrate this without the use of matrices for the simple case of a single explanatory variable, X_t. Consider first the use of "detrended" series. We regress Y and X in turn on a linear time trend and take the residuals as the "detrended" versions of Y and X, which we will denote by Y^* and X^*. Expressing all variables in terms of deviations from their respective means and using the moment notation of

p. 109, we can write

$$Y_t^* - \bar{Y}^* = (Y_t - \bar{Y}) - (t - \bar{t}) \frac{m_{yt}}{m_{tt}}$$

$$X_t^* - \bar{X}^* = (X_t - \bar{X}) - (t - \bar{t}) \frac{m_{xt}}{m_{tt}}.$$

(Notice that for strict compatibility with the general case considered above in matrix notation these regressions should have excluded constant terms. However we shall see that this will not affect the final slope coefficient. Note also that $\bar{Y}^*$ and $\bar{X}^*$ are in fact both zero.)

Regression of Y^* on X^* then gives an estimated slope coefficient of

$$\hat{\theta} = \frac{\Sigma(Y_t^* - \bar{Y}^*)(X_t^* - \bar{X}^*)}{\Sigma(X_t^* - \bar{X}^*)^2}$$

$$= \frac{\Sigma\left\{Y_t - \bar{Y} - (t - \bar{t})\frac{m_{yt}}{m_{tt}}\right\}\left\{X_t - \bar{X} - (t - \bar{t})\frac{m_{xt}}{m_{tt}}\right\}}{\Sigma\left\{X_t - \bar{X} - (t - \bar{t})\frac{m_{xt}}{m_{tt}}\right\}^2}$$

$$= \frac{m_{yx} - (m_{yt}m_{xt}/m_{tt})}{m_{xx} - (m_{xt}^2/m_{tt})}$$

$$= \frac{m_{yx}m_{tt} - m_{yt}m_{xt}}{m_{xx}m_{tt} - m_{xt}^2}.$$

Next consider direct estimation of the equation

$$Y_t = \alpha + \beta X_t + \gamma t + u_t$$

From section 6.1 the normal equations for the slope coefficients can be written (see p. 147)

$$m_{yx} = \hat{\beta}m_{xx} + \hat{\gamma}m_{xt}$$

$$m_{yt} = \hat{\beta}m_{xt} + \hat{\gamma}m_{tt}.$$

Solving these for $\hat{\beta}$ gives

$$\hat{\beta} = \frac{m_{yx}m_{tt} - m_{yt}m_{xt}}{m_{xx}m_{tt} - m_{xt}^2}$$

which is the same as the expression for $\hat{\theta}$ derived above.

Another useful application of these results arises when we are interested in allowing for seasonal variation. This will be examined in section 7.1.

6.6 CONSEQUENCES OF MISSPECIFICATION OF THE EQUATION

Correct inference in econometrics is heavily dependent on the implicit assumption that our equation is correctly specified. In this section we examine this assumption in relation to the deterministic part of the equation, where it is largely a question of whether or not our equation contains the correct variables and whether or not we have the correct functional form. Economic theory may suggest for example that an important variable has been left out (possibly due to the data not being available). We will also see later (in chapters 8 and 9) that the presence of autocorrelated or heteroscedastic residuals can be an indication of misspecification of the variables that should be included in the equation. Here we will look at the consequences of such misspecification.

(1) *A relevant explanatory variable left out*

We consider first the misspecification of not including some relevant explanatory variable. To take the simplest illustration, suppose that the "true" relationship between the variables is given by

$$Y_t = \beta_1 + \beta_2 X_{2t} + \beta_3 X_{3t} + u_t$$

where the u_t satisfy the full set of classical assumptions. However, we overlook X_3 and instead estimate the equation

$$Y_t = \beta_1 + \beta_2 X_{2t} + u_t^*$$

What are the consequences of this for the OLS estimates of β_1 and β_2? In general they are biased and inconsistent. To see why consider the estimate of β_2:

$$\hat{\beta}_2 = \frac{\Sigma(X_{2t} - \bar{X}_2)(Y_t - \bar{Y})}{\Sigma(X_{2t} - \bar{X}_2)^2}.$$

From the true relationship we can see that

$$(Y_t - \bar{Y}) = \beta_2(X_{2t} - \bar{X}_2) + \beta_3(X_{3t} - \bar{X}_3) + (u_t - \bar{u}).$$

Substitution of this into the expression for $\hat{\beta}_2$ gives

$$\hat{\beta}_2 = \beta_2 + \beta_3 \frac{\Sigma(X_{2t} - \bar{X}_2)(X_{3t} - \bar{X}_3)}{\Sigma(X_{2t} - \bar{X}_2)^2} + \frac{\Sigma(X_{2t} - \bar{X}_2)(u_t - \bar{u})}{\Sigma(X_{2t} - \bar{X}_2)^2}.$$

Hence

$$E(\hat{\beta}_2) = \beta_2 + \beta_3 \hat{\lambda}_2$$

where

$$\hat{\lambda}_2 = \frac{\Sigma(X_{2t} - \bar{X}_2)(X_{3t} - \bar{X}_3)}{\Sigma(X_{2t} - \bar{X}_2)^2}$$

is the slope coefficient from a hypothetical regression of X_3 on X_2:

$$X_{3t} = \lambda_1 + \lambda_2 X_{2t} + \text{an error term.}$$

Similarly we can show that

$$E(\hat{\beta}_1) = \beta_1 + \beta_3 \hat{\lambda}_1.$$

Given that $\beta_3 \neq 0$, $\hat{\beta}_2$ is biased unless $\hat{\lambda}_2 = 0$, that is unless X_2 and X_3 are uncorrelated. The direction of the bias in $\hat{\beta}_2$ depends on the sign of the effect of the omitted variable on the dependent variable (β_3) and the sign of the correlation between the omitted variable and the included explanatory variable $(\hat{\lambda}_2)$. If these have the same sign, $\hat{\beta}_2$ is biased upwards and if they have opposite signs it is biased downwards. Unless $\hat{\lambda}_2 \to 0$ as the sample size increases, $\hat{\beta}_2$ is also inconsistent.

These results extend in a straightforward manner to the multiple regression case. Suppose that the "true" relationship is given by

$$y = X\beta + \gamma z + u$$

where y, X, β and u are as defined at the start of the chapter and z is the vector of observations on the omitted variable. The equation actually estimated is

$$y = X\beta + u^*.$$

The OLS estimate of β is given by

$$\hat{\beta} = (X'X)^{-1}X'y.$$

Substituting from the "true" relationship

$$\hat{\beta} = (X'X)^{-1}X'(X\beta + \gamma z + u)$$
$$= \beta + \gamma(X'X)^{-1}X'z + (X'X)^{-1}X'u.$$

Hence, taking expectations,

$$E(\hat{\beta}) = \beta + \gamma \{(X'X)^{-1}X'z\}$$

and the bias in $\hat{\beta}$ given by the coefficient in the "true" relationship on the omitted variable multiplied by the estimated coefficient vector in a regression of z on X. The bias in the coefficient on any particular variable is therefore equal to the coefficient in the "true" relationship on the omitted variable multiplied by the regression coefficient on that variable in a regression of the omitted variable on all the included variables.

(2) *An irrelevant explanatory variable included*

We consider next the misspecification of including an irrelevant explanatory variable. Once again we start with a simple equation and then proceed to examination of the general multiple regression equation.

Suppose initially that the "true" relationship is

$$Y_t = \beta_1 + \beta_2 X_{2t} + u_t$$

whilst the equation that is estimated is

$$Y_t = \beta_1 + \beta_2 X_{2t} + \beta_3 X_{3t} + u_t^*.$$

The estimates of β_1 and β_2 will in general be different from those that would have been obtained if the "true" model had been estimated, i.e. if X_3 had not been included, and the estimate of β_3 will be different from its "true" value of zero. However, since the proofs of the unbiasedness and consistency of OLS estimates hold irrespective of the numerical values of the parameters, the standard results tell us that OLS will provide unbiased and consistent estimates of β_1, β_2 and 0. Furthermore the estimated variances are unbiased even if X_2 and X_3 are correlated. So the usual t-tests are still valid. The only problem is one of inefficiency. If $\tilde{\beta}_2$ is the estimate we would have obtained if we had estimated the "true" relationship, then it can be shown that

$$\frac{\text{var}(\hat{\beta}_2)}{\text{var}(\tilde{\beta}_2)} = \frac{1}{1 - r^2} \geqslant 1$$

where r is the coefficient of correlation between X_2 and X_3. Hence if X_2 and X_3 are correlated $\hat{\beta}$ is inefficient. In other words, the inclusion of X_3 (if it is correlated with X_2) causes the estimate of β_2 to be *less reliable* than it would have been.

Turning now to the multiple regression case, suppose that the "true" relationship is given by

$$y = X\beta + u.$$

whilst the estimated equation is given by

$$y = X\beta + \gamma z + u^*.$$

Then, from section 6.5, the OLS estimate of β is given by

$$\hat{\beta} = (X'MX)^{-1}X'My$$

where $M = I - z(z'z)^{-1}z'$. This is clearly different from what would have been obtained by estimating the "true" equation:

$$\hat{\beta} = (X'X)^{-1}X'y.$$

However, it is still an unbiased estimate. Substituting from the "true" relationship,

$$\hat{\beta} = (X'MX)^{-1}X'MX\beta + (X'MX)^{-1}X'Mu.$$

Thus

$$E(\hat{\beta}) = \beta.$$

Similarly, the estimate of γ will be unbiased.

$$\hat{\gamma} = (z'Qz)^{-1}z'Qy$$

where $Q = I - X(X'X)^{-1}X'$ the counterpart of the matrix M. Substituting from the "true" relationship again gives

$$\hat{\gamma} = (z'Qz)^{-1}z'QX\beta + (z'Qz)^{-1}z'Qu.$$

However,

$$QX = X - X = 0.$$

Thus

$$E(\hat{\gamma}) = 0.$$

(3) *Incorrect functional form*

The equations estimated in applied economics are most commonly linear in both parameters and variables. However the underlying "true" relationship may well be nonlinear and our estimating equation should probably be regarded as simply a linear *approximation* to the "true" relationship. What will be the consequences of this approximation for our coefficient estimates?

Providing the functional form in the relationship between two variables is continuous and differentiable a sufficient number of times, it can be approximated to any required degree of accuracy by a polynomial of sufficiently high order. Thus we may suppose the underlying relationship between two variables to be given by

$$Y_t = \beta_1 + \beta_2 X_t + \beta_3 X_t^2 + \ldots + u_t.$$

If we then estimate a linear approximation of this

$$Y_t = \beta_1 + \beta_2 X_t + u_t^*$$

relevant explanatory variables have been omitted. The implications, however, are not quite the same as in the general case in (1) above. To illustrate, suppose that the correctly specified equation is quadratic

$$Y_t = \beta_1 + \beta_2 X_t + \beta_3 X_t^2 + u_t$$

and that we estimate a linear approximation. Then by the analysis in (1) above

$$E(\hat{\beta}_2) = \beta_2 + \beta_3 \hat{\lambda}_2$$

where $\hat{\lambda}_2$ is the estimated slope coefficient from a hypothetical regression of X_t^2 on X_t. Thus $\hat{\beta}_2$ will be a biased estimate of β_2. However

$$\frac{dY}{dX} = \beta_2 + 2\beta_3 X$$

and hence β_2 measures the effect of X on Y only when X equals zero. So we are probably not very interested in whether $\hat{\beta}_2$ is an unbiased estimate of this quantity.

It can be shown by simple manipulation that

$$\hat{\lambda}_2 = \frac{\Sigma(X_t - \bar{X})^3}{\Sigma(X_t - \bar{X})^2} + 2\bar{X}.$$

If the observations on X are *symmetric* about the mean, $\bar{X}$, then the first of these terms is zero and

$$\hat{\lambda}_2 = 2\bar{X}.$$

Thus

$$E(\hat{\beta}_2) = \beta_2 + 2\beta_3 \bar{X} = \frac{dY}{dX}\bigg|_{X=\bar{X}}$$

Hence $\hat{\beta}_2$ is an unbiased estimate of dY/dX evaluated at the mean of X.

If the observations on X are *not symmetric* about their mean (the general case) then $\hat{\lambda}_2 \neq 2\bar{X}$ and so $\hat{\beta}_2$ will be a biased estimate of

$$\frac{dY}{dX}\bigg|_{X=\bar{X}}$$

EXERCISES

6.1 Estimate the slope coefficients of the equation

$$Y_t = \beta_1 + \beta_2 X_{2t} + \beta_3 X_{3t} + u_t$$

given the following sample moments

	Y	X_2	X_3
Y	1	3	7
X_2	3	20	30
X_3	7	30	50

6.2 Use the data from exercise 5.1 to estimate the equation

$$C_t = \beta_1 + \beta_2 DI_t + \beta_3 C_{t-4} + u_t$$

Discuss the specification and compare the results with those in exercise 5.1.

6.3 Consider the equations

$$\log Y_i = \beta_1 + \beta_2 \log W_i + \beta_3 S_i + u_i$$

$$(i = 1, \ldots, n)$$

$$\log (Y_i/W_i) = \gamma_1 + \gamma_2 \log W_i + \gamma_3 S_i + u_i$$

where Y_i = the annual income of the ith individual in the sample, W_i = the number of weeks worked in the year by the ith individual, and S_i = the number of years of full-time education received by the ith individual.

(a) Show that OLS estimation will give $\hat{\gamma}_1 = \hat{\beta}_1$, $\hat{\gamma}_3 = \hat{\beta}_3$ and $\hat{\gamma}_2 = \hat{\beta}_2 - 1$.

(b) Show that the residuals from the two regressions will be identical.

(c) What light does the second formulation throw on the implicit assumption that W is exogenous in the first?

(d) Under what conditions will the R^2 for the first formulation exceed that for the second and what does it tell us about the goodness of fit?

6.4 Which of the parameters in the following equation can be estimated?

$$Y_t = \beta_1 + \beta_2 X_{2t} + \beta_3 X_{3t} + \beta_4 (X_{2t} - X_{3t}) + \beta_5 X_{5t} + u_t$$

6.5 Show that, for the case of a single explanatory variable, to the list on p. 160 can be added

(iv) regress y on "detrended X" and a time trend.

6.6 Use the equation estimated in exercise 6.2 to construct a 95% prediction interval for C given the value of DI in the first quarter of 1977 is £17,803 m.

VII

SOME USES OF THE REGRESSION MODEL

7.1 DUMMY VARIABLES

So far we have dealt only with variables that can be measured quantitatively. For example, consumption, disposable income, investment and prices can all be measured in units of money, whilst interest rates can be measured in percentage terms. Sometimes in economics, however, we are interested in *qualitative* variables; that is variables which do not have a natural scale of measurement. Some examples will help to illustrate the distinction being made.

(i) In a time series analysis of consumption we might think of consumers' expenditure as depending not only on disposable income, but also on whether or not the country was in a period of war or peace at the time. During wartime there is rationing and other restrictions on consumption. Hence we might expect a lower level of consumption for any given level of disposable income than in peacetime.

(ii) If we were conducting an analysis of consumption over a cross-section of households, we might wish to argue that households in urban and rural areas would have different patterns of consumption at any given income level; that consumption behaviour would vary between the north and the south of the country; or that the expenditures of single people will differ from those of married couples.

(iii) If examining the determinants of the rate of change of money wages, we may wish to investigate the possibility that the rate is, *ceteris paribus,* lower when an incomes policy is being enforced.

(iv) Finally, suppose we were examining inter-personal differences in earnings across a cross-section of individuals. In addition to the effects of age at completion of full-time education and the number of years of labour market experience, we might expect differences by sex, race, qualifications and whether the individual was single or married.

In all of these instances dummy variables can be used to model the effects we wish to examine. We start with the simplest way in which a dummy variable can be introduced into an equation.

The additive case

Suppose intitially that our qualitative variable changes the intercept but not the slope of the relationship. To illustrate, consider the third example above of the effect of an incomes policy on the rate of change of money wages. We suppose a simple wage equation where the rate of change of wages in period t, $\dot{W}_t$, is determined by the rate of change of prices in the preceding period, $\dot{P}_{t-1}$.

We suppose (as illustrated in Figure 7.1) that the imposition of an incomes policy reduces the rate of wage inflation, but does not alter the effect of $\dot{P}$ on $\dot{W}$, i.e. the wage equation during periods with an incomes policy has the same slope as that during periods without, but a lower intercept. In this case we can express both the policy-on and

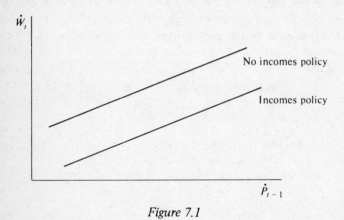

Figure 7.1

the policy-off wage equations in terms of a single equation:

$$\dot{W}_t = \beta_1 + \beta_2 \dot{P}_{t-1} + \beta_3 D_t + u_t, \qquad t = 1, \ldots, n$$

where

$$D_t = \begin{cases} 1 \text{ if } t \text{ was a period of incomes policy} \\ 0 \text{ if not} \end{cases}$$

D_t is called a *dummy variable* (or sometimes an *indicator variable*).

The interpretation of this equation is as follows. During periods without an incomes policy $(D_t = 0)$ the relationship between wage changes and price changes is given by

$$\dot{W}_t = \beta_1 + \beta_2 \dot{P}_{t-1} + u_t$$

whereas during periods of incomes policy $(D_t = 1)$ it is given by

$$\dot{W}_t = (\beta_1 + \beta_3) + \beta_2 \dot{P}_{t-1} + u_t$$

and hence we would presumably expect β_3 to be negative. The coefficients can be estimated in the usual way using the regression technique of the previous section just as if D was a continuous variable. Notice that, in addition to the assumption of equal slopes, two other important implicit assumptions are also being made in this simple formulation. Firstly we are assuming that our equation is a reduced form equation, and in particular that D is exogenous. This carries with it the implicit assumption that the level of $\dot{W}$ does not affect the government's decision of whether or not to impose an incomes policy. Secondly we are assuming that the effect of an incomes policy on $\dot{W}$ is constant throughout the policy and the same for any separate policies during the sample period $t = 1, \ldots, n$. (It is β_3 at all times).

To consider the interpretation of estimated equations with dummy variables, suppose the following results were obtained for the equation we have been discussing

$$\hat{\dot{W}}_t = 6 + 0.7 \dot{P}_{t-1} - 4D$$
$$(7.4) \quad (9.2) \quad (-4.9)$$

where the numbers in parentheses are t-ratios and $\dot{W}$ and $\dot{P}$ are measured in percentage terms. There is a test statistic of -4.9 on the hypothesis $\beta_3 = 0$. Hence β_3 is significantly different from zero. Thus we would conclude that during the sample period incomes policy had a significant negative effect on the rate of change of money wages. The estimated wage equation is given by

$$\hat{\dot{W}}_t = 6 + 0.7\,\dot{P}_{t-1} \qquad \text{for policy-off periods}$$

$$\hat{\dot{W}}_t = 2 + 0.7\,\dot{P}_{t-1} \qquad \text{for policy-on periods.}$$

The effect of incomes policy has been modelled as a parallel downward shift in the wage-price relationship.

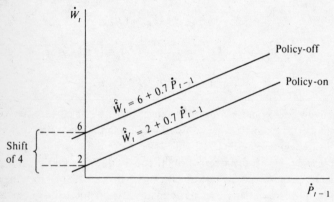

Figure 7.2

The multiplicative case

Alternatively we might wish to hypothesise that incomes policy affects the slope with respect to $\dot{P}$ rather than the intercept. In this case we can write our single regression equation as

$$\dot{W}_t = \beta_1 + \beta_2\dot{P}_{t-1} + \beta_4(\dot{P}_{t-1}D_t) + u_t$$

where D_t is defined exactly as before and is now being used as a *multiplicative dummy variable*. The interpretation is now as follows. During periods without an incomes policy $(D_t = 0)$ the relationship between $\dot{W}$ and $\dot{P}$ is given by

$$\dot{W}_t = \beta_1 + \beta_2 \dot{P}_{t-1} + u_t$$

whereas during periods of incomes policy $(D_t = 1)$ it is given by

$$\dot{W}_t = \beta_1 + (\beta_2 + \beta_4) \dot{P}_{t-1} + u_t$$

This is illustrated in Figure 7.3 for the case where β_4 is negative. The single equation can be estimated as in the continuous case, with $(\dot{P}_{t-1} D_t)$ taken as a separate variable which has the value zero when $D_t = 0$ and is equal to $\dot{P}_{t-1}$ when $D_t = 1$. The interpretation is analogous to the additive case.

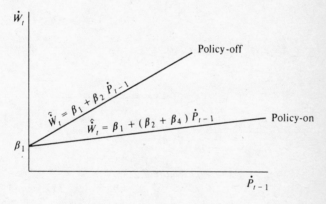

Figure 7.3

The combined case

We can combine these two methods and have both additive and multiplicative dummy variables in the same equation. If we hypothesised that both the slope and the intercept of the relationship were different between policy-off and policy-on periods, then we would formulate our equation as

$$\dot{W}_t = \beta_1 + \beta_2\dot{P}_{t-1} + \beta_3 D_t + \beta_4(\dot{P}_{t-1}D_t) + u_t, \qquad t = 1, \ldots, n$$

This is the combination of:

$$\text{Policy-off: } \dot{W}_t = \beta_1 + \beta_2\dot{P}_{t-1} + u_t$$
$$\text{Policy-on: } \dot{W}_t = (\beta_1 + \beta_3) + (\beta_2 + \beta_4)\dot{P}_{t-1} + u_t.$$

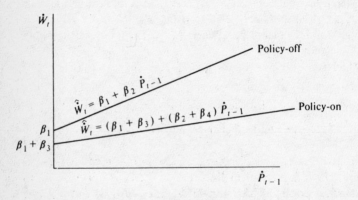

Figure 7.4

The single equation can be estimated in the usual way and the interpretation of the results is as in the additive and multiplicative only cases.

Alternatively, since both slope and intercept differ between policy-on and policy-off periods, we could split the sample and estimate two separate equations:

$$\hat{\dot{W}}_t = \hat{\alpha}_1 + \hat{\alpha}_2\dot{P}_{t-1} \qquad \text{estimated for policy-on periods } (D_t = 1)$$
$$\hat{\dot{W}}_t = \hat{\gamma}_1 + \hat{\gamma}_2\dot{P}_{t-1} \qquad \text{estimated for policy-off periods } (D_t = 0)$$

It can be shown that the two methods give exactly equivalent coefficient estimates:

$$\text{Policy-on: intercept: } \hat{\alpha}_1 = \hat{\beta}_1 + \hat{\beta}_3$$
$$\text{slope} \quad : \hat{\alpha}_2 = \hat{\beta}_2 + \hat{\beta}_4$$
$$\text{Policy-off: intercept: } \hat{\gamma}_1 = \hat{\beta}_1$$
$$\text{slope} \quad : \hat{\gamma}_2 = \hat{\beta}_2$$

Hence $\hat{\beta}_3 = \hat{\alpha}_1 - \hat{\gamma}_1$ and $\hat{\beta}_4 = \hat{\alpha}_2 - \hat{\gamma}_2$ and so the single equation is given by

$$\hat{\dot{W}}_t = \hat{\gamma}_1 + \hat{\gamma}_2 \dot{P}_{t-1} + (\hat{\alpha}_1 - \hat{\gamma}_1) D_t + (\hat{\alpha}_2 - \hat{\gamma}_2)(\dot{P}_{t-1} D_t)$$

which is the same as the result of taking:

$$D_t \times \text{policy-on equation: } \hat{\dot{W}}_t = \hat{\alpha}_1 + \hat{\alpha}_2 \dot{P}_{t-1}$$
$$+ (1 - D_t) \times \text{policy-off equation: } \hat{\dot{W}}_t = \hat{\gamma}_1 + \hat{\gamma}_2 \dot{P}_{t-1}.$$

If attention is being focussed on testing for shifts, estimation on the full sample is convenient since it gives direct estimates (and associated standard errors) of the shift in the intercept (β_3) and the shift in the slope (β_4). If attention is being focussed on the actual equations in the two periods then estimation on the separate samples may be more convenient. The equivalence of the results still holds when the method is extended to several explanatory variables: inclusion of an additive dummy and multiplicative dummies for each of the explanatory variables will give coefficient estimates that correspond exactly to those obtained by splitting the sample and estimating separate equations. Notice however that estimation on the full sample with dummy variables assumes that the error terms in the policy-on and policy-off equations have the same variance. This is not the case when separate regressions are run. Thus in general the standard error of the equation, σ_u, for the full sample will differ from those for the separate equations. (Note however that each estimate $\hat{\sigma}_u^2$ will be an unbiased estimate of σ_u^2, under the assumptions of chapter 5.) Thus, although the coefficient estimates from the two methods will be the same, the t-ratios will not be.

The combination rule of dummy variables

We can use several dummy variables for several qualitative factors in the same equation providing we observe the following rules.

Additive dummy variables: If a constant is included in the equation then no sub-group of the additive dummy variables should sum identically to a constant value.

Multiplicative dummy variables: For any continuous variable included in the equation, no sub-group of the multiplicative dummy variables in product with it should sum identically to a constant multiple of the continuous variable itself.

In both cases the object of the rule is to avoid perfect multicollinearity. Suppose that in addition to the dummy variable, D_t, defined above we also defined:

$$E_t = \begin{cases} 1 \text{ if } t \text{ was a period without incomes policy} \\ 0 \text{ otherwise} \end{cases}$$

Then $D_t + E_t = 1$ for all t, i.e. D_t and E_t sum to the unit constant. Thus if we were to include D_t, E_t and a constant in the same equation we would have perfect multicollinearity and be unable to estimate the coefficients concerned.

The use of dummy variables for seasonal adjustment

Many economic time-series show marked seasonal fluctuations. For example industrial production usually declines in the third quarter of the year and non-durable consumption is usually highest in the fourth quarter. Two main methods are used to take account of seasonal fluctuations when estimating economic relationships. The first is to "de-seasonalise" the data (by, for example, a moving average method) before estimation. The second is to use particular dummy variables during estimation. The first method can be criticised on several counts. Firstly, it will induce autocorrelation. Secondly, if different techniques of seasonal adjustment are used on the different series (e.g. by different statistics-gathering organisations) then this may distort the relationships between the series. Thirdly, one does not know the degrees of freedom used up in the adjustment technique and so cannot adjust for it when conducting tests, etc., in the later estimation. Finally cumulative averaging is a smoothing device and may tend to obscure some of the finer movements in the series we are considering.

The alternative technique of using dummy variables is an attempt to overcome these difficulties. If using quarterly data we would define the following variables (using only three variables to avoid perfect multicollinearity):

$$Q_{1t} = \begin{cases} 1 \text{ if } t \text{ is the 1st quarter of the year} \\ 0 \text{ otherwise} \end{cases}$$

$$Q_{2t} = \begin{cases} 1 \text{ if } t \text{ is the 2nd quarter of the year} \\ 0 \text{ otherwise} \end{cases}$$

$$Q_{3t} = \begin{cases} 1 \text{ if } t \text{ is the 3rd quarter of the year} \\ 0 \text{ otherwise} \end{cases}$$

These three variables would then be included in the regression. For example if estimating a simple consumption function and wishing to take account of seasonal fluctuations in this way we might estimate the equation

$$C_t = \beta_1 + \beta_2 Y_t^d + \beta_3 Q_{1t} + \beta_4 Q_{2t} + \beta_5 Q_{3t} + u_t$$

Notice that in including the three dummy variables in this way we are making the implicit assumption that the seasonal fluctuations in consumption can be regarded as additive, only effecting the intercept in the relations. We are assuming, for example, that the marginal propensity to consume (β_2) is constant across the quarters. If we wished to allow for a seasonal component in the marginal propensity to consume, we would have to include multiplicative dummies.

The question obviously raised is how do the estimates obtained when seasonal dummy variables are included in the regression compare with those when deseasonalised data are used. Suppose we obtained deseasonalised series for C and Y^d, call them $\tilde{C}$ and $\tilde{Y}^d$, and then estimated the regression

$$\tilde{C}_t = \alpha_1 + \alpha_2 \tilde{Y}_t^d + \text{an error term}$$

How would $\hat{\alpha}_2$ compare with $\hat{\beta}_2$? From the properties of partitioned regression discussed in section 6.5 we can say that if the deseasonalised series were obtained by regression on seasonal dummies, the two techniques would give exactly the same estimate of the marginal propensity to consume: $\hat{\alpha}_2 = \hat{\beta}_2$. However if the deseasonalised series were obtained by another method, for example by a moving average method, then $\hat{\alpha}_2$ and $\hat{\beta}_2$ will in general not be the same. If there is only little cyclical variation in C and Y^d, i.e. if both follow a fairly steady growth path, then the difference between $\hat{\alpha}_2$ and $\hat{\beta}_2$ will be negligible. The greater are the cyclical effects the less will be the agreement between $\hat{\alpha}_2$ and $\hat{\beta}_2$.

Dummy variables as the only explanatory variables

Although equations containing only dummy variables are hardly ever estimated, brief consideration of such equations is a useful aid to understanding the interpretation of the coefficients of dummy variables in equations that also contain continuous variables. Consider first the simple case of a single explanatory variable which is a dummy variable.

As an illustration, suppose we have data on a cross-section of individuals, some of whom have A-level or an equivalent qualification and some of whom do not.

Let

Y_i = the average weekly earnings of the ith individual

and

$$D_i = \begin{cases} 1 \text{ if the } i\text{th individual has A-level or equivalent} \\ 0 \text{ if not} \end{cases}$$

Then consider the regression equation

$$Y_i = \beta_1 + \beta_2 D_i + u_i$$

Let

$\bar{Y}_1$ = the mean earnings of the individuals in the sample with A-level or equivalent,

and

$\bar{Y}_0$ = the mean earnings of the individuals in the sample without.

Then we can show that the OLS estimates will be

$$\hat{\beta}_1 = \bar{Y}_0$$
$$\hat{\beta}_2 = \bar{Y}_1 - \bar{Y}_0.$$

The coefficient on the dummy variable is simply the difference in mean earnings between the two groups.

Suppose now that we wanted to consider a three-way breakdown of the sample according to the highest qualification that an individual has: (i) those with a degree, (ii) those without a degree but with A-level or equivalent, and (iii) those without either. We could formulate the effect of this on earnings by considering two dummy variables:

$$D_{1i} = \begin{cases} 1 \text{ if the } i\text{th individual has A-level or equivalent} \\ \quad \text{as highest qualification (i.e. and } no \text{ degree)} \\ 0 \text{ if not} \end{cases}$$

$$D_{2i} = \begin{cases} 1 \text{ if the } i\text{th individual has a degree} \\ 0 \text{ if not} \end{cases}$$

and considering the regression

$$Y_i = \beta_1 + \beta_2 D_{1i} + \beta_3 D_{2i} + u_i.$$

Let

$\bar{Y}_2$ = the mean earnings of the individuals in the sample with a degree,

$\bar{Y}_1$ = the mean earnings of the individuals in the sample with A-level or equivalent but without a degree,

and

$\bar{Y}_0$ = the mean earnings of the individuals in the sample without either A-level or a degree.

Then we can show that the OLS estimates will be

$$\hat{\beta}_1 = \bar{Y}_0$$
$$\hat{\beta}_2 = \bar{Y}_1 - \bar{Y}_0$$
$$\hat{\beta}_3 = \bar{Y}_2 - \bar{Y}_0.$$

Note that this is only true in the case where the properties represented by D_1 and D_2 are mutually exclusive. An equivalent result holds for higher-order breakdowns of the sample.

We consider next the case of overlapping categories. Suppose we now wish to use the dummy variables

$$D_{1i} = \begin{cases} 1 \text{ if the } i\text{th individual has A-level or equivalent} \\ 0 \text{ if not} \end{cases}$$

$$D_{2i} = \begin{cases} 1 \text{ if the } i\text{th individual is male} \\ 0 \text{ if the } i\text{th individual is female} \end{cases}$$

and suppose that the mean earnings in each of the four possible categories is given by:

Highest qualification		Without A-level or equivalent	With A-level or equivalent
Sex	D_1	0	1
	D_2		
Female	0	$\bar{Y}_1$	$\bar{Y}_2$
Male	1	$\bar{Y}_3$	$\bar{Y}_4$

If we now formulate and estimate the regression

$$Y_i = \beta_1 + \beta_2 D_{1i} + \beta_3 D_{2i} + u_i$$

we are making the implicit assumption that the increase in earnings due to having A-level is the same for men and women (β_2 in both cases). If this is true in the sample, then the OLS estimate of β_2 will be given by

$$\hat{\beta}_2 = \bar{Y}_2 - \bar{Y}_1 = \bar{Y}_4 - \bar{Y}_3.$$

If not, then it will be a weighted average of $(\bar{Y}_2 - \bar{Y}_1)$ and $(\bar{Y}_4 - \bar{Y}_3)$ and equal to neither.

If instead we set up the regression

$$Y_i = \beta_1 + \beta_2 D_{1i} + \beta_3 D_{2i} + \beta_4 (D_{1i} D_{2i}) + u_i$$

we are no longer assuming that the possession of A-level or equivalent has the same effect on earnings for both men and women. Now the mean difference in earnings due to A-level is $(\beta_2 + \beta_4)$ for men and β_2

for women, and we can show that the OLS estimates will be

$$\hat{\beta}_1 = \bar{Y}_1$$

$$\hat{\beta}_2 = \bar{Y}_2 - \bar{Y}_1$$

$$\hat{\beta}_3 = \bar{Y}_3 - \bar{Y}_1$$

$$\hat{\beta}_4 = (\bar{Y}_4 - \bar{Y}_3) - (\bar{Y}_2 - \bar{Y}_1).$$

The significance test on $\hat{\beta}_4$ is a test of the equality of the mean difference in earnings due to A-level between men and women. This equality was implicitly assumed in the previous equation, in which $\beta_4 = 0$.

Notice also, and equivalently, that in the previous equation the sex difference in earnings is assumed to be the same for those with A-level and those without (β_3 for both groups). This implicit assumption is not made in this equation. The sex difference in earnings is β_3 for those without A-level and ($\beta_3 + \beta_4$) for those with.

In conclusion, if we have as our explanatory variables in a regression a set of dummy variables together with a complete set of interactions and no other variables, then OLS is equivalent to taking the mean of the dependent variable in each cell of a multi-dimensional cross-tabulation. If the interactions are omitted and the dummy variables are not mutually exclusive then a number of implicit assumptions of the type discussed above are being made.

In general, of course, our regression equations will not consist of dummy explanatory variables alone, but will also contain continuous variables on the right-hand side. The interpretation of coefficient estimates obtained in such situations is a natural extension of the illustrations discussed above. The coefficient on a dummy variable now represents the difference in the mean of the dependent variable adjusted for the right-hand side continuous variables, i.e. given the other right-hand side variables. For example suppose Y and D_1 are as defined in the previous example, A_i = the age of the ith individual, and we estimate the equation

$$Y_i = \beta_1 + \beta_2 D_{1i} + \beta_3 A_i + u_i.$$

Then $\hat{\beta}_2$ is the difference in the mean of earnings adjusted for age between those with A-level and those without, i.e. it is the average effect of having A-level on earnings, holding age constant.

A dummy variable as dependent variable

Ordinary Least Squares estimation runs into several difficulties when the dependent variable is a dummy variable. As an illustration suppose we wish to explain the incidence of car ownership among a sample of families. Let

$$Y_i = \begin{cases} 1 \text{ if the } i\text{th family own a car} \\ 0 \text{ if they do not} \end{cases}$$

and let X_i = the income of the ith family. If we then use OLS to estimate the equation

$$Y_i = \beta_1 + \beta_2 X_i + u_i$$

several problems arise.

(i) The disturbances u_i cannot be normally distributed. They are given by

$$u_i = Y_i - \beta_1 - \beta_2 X_i$$

and Y_i can only take the values 1 or 0. Hence, for any given X_i, u_i can only equal $(1 - \beta_1 - \beta_2 X_i)$ or $(-\beta_1 - \beta_2 X_i)$. Thus, given X_i, u_i will have a discrete probability distribution of the form

u_i	Prob (u_i)
$1 - \beta_1 - \beta_2 X_i$	p_i
$-\beta_1 - \beta_2 X_i$	$1 - p_i$
	1

where p_i is the probability of owning a car given income X_i. So clearly the distribution of u_i given X_i is *not* normal.

(ii) The second problem is a question of interpretation and prediction. Y_i takes on the value 1 with probability p_i and the value 0 with probability $(1 - p_i)$. Hence $E(Y_i) = p_i$. Thus in our linear equation $E(Y_i) = \beta_1 + \beta_2 X_i$ is to be interpreted as a probability. (In the illustration above the probability of a family with income X_i owning a car.) So its value is confined to the range $(0, 1)$. However its estimate (the predicted value of Y_i) is given by

$$\hat{Y}_i = \hat{\beta}_1 + \hat{\beta}_2 X_i$$

and is not bounded and so may take a value outside the range $(0, 1)$.

(iii) Finally, the u_i will be heteroscedastic, i.e. will have non-constant variance. From (ii) we have that

$$p_i = E(Y_i) = \beta_1 + \beta_2 X_i$$

Thus, given X_i, u_i has two possible values which it takes with probabilities depending on X_i. Hence the variance of u_i will depend on X_i.

Because of these problems OLS should not be used to estimate this linear model. Either certain modifications are required or alternatively a more appropriate model which avoids the second problem should be formulated.

7.2 FUNCTIONAL FORM

The assumption of linearity in our regression model refers to linearity in the parameters, not the variables. Sometimes the relationship we wish to estimate is inherently non-linear and sometimes consideration of the data will suggest a non-linear function form. Providing the equation is still linear in the parameters our method for estimating the linear model is still applicable. We have in fact already seen a case of this in the previous section where the incomes policy illustration used the variable $\dot{W}_t$ as dependent variable and P_{t-1} as an explanatory variable. Both are in fact non-linear functions of the original data on the levels of wages and prices, for example

$$\dot{W}_t = \frac{W_t - W_{t-1}}{W_{t-1}} \cdot 100.$$

However since the equation being estimated was still linear in the parameters it was still amenable to estimation by OLS. Some examples of useful transformations commonly encountered in the estimation of economic relationships are given below.

(i) *The Phillips curve* (the reciprocal transformation)

Phillips observed that the relationship between the percentage change in wages ($\dot{W}$) and the rate of unemployment (N) was non-linear and of the shape shown in Figure 7.5.

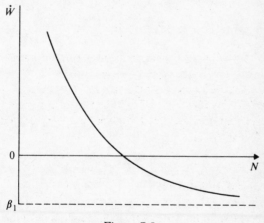

Figure 7.5

We can estimate a curve like this by using the reciprocal transformation to given an equation of the form

$$\dot{W}_t = \beta_1 + \beta_2\left(\frac{1}{N_t}\right) + u_t$$

Despite the fact that this equation is non-linear in the original variables, OLS is applicable since it is linear in the parameters. We simply need to construct the transformed variables $\dot{W}_t$ and $1/N_t$ and then proceed with OLS estimation using the transformed data.

(ii)   *The Cobb-Douglas Production Function* (full logarithmic transformation of the equation)

Consider the production function

$$Q_t = AL_t^{\beta_1} K_t^{\beta_2} e^{u_t}$$

where Q_t = output and L and K are the inputs of labour and capital respectively. (e is the base of natural logarithms).

The equation is clearly not linear as it stands. However if we take natural logarithms of both sides of the equation we will get

$$\log Q_t = \log A + \beta_1 \log L_t + \beta_2 \log K_t + u_t$$

which we can write as

$$Q_t^* = \alpha + \beta_1 L_t^* + \beta_2 K_t^* + u_t$$

where

$$Q_t^* = \log Q_t,\ L_t^* = \log L_t,\ K_t^* = \log K_t \text{ and } \alpha = \log A.$$

This equation is now clearly linear and once we have constructed the starred variables can be estimated by OLS in the usual way. Note that β_1 and β_2 are the elasticities which can therefore be directly estimated. This can be advantageous. However the implicit assumption of their constancy may also be a limitation of this functional form.

An important point to notice, which is relevant to any situation where a complete equation is transformed, is the form of the error term in the original equation. In this case an exponential form for the error term was necessary to allow this transformation of the equation. An equation of the form

$$Q_t = AL_t^{\beta_1} K_t^{\beta_2} + u_t$$

cannot be transformed into an equation linear in the parameters and hence amenable to estimation by OLS.

(iii) *Age-Earnings Profiles* (logarithmic and polynomial transformations).

Examination of cross-section data on the earnings, age and other characteristics of individuals suggests that age-earnings profiles are of the shape shown in Figure 7.6.

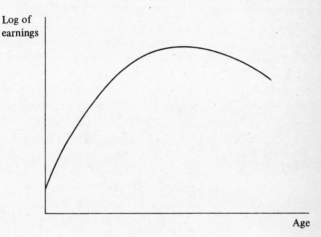

Figure 7.6

Given this evidence we might fit a quadratic rather than linear relationship between the log of earnings and age

$$\log Y_i = \beta_1 + \beta_2 A_i + \beta_3 A_i^2 + \beta_4 S_i + \beta_5 X_{5i} + \ldots + \beta_k X_{ki} + u_i$$

where Y = earnings, A = age, S = years of full-time education and $X_5, \ldots, X_k$ are other earnings-determining characteristics.

Notice that we have combined different transformations of variables in the same equation. This is very common and is often useful in increasing the plausibility of the economic interpretation of the equation. For example, in the above equation we have combined a quadratic in A with a dependent variable in logarithmic form. One reason for choosing to do this can be seen by differentiating the equation with respect to S. This gives

$$\frac{1}{Y} \cdot \frac{\partial Y}{\partial S} = \beta_4$$

i.e. β_4 represents the *proportional* change in Y as a result of a change in S. In particular it represents the proportional return to having an additional year of education given age and other characteristics. The implicit assumption here that an extra year of education gives rise to a (constant) proportional change in earnings might be regarded as more reasonable than assuming the effect to be a constant absolute number of pounds, which is what would be implied by using Y rather than log Y as the dependent variable.

Quadratic terms can be used whenever we wish the effect of a certain variable, here A, to vary across its own range. However it should be noted that the variation introduced is of a fairly limited nature. The assumption that the effect of A is constant is replaced by the assumption that the effect (i.e. the partial derivative of Y with respect to A) is a linear function of A. An alternative, and more flexible, approach to allowing the effect of a variable to vary over its own range is by means of what are called *spline functions*. These are discussed in section 7.5.

Finally, it is worth noting that the usual t-test of $\beta_3 = 0$ can be used as a partial test of the linearity of the relationship between log Y and A.

In general, any combination of functional forms that is linear in the parameters is amenable to OLS estimation. For example any equation of the form

$$f_1(Y_t) = \beta_1 + \beta_2 f_2(X_{2t}) + \beta_3 f_3(X_{3t}) + \ldots + \beta_k f_k(X_{kt}) + u_t$$

where $f_1, f_2, \ldots, f_k$ are any known functions not containing unknown parameters can be so estimated. The Ordinary Least Squares technique can in fact cope with even more general functional forms than this. The f_j can be functions of more than one of the X variables. A particularly useful example of this is the use of *interaction terms*.

Consider the equation

$$Y_t = \beta_1 + \beta_2 X_{2t} + \beta_3 X_{3t} + u_t.$$

As usual this equation implicitly assumes that the effect of X_2 on Y is constant across the sample and in particular is independent of what value X_3 takes. In certain situations we may feel that this is an unrealistic assumption, and so might formulate the more general model

$$Y_t = \beta_1 + \gamma_t X_{2t} + \beta_3 X_{3t} + u_t$$

where $\gamma = \partial Y/\partial X_2$ is the effect of X_2 on Y. This might then be assumed· to depend on X_3, for example:

$$\gamma_t = \beta_4 + \beta_5 X_{3t}.$$

Substitution gives the regression equation

$$Y_t = \beta_1 + \beta_3 X_{3t} + \beta_4 X_{2t} + \beta_5 (X_{2t} X_{3t}) + u_t,$$

which contains the interaction term $(X_{2t} X_{3t})$ but is still linear in the parameters and hence amenable to estimation by OLS. Notice that the usual t-test on the significance of β_5 tests the hypothesis that γ does not vary with X_3, i.e. that the effect of X_2 on Y is independent of X_3.

7.3 LINEAR RESTRICTIONS

Estimation subject to linear restrictions

To illustrate, suppose we wish to estimate the equation

$$Y_t = \beta_1 + \beta_2 X_{2t} + \beta_3 X_{3t} + u_t$$

subject to the linear restriction on the parameters

$$\beta_2 + \beta_3 = 1.$$

The most obvious example of this is the case where Y_t is the logarithm of output, X_{2t} is the logarithm of labour input and X_{3t} is the logarithm of capital input. The model being estimated is then a Cobb-Doublas production function and the linear restriction being imposed is an assumption of constant returns to scale.

A natural extension of the least squares method of estimation seen so far would be to minimise the residual sum of squares

$$S = \sum_{t=1}^{n} (Y_t - \hat{\beta}_1 - \hat{\beta}_2 X_{2t} - \hat{\beta}_3 X_{3t})^2$$

subject to $\hat{\beta}_2 + \hat{\beta}_3 = 1$. To perform such a constrained minimisation we might employ the Lagrangean multiplier technique or we might simply substitute the constraint into the minimand and then perform ordinary unconstrained minimisation. It is a well known result that the two methods are equivalent. We will employ the latter. Hence we now need to minimise

$$S^* = \sum_{t=1}^{n} (Y_t - \hat{\beta}_1 - \hat{\beta}_2 X_{2t} - (1 - \hat{\beta}_2) X_{3t})^2$$

with respect to $\hat{\beta}_1$ and $\hat{\beta}_2$. But S^* can be rewritten as

$$S^* = \sum_{t=1}^{n} (Y_t - X_{3t} - \hat{\beta}_1 - \hat{\beta}_2 (X_{2t} - X_{3t}))^2$$

and minimisation of this with respect to $\hat{\beta}_1$ and $\hat{\beta}_2$ is equivalent to the estimation by OLS of

$$(Y_t - X_{3t}) = \beta_1 + \beta_2 (X_{2t} - X_{3t}) + u_t.$$

Thus to estimate the original equation subject to the restriction $\beta_2 + \beta_3 = 1$ we simply regress $(Y_t - X_{3t})$ on $(X_{2t} - X_{3t})$ and a constant. This yields estimates $\hat{\beta}_1$ and $\hat{\beta}_2$, and our estimate of β_3 is then calculated as $\hat{\beta}_3 = 1 - \hat{\beta}_2$. Note that we could equally well estimate the equation

$$(Y_t - X_{2t}) = \beta_1 + \beta_3 (X_{3t} - X_{2t}) + u_t$$

yielding estimates of $\hat{\beta}_1$ and $\hat{\beta}_3$, from which we would calculate $\hat{\beta}_2 = 1 - \hat{\beta}_3$. These methods are equivalent (checking this is left as an exercise for the reader). This method applies to estimation subject to any set of linear restrictions (providing they are not mutually contradictory):

(i) substitute the restrictions into the equation,
(ii) rearrange the equation so that each parameter appears only once, and
(iii) create new variables where necessary and estimate by OLS.

As another example, suppose we wish to estimate

$$Y_t = \beta_1 + \beta_2 X_{2t} + \beta_3 X_{3t} + u_t$$

again, but this time subject to the restriction

$$\beta_2 = \beta_3.$$

Then applying the method just outlined we would need to estimate the equation

$$Y_t = \beta_1 + \beta_2(X_{2t} + X_{3t}) + u_t.$$

Testing a set of linear restrictions – the general procedure

One of the most common reasons for estimating an equation subject to a set of linear restrictions is to provide a test of the validity of the restrictions. We will now consider a very straightforward procedure for performing this test. One of its most common usages is on the simplest restrictions of all (so simple that they didn't even merit mention under estimation subject to restrictions), namely a set of zero restrictions. As an illustration, suppose we are estimating the equation

$$Y_t = \beta_1 + \beta_2 X_{2t} + \beta_3 X_{3t} + \gamma_1 Q_{1t} + \gamma_2 Q_{2t} + \gamma_3 Q_{3t} + u_t$$

where Q_1, Q_2, Q_3 are three quarterly dummy variables to allow for seasonal variation (as discussed in section 7.1). We might wish to test the hypothesis that there is no seasonal variation in the intercept. This would be done by testing the set of restrictions

$$\gamma_1 = \gamma_2 = \gamma_3 = 0.$$

Estimation subject to this set of restrictions is very simple. The restricted equation is given by

$$Y_t = \beta_1 + \beta_2 X_{2t} + \beta_3 X_{3t} + u_t.$$

Bearing this illustration in mind, we now proceed to outline the general test procedure.

Test Procedure

(1) Impose the restrictions to be tested on the equation to obtain the *restricted form* of the equation. Estimate this restricted form by OLS and calculate the residual sum of squares,

$$\sum_{t=1}^{n} e_t^2.$$

Call this RSS_R.

(2) Next estimate the *unrestricted form* of the equation (i.e. the original equation), and calculate here the residual sum of squares. Call this RSS_U.

(3) Finally calculate the ratio

$$F = \frac{(RSS_R - RSS_U)/d}{RSS_U/(n-k)}$$

where

d = the difference in the number of parameters between the restricted and unrestricted equations (i.e. the number of restrictions),

k = the number of parameters in the original (i.e. unrestricted) equation, and

n = the number of observations used in the estimation of the equations.

This will be our *test-statistic*.

It can be shown that under the null hypothesis that the restrictions are true, this ratio has a Fisher's F-distribution with d and $(n - k)$ degrees of freedom (written variously as $F(d, n - k)$ or F_{n-k}^{d} or $F_{d,n-k}$).

If the restrictions are satisfied (i.e. if the null hypothesis holds true) then we would expect the restricted and unrestricted forms of the equation to give very similar results. So we would expect RSS_R and RSS_U to be very similar. Thus we expect our test statistic to take a rather small (positive) value, i.e. to be "close" to zero. (Note that imposing a restriction on an equation can never reduce the residual sum of squares.) So we will want to accept the null hypothesis when the test-statistic gives a small value. If on the other hand one or more of the restrictions does not hold (i.e. the null hypothesis is not true) then the restricted form of the equation will have had an invalid restriction imposed upon it and hence will be misspecified. Thus extra residual variation will be introduced into the equation and hence we would expect RSS_R to be considerably greater than RSS_U and so our test statistic to be considerably greater than zero. Therefore we will want to reject the null hypothesis when the test-statistic gives a large value.

Given the distribution of the test-statistic therefore, we will accept the null hypothesis at the 5% significance level if

$$F < F_{d,n-k}^{0.05}$$

where $P(F_{d,n-k} > F_{d,n-k}^{0.05}) = 0.05$ and reject it otherwise. ($F_{d,n-k}^{0.05}$ is obtained by consulting the table of critical points of the F-distribution.)

Testing a single restriction – an alternative procedure

In the case where we wish to test only a single linear restriction, there is an alternative procedure available that avoids the necessity of estimating the restricted form of the equation but at the cost of requiring the estimation of certain covariances. Since the required covariances are automatically output by some computer regression packages this procedure is sometimes simpler to perform than the general procedure already outlined.

To illustrate the procedure consider again the example examined at the start of this section. Suppose we are estimating the equation

$$Y_t = \beta_1 + \beta_2 X_{2t} + \beta_3 X_{3t} + u_t$$

and wish to test the hypothesis $\beta_2 + \beta_3 = 1$. The procedure we are going to examine is a simple extension of the significance testing procedure. Recall that if we wish to test a hypothesis about a parameter in a linear regression, say γ, we make use of the fact that the OLS estimate $\hat{\gamma}$, can be shown to be normally distributed and take as our test statistic

$$\frac{\hat{\gamma} - \gamma_0}{\text{SE}(\hat{\gamma})}$$

This statistic will have a t-distribution under the null hypothesis $H_0 : \gamma = \gamma_0$ (see sections 5.3 and 6.2).

Here we simply take $\gamma = \beta_2 + \beta_3$. Under the classical assumptions the OLS estimators $\hat{\beta}_2$ and $\hat{\beta}_3$ are unbiased. Hence $\hat{\beta}_2 + \hat{\beta}_3$ will be an unbiased estimator of $\beta_2 + \beta_3$. Since $\hat{\beta}_2$ and $\hat{\beta}_3$ are both normally distributed $\hat{\beta}_2 + \hat{\beta}_3$ will be also. Thus

$$\frac{(\hat{\beta}_2 + \hat{\beta}_3) - (\beta_2 + \beta_3)}{\sqrt{\text{var}\,(\hat{\beta}_2 + \hat{\beta}_3)}} \sim N(0, 1)$$

and $\text{var}\,(\hat{\beta}_2 + \hat{\beta}_3) = \text{var}\,(\hat{\beta}_2) + \text{var}\,(\hat{\beta}_3) + 2\,\text{cov}\,(\hat{\beta}_2, \hat{\beta}_3)$ with all three terms in this expression being given by the appropriate elements in the variance-covariance matrix of the parameter estimates, $\sigma_u^2(\mathbf{X}'\mathbf{X})^{-1}$. (See Section 6.2). These variances and covariances are of course unobservable since σ_u^2 is, but they can be estimated unbiasedly using the unbiased estimate of $\sigma_u{}^2$ given in section 6.2. Then

$$\frac{(\hat{\beta}_2 + \hat{\beta}_3) - (\beta_2 + \beta_3)}{s} \sim t_{n-k}$$

where $s^2 = \hat{var}(\hat{\beta}_2) + \hat{var}(\hat{\beta}_3) + 2\hat{cov}(\hat{\beta}_2, \hat{\beta}_3)$, with each of these elements being given by the appropriate entries in the estimated variance − covariance matrix, $\hat{\sigma}_u{}^2(\mathbf{X'X})^{-1}$. From this it can be seen that under the null hypothesis $H_0 : \beta_2 + \beta_3 = 1$, the quantity

$$\frac{\hat{\beta}_2 + \hat{\beta}_3 - 1}{s}$$

will have a t-distribution with $n - k$ degrees of freedom. Hence this is what we take as our test statistic. It can be shown that this will be exactly equal to the square root of the F-test statistic from the general procedure described earlier. Thus the two tests are equivalent, since any critical point of the t-distribution with $n - k$ degrees of freedom is exactly the square root of the corresponding critical point of the F-distribution with $(1, n - k)$ degrees of freedom.

The procedure extends quite naturally to any hypothesis involving a linear combination of parameters. In the case of the hypothesis being that a single parameter is equal to zero, the test-statistic reduces to the familiar t-ratio.

A special case: homogeneous restrictions

Consider our earlier example with seasonal dummy variables. The unrestricted form of the equation is given by

$$Y_t = \beta_1 + \beta_2 X_{2t} + \beta_3 X_{3t} + \gamma_1 Q_{1t} + \gamma_2 Q_{2t} + \gamma_3 Q_{3t} + u_t$$

whilst the restricted form under the null hypothesis of no seasonal variation in the intercept is given by

$$Y_t = \beta_1 + \beta_2 X_{2t} + \beta_3 X_{3t} + u_t.$$

Because the set of restrictions being tested are all homogeneous, the dependent variable is the same in both the restricted and unrestricted forms. In such a situation we can rewrite our F-ratio test-statistic in terms of R^2s. Recall that for any equation

$$R^2 = 1 - \frac{RSS}{TSS}$$

where TSS = the total sum of squares of the dependent variable, and so

$$RSS = (1 - R^2)\,TSS.$$

Let $R_R{}^2$ be the value calculated from estimation of the restricted form of the equation and $R_U{}^2$ be that calculated from estimation of the unrestricted form of the equation. Then

$$RSS_R = (1 - R_R{}^2)\,TSS,$$
$$RSS_U = (1 - R_U{}^2)\,TSS.$$

The total sum of squares is the same in both cases since the dependent variable is the same in the two equations. Thus our test-statistic can be rewritten in this case as

$$F = \frac{[(1 - R_R{}^2)\,TSS - (1 - R_U{}^2)\,TSS]/d}{[(1 - R_U{}^2)\,TSS]/(n - k)}$$

$$= \frac{(R_U{}^2 - R_R{}^2)/d}{(1 - R_U{}^2)/(n - k)}$$

This alternative formulation of the test statistic can be used in any circumstances where the dependent variable is the same in the restricted and unrestricted forms.

Another special case: testing for the existence of a relationship

A particular case of the previous test of homogeneous restrictions is where we want to test the hypothesis that *all* the slope coefficients are zero, i.e. to test whether or not the explanatory variables taken together, have a significant influence on the dependent variable:

$$Y_t = \beta_1 + \beta_2 X_{2t} + \ldots + \beta_k X_{kt} + u_t$$

$$H_0 : \beta_2 = \beta_3 = \ldots = \beta_k = 0.$$

In this case the restricted form of the equation does no explaining at all and hence has zero R^2. Thus the test-statistic for this hypothesis can be written as

$$F = \frac{R^2/(k-1)}{(1-R^2)/(n-k)} = \frac{(n-k)R^2}{(k-1)(1-R^2)}$$

where R^2 is that from the unrestricted equation.

If the equation does not contain a constant term the test ceases to be very interesting, since the null hypothesis in this case includes that of a zero mean for the dependent variable. Finally note that if there is only one explanatory variable the test-statistic is just the square of the t-ratio again.

7.4 TESTING FOR STRUCTURAL CHANGE

We can apply the general procedure derived for the testing of linear restrictions to the problem of testing for structural change.

Suppose we have a regression equation

$$Y_t = \beta_1 + \beta_2 X_{2t} + \beta_3 X_{3t} + \ldots + \beta_k X_{kt} + u_t, \qquad t = 1, \ldots, n$$

which has been estimated using a sample of n observations. Suppose now that we obtain m additional observations and want to test the hypothesis that they come from the same structure. (Assume for the moment that $m > k$. We will consider later the appropriate course of action if this is not the case). If we write

$$Y_t = \gamma_1 + \gamma_2 X_{2t} + \gamma_3 X_{3t} + \ldots + \gamma_k X_{kt} + u_t, \qquad t = n+1, \ldots, n+m$$

then the hypothesis to be tested would be

$$H_0 : \beta_1 = \gamma_1, \beta_2 = \gamma_2, \ldots, \beta_k = \gamma_k.$$

If we define a dummy variable $D_t = 0$ if $t \leqslant n$ and $D_t = 1$ if $t > n$ then our unrestricted form could be written as

$$Y_t = \beta_1 + \beta_2 X_{2t} + \ldots + \beta_k X_{kt} + \beta_1' D_t + \beta_2' X_{2t} D_t + \ldots + \beta_k' X_{kt} D_t + u_t,$$
$$t = 1, \ldots, n + m.$$

However, recall from section 7.1 that since we have a complete set of interactions with D_t, we would get the same coefficient estimates by estimating separate equations for $D = 1$ and $D = 0$. Also the sum of the residual sum of squares from the two separate regressions will be the same as the residual sum of squares from the equation with the complete set of dummy variables.

Thus the test procedure is:

(1) Run the regression on the first set of data $(t = 1, \ldots, n)$. Let the residual sum of squares from this estimation be RSS_1.

(2) Run the regression on the second set of data $(t = n + 1, \ldots, n + m)$ to get RSS_2. (The unrestricted residual sum of squares is then given by $RSS_U = RSS_1 + RSS_2$.)

(3) Run the regression on the two sets of data combined $(t = 1, \ldots, n + m)$ to get RSS_C. (This is of course the restricted form under the null hypothesis of no structural change.)

(4) Applying the expression from section 7.3 gives as our test-statistic:

$$F = \frac{(RSS_C - RSS_1 - RSS_2)/k}{(RSS_1 + RSS_2)/(n + m - 2k)}$$

which has a Fisher's F-distribution with $(k, n + m - 2k)$ degrees of freedom if H_0 is true.

Two possible modifications are of interest:

(i) In deriving this test we made the assumption that $m > k$. If we do not have sufficient "extra" observations to estimate the regression from the second set of data alone, stage (2) of the outlined test procedure will not be possible. The appropriate test procedure in this situation is to do stages (1) and (3) above and then set up the test-statistic:

$$F' = \frac{(RSS_C - RSS_1)/m}{RSS_1/(n-k)}$$

Under the null hypothesis of no structural change F' has a Fisher's F-distribution with $(m, n-k)$ degrees of freedom.

(ii) The hypothesis being tested here is formulated in such a way that the alternative allows for *all* of the regression parameters to change as we move from one set of data to the other. If we want to hold some fixed and test for structural change only in a subset, then we must explicitly set up our unrestricted form with multiplicative dummy variables on only the chosen subset. We estimate this and the restricted form (which contains no additive dummy variable or interactions) both on the combined $n+m$ observations, and use the general test of section 7.3.

7.5. SPLINE FUNCTIONS

All the functional forms considered in section 7.2 allow us to move away from the restrictive assumption, embodied in the equations that are linear in the variables, that the effect of a given variable is constant. For example one way to allow the effect of a variable to vary across its own range is to include a quadratic term as was discussed in section 7.2. However this imposes quite a restrictive form on the relationship between dependent and explanatory variable. A more flexible approach is based on what are known as *spline functions*. These are made up of segments of curves which are spliced together to form a single continuous function. The most commonly used types are *linear splines* and *cubic splines*. Only the former will be considered here.

Linear splines

A linear spline is simply a continuous piecewise-linear function such as, for example, that illustrated in Figure 7.7.

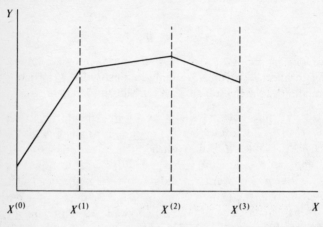

Figure 7.7

The range of X is divided into three intervals with interval boundaries $X^{(0)}$, $X^{(1)}$, $X^{(2)}$ and $X^{(3)}$. The X profile consists of a set of three line segments constrained in such a way that consecutive segments meet at the boundary. The line segments can be defined by

$$Y_t = [\alpha_1 + \beta_1(X_t - X^{(0)})]D_{1t} + [\alpha_2 + \beta_2(X_t - X^{(1)})]D_{2t}$$
$$+ [\alpha_3 + \beta_3(X_t - X^{(2)})]D_{3t} + u_t$$

where

$$D_{jt} = \begin{cases} 1 \text{ if } X^{(j-1)} \leqslant X_t \leqslant X^{(j)} \\ 0 \text{ otherwise.} \end{cases}$$

This function must then be constrained to ensure continuity, i.e. the meeting of consecutive segments at the boundary. At $X^{(1)}$ the condition for continuity is

$$\alpha_1 + \beta_1(X^{(1)} - X^{(0)}) = \alpha_2$$

and at $X^{(2)}$ the condition is

$$\alpha_2 + \beta_2(X^{(2)} - X^{(1)}) = \alpha_3.$$

As we saw in section 7.3 the easiest way to estimate an equation subject to linear restrictions is simply to substitute the restrictions into the equation and then estimate as usual. Substitution here gives

$$Y_t = [\alpha_1 + \beta_1(X_t - X^{(0)})] D_{1t}$$
$$+ [\alpha_1 + \beta_1(X^{(1)} - X^{(0)}) + \beta_2(X_t - X^{(1)})] D_{2t}$$
$$+ [\alpha_1 + \beta_1(X^{(1)} - X^{(0)}) + \beta_2(X^{(2)} - X^{(1)}) + \beta_3(X_t - X^{(2)})] D_{3t} + u_t.$$

Collecting terms in each parameter gives

$$Y_t = \alpha_1 + \beta_1 [(X_t - X^{(0)})D_{1t} + (X^{(1)} - X^{(0)})(D_{2t} + D_{3t})]$$
$$+ \beta_2 [(X_t - X^{(1)})D_{2t} + (X^{(2)} - X^{(1)})D_{3t}] + \beta_3 [(X_t - X^{(2)})D_{3t}] + u_t$$

which we can write as

$$Y_t = \alpha_1 + \beta_1 Z_{1t} + \beta_2 Z_{2t} + \beta_3 Z_{3t} + u_t$$

where

$$Z_{1t} = \begin{cases} X_t - X^{(0)} & \text{if} \quad X^{(0)} \leqslant X_t < X^{(1)} \\ X^{(1)} - X^{(0)} & \text{if} \quad X^{(1)} \leqslant X_t \end{cases}$$

$$Z_{2t} = \begin{cases} 0 & \text{if} \quad X_t < X^{(1)} \\ X_t - X^{(1)} & \text{if} \quad X^{(1)} \leqslant X_t < X^{(2)} \\ X^{(2)} - X^{(1)} & \text{if} \quad X^{(2)} \leqslant X_t \end{cases}$$

$$Z_{3t} = \begin{cases} 0 & \text{if} \quad X_t < X^{(2)} \\ X_t - X^{(2)} & \text{if} \quad X^{(2)} \leqslant X_t \end{cases}$$

which we can write in general as

$$Z_{jt} = \begin{cases} 0 & \text{if} \quad X_t < X^{(j-1)} \\ X_t - X^{(j-1)} & \text{if} \quad X^{(j-1)} \leqslant X_t < X^{(j)} \\ X^{(j)} - X^{(j-1)} & \text{if} \quad X^{(j)} \leqslant X_t \end{cases}$$

for $j = 1, 2, 3$. Thus to estimate the parameters of the linear spline we simply construct the variables Z_1, Z_2, Z_3 and estimate this equation. Generalisation to include other explanatory variables in the equation and/or to more segments are both extremely straightforward. The general definition of Z_j still holds in both cases.

Finally notice that if $\beta_1 = \beta_2 = \beta_3$ the equation collapses back to a simple linear relationship between Y and X since $Z_{1t} + Z_{2t} + Z_{3t} = X_t - X^{(0)}$ for all values of X_t. Hence a hypothesis of a single linear relation can be tested using the F-statistic discussed in section 7.3 calculated from the residual sums of squares or R^2s from the simple linear equation and the linear spline function.

7.6 DISTRIBUTED LAG MODELS

The concept of a distributed lag was introduced and discussed in section 3.2. Here we examine some of the difficulties in estimating equations with distributed lags. Consider the general distributed lag formulation

$$Y_t = \alpha + \beta_0 X_t + \beta_1 X_{t-1} + \beta_2 X_{t-2} + \ldots + \beta_m X_{t-m} + u_t$$

where the number of lags, m, may be either finite or infinite. There are two main difficulties in attempting to estimate an equation of this form. Firstly we lose the use of m observations from our data set. For example, suppose we have annual data for 1950 to 1979 inclusive (30 years) and want to estimate a distributed lag formulation of the type given above with $m = 12$. We would only be able to estimate it for the period 1962 to 1979 (18 years) since it is not until 1962 that we have observations in our data set for X_{t-12}. Thus we would have only

4 degrees of freedom. This problem can sometimes be overcome by getting additional earlier observations on X. However, there is a second more serious difficulty. It is likely with economic time-series that $X_t, X_{t-1}, \ldots, X_{t-m}$ will be highly correlated with one-another. This multicollinearity will result in large standard errors and hence make it extremely difficult to separate out the effects of the different lags. It is in response to these two basic problems that various distributed lag models have been developed which, in various ways, restrict the form that the β_j can take. One such model, based on the Koyck transformation, was seen in section 3.2.

The Koyck geometric lag model assumes that the coefficients decline geometrically indefinitely into the past, i.e.

$$\beta_j = \lambda^j \beta \qquad j = 0, 1, \ldots \qquad 0 < \lambda < 1.$$

Imposition of this form for the coefficients on the general distributed lag formulation above and application of the Koyck transformation was shown in section 3.2 to result in the equation

$$Y_t = \alpha(1 - \lambda) + \beta X_t + \lambda Y_{t-1} + v_t.$$

Notice that the error term u_t will be transformed along with the rest of the equation. Hence the error term in the final equation will be given by

$$v_t = u_t - \lambda u_{t-1}$$

and so will be autocorrelated as demonstrated in section 3.7 (see p. 64). Thus the final equation contains both a lagged dependent variable and an autocorrelated error term. This combination means that the OLS estimates of the coefficients will be inconsistent as well as biased.

The Almon Polynomial Lag

In addition to the inappropriateness of its estimation by OLS the coefficient restrictions specified by the Koyck geometric lag may also be thought inappropriate in many situations. For example, rather than assuming that the weights decline geometrically we may want a model where the weights initially increase, reach a peak and then decline. The Almon polynomial lag allows for this possibility, amongst others.

As the name suggests, the Almon polynomial lag imposes some form of polynomial on the β_j. For example if it was felt that the weights were of the form described above then we could impose a quadratic on the β_j

$$\beta_j = \alpha_0 + \alpha_1 j + \alpha_2 j^2 \qquad j = 0, 1, \ldots, m$$

where $\alpha_0, \alpha_1, \alpha_2$ are parameters to be estimated.

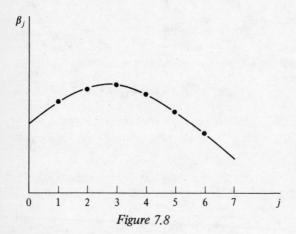

Figure 7.8

Substitution into the original equation gives

$$Y_t = \gamma + \alpha_0 X_t + (\alpha_0 + \alpha_1 + \alpha_2) X_{t-1} + (\alpha_0 + 2\alpha_1 + 4\alpha_2) X_{t-2} + \ldots$$
$$+ (\alpha_0 + m\alpha_1 + m^2\alpha_2) X_{t-m} + u_t.$$

Collecting terms in each parameter gives

$$Y_t = \gamma + \alpha_0 Z_{0t} + \alpha_1 Z_{1t} + \alpha_2 Z_{2t} + u_t$$

where

$$Z_{0t} = \sum_{j=0}^{m} X_{t-j}; \; Z_{1t} = \sum_{j=0}^{m} jX_{t-j}; \; Z_{2t} = \sum_{j=0}^{m} j^2 X_{t-j};$$

$$t = m + 1, \ldots, n.$$

Having constructed the variables Z_0, Z_1, Z_2 from the original data on X we can then estimate $\gamma, \alpha_0, \alpha_1, \alpha_2$ by OLS. Having estimated the α_j we can then obtain estimates of the β_j as follows:

$$\hat{\beta}_0 = \hat{\alpha}_0$$
$$\hat{\beta}_1 = \hat{\alpha}_0 + \hat{\alpha}_1 + \hat{\alpha}_2$$
$$\hat{\beta}_2 = \hat{\alpha}_0 + 2\hat{\alpha}_1 + 4\hat{\alpha}_2$$

$$\vdots$$

$$\hat{\beta}_m = \hat{\alpha}_0 + m\hat{\alpha}_1 + m^2\hat{\alpha}_2.$$

Thus the Almon method obtains estimates of the $(m+1)$ β's by estimating only three α's. Hence it reduces the number of parameters estimated directly by $m-2$ and thereby reduces the multicollinearity problems. Notice however that, unlike the Koyck lag, it does not reduce the number of observations lost. Also unlike the Koyck lag it does not induce autocorrelation: the error term in the estimating equation is the original u_t. Generalisation to any other order of polynomial and the inclusion of other variables in the equation is straightforward.

The reduction in parameters is equivalent to imposing linear restrictions

As was stated above, in the quadratic case the Almon method reduces the number of parameters to be estimated by $m-2$. It can be shown that the method is equivalent to imposing a certain set of $m - 2$ linear restrictions on the equation. To illustrate, suppose $m = 3$ and we impose a quadratic on the β's:

$$Y_t = \gamma + \beta_0 X_t + \beta_1 X_{t-1} + \beta_2 X_{t-2} + \beta_3 X_{t-3} + u_t,$$

$$\beta_j = \alpha_0 + \alpha_1 j + \alpha_2 j^2.$$

Thus, the coefficients of X_t, X_{t-1}, and X_{t-2} are given as

$$\beta_0 = \alpha_0$$

$$\beta_1 = \alpha_0 + \alpha_1 + \alpha_2$$

$$\beta_2 = \alpha_0 + 2\alpha_1 + 4\alpha_2$$

which yields a one-to-one relation between α_0, α_1, α_2 and β_0, β_1, β_2. Thus the addition of the expression for the coefficient of X_{t-3},

$$\beta_3 = \alpha_0 + 3\alpha_1 + 9\alpha_2,$$

imposes a restriction on the relationship between β_3 and β_0, β_1, β_2. Substitution of the expressions for $\alpha_0, \alpha_1, \alpha_2$ shows that the restriction is

$$\beta_3 - 3\beta_2 + 3\beta_1 - \beta_0 = 0.$$

Thus in this particular case, estimation by the Almon technique is equivalent to estimation subject to this linear restriction. Thus the quadratic form for the β's can be tested using the procedures of section 7.3.

In general, estimation of an equation such as our original equation with longest lag m by the Almon technique assuming a polynomial of degree q is equivalent to estimation subject to a set of $(m - q)$ restrictions of this form.

Imposition of endpoint restrictions

We may wish to impose some form of "endpoint" restrictions on the values of the β's. These usually take the form of zero restrictions, i.e. requiring that the polynomial reaches the horizontal axis at certain points. For the cubic illustrated in Figure 7.9 we may feel that the effect has exhausted itself after the pth period and so want to impose the restriction

$$\beta_{p+1} = 0.$$

For the quadratic illustrated in Figure 7.9 we might want to impose zero restrictions at both ends:

$$\beta_{-1} = \beta_{m+1} = 0.$$

Notice that these coefficients do not actually appear in the model even if we do not impose these restrictions. We are merely specifying where the polynomial would, if extended, cut the horizontal axis. (In reality of course there is no reason why the polynomial should cut the axis at an integer point).

To illustrate, suppose that we wish to impose zero endpoint restrictions at both ends of the quadratic for which the Almon technique was demonstrated above:

$$\beta_j = \alpha_0 + \alpha_1 j + \alpha_2 j^2 \qquad j = 0, 1, \ldots, m$$

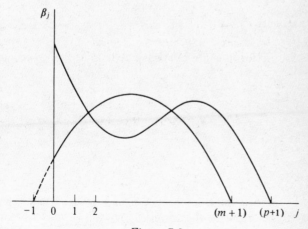

Figure 7.9

and we wish to impose the restrictions

$$\beta_{-1} = \beta_{m+1} = 0.$$

Thus the restrictions to be imposed on the αs are

$$\alpha_0 - \alpha_1 + \alpha_2 = 0,$$
$$\alpha_0 + \alpha_1(m+1) + \alpha_2(m+1)^2 = 0.$$

Substitution of α_1 from the first into the second gives

$$\alpha_0 = -\alpha_2(m+1)$$

and therefore, reusing the first restriction, we have

$$\alpha_1 = -\alpha_2 m.$$

Imposition of these involves merely substituting them into the estimating equation. This gives

$$Y_t = \gamma - \alpha_2(m+1)Z_{0t} - \alpha_2 m Z_{1t} + \alpha_2 Z_{2t} + u_t.$$

Hence we would estimate

$$Y_t = \gamma + \alpha_2 Z_t^* + u_t$$

where

$$Z_t^* = Z_{2t} - m Z_{1t} - (m+1)Z_{0t}$$

$$= \sum_{j=0}^{m} (j^2 - mj - m - 1)X_{t-j}.$$

Imposition of two end-point restrictions has reduced the number of coefficients estimated in the regression equation from three to one. Estimation of this equation gives $\hat{\alpha}_2$. The remaining two coefficient values are then deduced from the restrictions:

$$\hat{\alpha}_0 = -\hat{\alpha}_2(m+1)$$

$$\hat{\alpha}_1 = -\hat{\alpha}_2 m.$$

Estimates of the β's are then obtained from $\hat{\alpha}_0$, $\hat{\alpha}_1$ and $\hat{\alpha}_2$ as before.

Finally, consider as another illustration imposing a single endpoint restriction in the case where a cubic has been used. Imposition of a cubic on the β's involves taking

$$\beta_j = \alpha_0 + \alpha_1 j + \alpha_2 j^2 + \alpha_3 j^3 \qquad j = 0, 1, \ldots, m.$$

Without the endpoint restriction, the Almon technique would require estimation of

$$Y_t = \gamma + \alpha_0 Z_{0t} + \alpha_1 Z_{1t} + \alpha_2 Z_{2t} + \alpha_3 Z_{3t} + u_t$$

where

$$Z_{0t} = \sum_{j=0}^{m} X_{t-j}$$

$$Z_{1t} = \sum_{j=0}^{m} j X_{t-j}$$

$$Z_{2t} = \sum_{j=0}^{m} j^2 X_{t-j}$$

$$Z_{3t} = \sum_{j=0}^{m} j^3 X_{t-j}.$$

To impose the endpoint restriction $\beta_{m+1} = 0$ we must impose the following restriction on the αs:

$$\alpha_0 + (m+1)\,\alpha_1 + (m+1)^2\,\alpha_2 + (m+1)^3\,\alpha_3 = 0$$

Substitution for α_0 and rearrangement yields the restricted estimating equation.

$$Y_t = \gamma + \alpha_1 W_{1t} + \alpha_2 W_{2t} + \alpha_3 W_{3t} + u_t$$

where

$$W_{1t} = Z_{1t} - (m + 1) Z_{0t},$$
$$W_{2t} = Z_{2t} - (m + 1)^2 Z_{0t},$$
$$W_{3t} = Z_{3t} - (m + 1)^3 Z_{0t}.$$

Estimation of this gives $\hat{\alpha}_1$, $\hat{\alpha}_2$ and $\hat{\alpha}_3$. From these we then obtain

$$\hat{\alpha}_0 = -(m + 1) \ \hat{\alpha}_1 - (m + 1)^2 \ \hat{\alpha}_2 - (m + 1)^3 \ \hat{\alpha}_3$$

and thence estimates of the β's in the usual way.

EXERCISES

7.1 Suppose that you want to estimate the simple linear consumption function $C_i = \alpha + \beta Y_i + u_i$ across n individuals. How would you take account of a possible shift in the function between urban and rural consumers if you felt that they had the same marginal propensity to consume but different average propensities to consume? How would you examine the hypothesis that the marginal propensity to consume of those with income below some level Y^* is different from that of those above.

7.2 Consider the regression equation

$$Y_i = \beta_1 + \beta_2 D_i + u_i, \qquad i = 1, \ldots, n$$

where D is a dummy variable. Let $\bar{Y}_1$ be the mean value of Y for the n_1 observations with $D = 1$ and let $\bar{Y}_0$ be the mean value of Y for the n_0 observations with $D = 0$ ($n_1 + n_2 = n$). Find var $(\hat{\beta}_1)$ and var $(\hat{\beta}_2)$.

7.3 Explain how you would test the linear spline formulation of section 7.5 against the unrestricted alternative of three disjoint linear segments.

7.4 Assume that the rate of investment in period t, I_t, depends on the interest rate in that period, r_t, sales in that period, S_t, and seven lagged values of sales. Assume that the weights corresponding to the lagged value of S are such that they first increase, reach a peak, and then decrease.

(a) Set up an unrestricted form of this model.

(b) Set up the Almon form of this model.

7.5 The following estimated equation was obtained by Ordinary Least Squares using quarterly data for 1971 to 1976 inclusive.

$$Y_t = 1.10 - 0.0096\,X_{1t} - 4.56\,X_{2t} + 0.034\,X_{3t}$$
$$(2.12)\ (0.0034)\qquad (3.35)\qquad (0.007)$$

The figures in brackets are standard errors.
Explained sum of squares = 109.24.
Residual sum of squares = 20.22.

(i) Test the significance of each of the slope coefficients.

(ii) Calculate the coefficient of determination.

(iii) Test the overall significance of the regression.

(iv) When 3 dummy variables representing the first 3 quarters of the year were added to the equation, the explained sum of squares rose to 117.09.
Test for the presence of seasonality stating what assumptions are being made concerning the form of the seasonality.

(v) Two further regressions using the original specification were run separately for the periods 1971 quarter 1–1975 quarter 1 and 1975 quarter 2–1976 quarter 4.

1971 (I) – 1975 (I) : Residual sum of squares = 11.09

1975 (II) – 1976 (IV) : Residual sum of squares = 2.17

Test the assertion that a "structural break" occurred between quarters 1 and 2 of 1975.

(vi) State the assumptions on which the validity of these tests rests.

VIII

AUTOCORRELATION

This chapter considers the situation where the errors of the reduced form equation that we are estimating are autocorrelated. That is when

$$E(u_t u_s) \neq 0 \text{ for } t \neq s$$

i.e., when the variance-covariance matrix is not diagonal.

8.1 THE CAUSES OF AUTOCORRELATION

There are several ways in which autocorrelated errors may arise. Firstly, recall that one of the reasons for including an error term in an equation is to represent the influence of omitted variables, (those that we do not know about, cannot measure or just do not have data on). Given that most economic time-series exhibit autocorrelation some of these omitted variables might do so also, in which case u_t will be autocorrelated too. A second, related, cause of autocorrelation in the errors is due to the fact that the effect of a random shock to the system may not be instantaneous but may still be felt several periods after its occurrence. A third way in which autocorrelated errors may arise is as a result of transformations applied to an equation in deriving the form that is estimated. We have seen an illustration of this in section 7.6. The application of the Koyck transformation to an equation with a general infinite distributed lag induces autocorrelation in the error term. Finally, autocorrelation can be the result of data adjustment such as the seasonal adjustment of data by moving average methods.

8.2 THE CONSEQUENCES FOR OLS

The consequences of autocorrelation in the errors depend on the nature of the explanatory variables in the equation. In the case where lagged endogenous variables are present on the right-hand side of the equation OLS estimates are both biased and inconsistent (as stated in section 5.2). The situation is very different when all the explanatory variables are exogenous. In this case OLS estimates remain unbiased and consistent (see section 5.2). However, several other problems arise.

(i) They are no longer the "best" estimators, in the sense of having minimum variance. There is now some other estimator, to be discussed below, which has a smaller sampling variance, i.e. is more efficient.

(ii) The way in which the variances and covariances of OLS estimates are calculated assuming serial independence is incorrect if the errors are autocorrelated. The OLS calculations are based on taking $\sigma_u^2 (\mathbf{X'X})^{-1}$ as the variance-covariance matrix of $\hat{\beta}$, whereas the true variance-covariance matrix in this case is given by $(\mathbf{X'X})^{-1} \mathbf{X'VX} (\mathbf{X'X})^{-1}$ where $\mathbf{V}$ is the variance-covariance matrix of the errors. If the u_t are positively autocorrelated then the OLS formula is likely to underestimate the true variances. Hence we may be overoptimistic about the significance of coefficients.

(iii) The OLS formulae for the various F-tests considered in the previous chapter are also incorrect.

(iv) Likewise the OLS estimator of the error variance gives an underestimate in the presence of positive of positive autocorrelation and so we are likely to get an overoptimistic value for R^2.

(v) Finally, we will obtain inefficient predictions, that is to say, predictions with larger variances than necessary.

8.3 REPRESENTATIONS OF AUTOCORRELATION

Examination of the problem of autocorrelation is considerably facilitated by assuming some formal representation of the process generating the autocorrelation. We seek a representation some of whose *autocovariances* are non-zero:

$$E(u_t u_{t-k}) \neq 0 \qquad (k \neq 0).$$

Testing for the presence of autocorrelation can be seen in terms of (directly or indirectly) calculating estimates of one or more of these autocovariances and comparing them with zero. Obvious estimators are the sample covariances of the estimated residuals. But for them to provide appropriate estimates requires that the error process be invariant with respect to time or what is known as *stationary*. In the present context this involves firstly the variances being time invariant:

$$E(u_t^2) = E(u_{t-k}^2) = \sigma_u^2,$$

i.e. the errors being homoscedastic, and secondly the covariances being time invariant:

$$E(u_t u_{t-k}) = E(u_s u_{s-k}),$$

i.e. the covariance between two u's depending only on their *relative* positions in time and not on their absolute positions. Combining the two we can define autocorrelations of the form

$$\frac{E(u_t u_{t-k})}{\sqrt{\{E(u_t^2) E(u_{t-k}^2)\}}}$$

which if the process is stationary will be given by

$$\rho_k = \frac{E(u_t u_{t-k})}{E(u_t^2)} = \rho_{-k}$$

and called the *autocorrelation with lag k*. The ρ_k as a function of k

are called the *autocorrelation function* for u and the graph of the autocorrelation function is called the *correlogram*.

We now seek a model for the u's that will represent the $n-1$ ρ's between them by a process involving a small number of parameters. These representations are usually autoregressive processes, moving-average processes or a combination of the two. We consider auto-regressive processes for u first. The simplest of these has already been considered in chapter 3: it is a *first-order autoregressive process*

$$u_t = \rho u_{t-1} + \epsilon_t$$

where $-1 < \rho < 1$ and the ϵ_t satisfy the classical assumptions including that of serial independence. This is denoted AR(1). A *second-order autoregressive process*, AR(2), is given by

$$u_t = \phi_1 u_{t-1} + \phi_2 u_{t-2} + \epsilon_t$$

and a *general autoregressive process*, AR(p), by

$$u_t = \phi_1 u_{t-1} + \phi_2 u_{t-2} + \ldots + \phi_p u_{t-p} + \epsilon_t.$$

The *general moving-average process*, MA(q), is given by

$$u_t = \epsilon_t - \theta_1 \epsilon_{t-1} - \theta_2 \epsilon_{t-2} - \ldots - \theta_q \epsilon_{t-q}$$

and the combination of the two, called a *mixed autoregressive moving-average process* and denoted ARMA(p, q) can be written

$$u_t - \phi_1 u_{t-1} - \ldots - \phi_p u_{t-p} = \epsilon_t - \theta_1 \epsilon_{t-1} - \ldots - \theta_q \epsilon_{t-q}.$$

Having seen the various representations used, the obvious question is what do they each imply about what we are actually interested in: the correlations between the u's? So we next consider the correlograms implied by some of the processes outlined above. We will assume throughout that they are stationary.

Consider first the AR(1) process. Repeated substitution gives

$$u_t = \rho u_{t-1} + \epsilon_t$$
$$= \rho(\rho u_{t-2} + \epsilon_{t-1}) + \epsilon_t$$

$$\vdots$$

$$= \epsilon_t + \rho \epsilon_{t-1} + \rho^2 \epsilon_{t-2} + \ldots$$

$$= \sum_{j=0}^{\infty} \rho^j \epsilon_{t-j} \qquad (-1 < \rho < 1)$$

This is called the moving average representation of u_t. Note that it is an infinite sum. From this we can see that u_{t-1} depends on ϵ_{t-1}, ϵ_{t-2}, ... Hence ϵ_t is independent of u_{t-1} and indeed all past u's. Thus

$$E(u_t u_{t-1}) = E(\rho u_{t-1}^2 + \epsilon_t u_{t-1})$$
$$= \rho E(u_{t-1}^2) + E(\epsilon_t u_{t-1})$$
$$= \rho E(u_{t-1}^2)$$

and therefore

$$\rho_1 = \rho.$$

In general

$$E(u_t u_{t-k}) = E(\rho u_{t-1} u_{t-k} + \epsilon_t u_{t-k})$$
$$= \rho E(u_{t-1} u_{t-k}).$$

Therefore

$$\rho_k = \rho \cdot \rho_{k-1}$$

and so

$$\rho_k = \rho^k, \qquad k = 0, 1, 2, \ldots$$

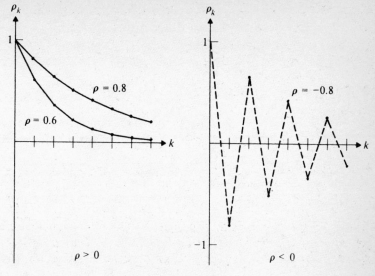

Figure 8.1

The correlogram for an AR(1) process $(-1 < \rho < 1)$ is sketched in Figure 8.1.

Next we consider the AR(2) process:

$$u_t = \phi_1 u_{t-1} + \phi_2 u_{t-2} + \epsilon_t.$$

Again we have that $E(\epsilon_t u_{t-k}) = 0$ for $k \geqslant 1$. Thus

$$E(u_t u_{t-k}) = \phi_1 E(u_{t-1} u_{t-k}) + \phi_2 E(u_{t-2} u_{t-k})$$

and on dividing through by the variance of u we obtain

$$\rho_k = \phi_1 \rho_{k-1} + \phi_2 \rho_{k-2}.$$

For $k = 1$ this gives

$$\rho_1 = \phi_1 \rho_0 + \phi_2 \rho_{-1}.$$

Assuming again that the process is stationary, $\rho_1 = \rho_{-1}$ and we have

$$\rho_1 = \frac{\phi_1}{1 - \phi_2}.$$

Taking $k = 2$, we have $\rho_2 = \phi_1 \rho_1 + \phi_2 \rho_0$, and so

$$\rho_2 = \frac{\phi_1{}^2}{1 - \phi_2} + \phi_2,$$

and similarly by repeated substitution in the general expression we obtain $\rho_k, k = 3, 4, \ldots$. An illustrative correlogram is shown in Fig. 8.2.

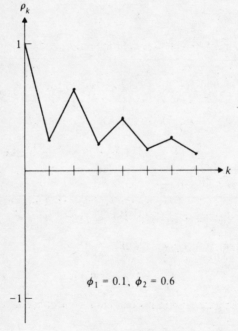

$\phi_1 = 0.1, \ \phi_2 = 0.6$

Figure 8.2

Finally we consider moving-average processes. For an MA(1) we have

$$E(u_t u_{t-1}) = E[(\epsilon_t - \theta_1 \epsilon_{t-1})(\epsilon_{t-1} - \theta_1 \epsilon_{t-2})]$$
$$= -\theta_1 E(\epsilon_{t-1}^2)$$
$$= -\theta_1 \sigma_\epsilon^2$$

since the ϵ_t are serially independent, and

$$E(u_t^2) = E(\epsilon_t^2 - 2\theta_1 \epsilon_t \epsilon_{t-1} + \theta_1^2 \epsilon_{t-1}^2)$$
$$= (1 + \theta_1^2)\sigma_\epsilon^2,$$

assuming stationarity. Thus

$$\rho_1 = \frac{-\theta_1}{1 + \theta_1^2}$$

The rest of the autocorrelation function is zero. For example

$$E(u_t u_{t-2}) = E[(\epsilon_t - \theta_1 \epsilon_{t-1})(\epsilon_{t-2} - \theta_1 \epsilon_{t-3})]$$
$$= E(\epsilon_t \epsilon_{t-2}) - \theta_1 E(\epsilon_{t-1}\epsilon_{t-2}) - \theta_1 E(\epsilon_t \epsilon_{t-3})$$
$$+ \theta_1^2 E(\epsilon_{t-1}\epsilon_{t-3})$$

and each of these terms is zero, since the ϵ_t are serially independent. So the correlogram for an MA(1) process looks like that shown in Figure 8.3.

This feature of the correlogram carries over to higher order moving-average processes. In general, for an MA(q) process

$$E(u_t u_{t-k}) = E[(\epsilon_t - \theta_1 \epsilon_{t-1} - \ldots - \theta_q \epsilon_{t-q})$$
$$\times (\epsilon_{t-k} - \theta_1 \epsilon_{t-k-1} - \ldots - \theta_q \epsilon_{t-k-q})].$$

For $k > q$ there are no ϵ-terms common to both bracketed expressions and hence

$$\rho_k = 0 \text{ for all } k > q.$$

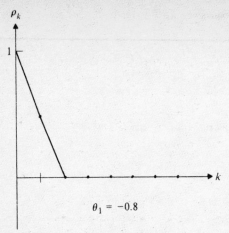

Figure 8.3

These theoretical correlograms generated by various error processes are useful for comparison when examining estimated residual correlograms for evidence of certain forms of autocorrelation.

8.4 TESTING FOR AUTOCORRELATION

Having seen earlier the consequences of autocorrelation it is clearly desirable to be able to test for its presence. A basic difficulty is that assumptions about the form of any autocorrelation are stated in terms of the errors which are unobservable. We therefore have to work with our estimates of the errors: the regression residuals, the e's. The most commonly used test employs what is known as the *Durbin-Watson statistic*. This is defined as the ratio of the sum of squares of the first differences of the residuals to the sum of squares of the residuals themselves:

$$d = \frac{\sum\limits_{t=2}^{n} (e_t - e_{t-1})^2}{\sum\limits_{t=1}^{n} e_t^2}.$$

To see what's going on when we use this statistic, suppose that the u's are generated by a first-order autoregressive process

$$u_t = \rho u_{t-1} + \epsilon_t.$$

The least squares estimator of ρ that we obtain if we use the residuals e_t in place of the unobservable error terms u_t is given by

$$\hat{\rho} = \frac{\sum\limits_{t=2}^{n} e_t e_{t-1}}{\sum\limits_{t=2}^{n} e_{t-1}^2}.$$

Clearly d and $\hat{\rho}$ are related. To see how expand the numerator of d to give

$$d = \frac{\sum\limits_{t=2}^{n} e_t{}^2 + \sum\limits_{t=2}^{n} e_{t-1}^2 - 2\sum\limits_{t=2}^{n} e_t e_{t-1}}{\sum\limits_{t=1}^{n} e_t{}^2}.$$

The first two terms in the numerator differ from the denominator only in so far as they contain $n - 1$ squared residuals, whereas the denominator is the sum of squares of all n residuals. If n is reasonably large we can neglect this difference. Hence

$$d \cong 2\left(1 - \frac{\sum\limits_{t=2}^{n} e_t e_{t-1}}{\sum\limits_{t=1}^{n} e_t{}^2}\right).$$

The ratio term differs from the expression for $\hat{\rho}$ given above only in the number of squared residuals summed in the denominator. Hence

$$d \cong 2(1 - \hat{\rho}).$$

Thus:

> If we have zero autocorrelation ($\rho = 0$) we would expect $d \cong 2$.
>
> If we have positive autocorrelation ($0 < \rho < 1$) we would expect $0 < d < 2$.
>
> If we have negative autocorrelation ($-1 < \rho < 0$) we would expect $2 < d < 4$.

So once we have calculated a value of d we have to decide whether it is sufficiently far away from 2 to force us to reject the null hypothesis that the errors are serially independent. We do this by comparing the calculated d with tabulated significance points. A problem with the Durbin-Watson statistic is that it does not have a single critical point, valid for all regression problems. This is because the distribution of d depends on the particular explanatory variables in the regression and when drawing up general tables these are of course not known. What Durbin and Watson did was to calculate upper and lower bounds (d_U and d_L) for the critical point in the one-sided test against an alternative hypothesis of positive autocorrelation. Providing all the explanatory variables in the equation are exogenous, the true critical point for d will lie between d_L and d_U. Therefore if one's calculated d is less than d_L it is probably too low to be explained by sampling variation alone and the null hypothesis of independence is rejected. Equally if the value is between d_U and 2 then the null hypothesis is accepted — such a small departure from 2 can be attributed to sampling error in a model with serially independent errors. If the computed d lies between d_L and d_U the test is unfortunately inconclusive. Most regression variables in economics are such that the actual critical value will be closer to the upper than the lower bound, so that when d falls in the inconclusive region one should nevertheless proceed with caution. If one is interested in the possibility of negative autocorrelation the tabulated significance points must be subtracted from 4, as d now varies between 2 and 4. Then if the calculated d lies between 2 and $(4 - d_U)$ the null hypothesis is accepted. If d lies between $(4 - d_L)$ and 4 there is evidence of significant negative autocorrelation. Finally, if the calculated d falls between $(4 - d_U)$ and $(4 - d_L)$ the test is again inconclusive.

The decision to be taken given a calculated value of d can be summarised as follows:

. Reject null .	. Accept null .	. Reject null .
. hypothesis in .	. hypothesis of .	. hypothesis in .
. favour of . Inconclusive	. serial . Inconclusive	. favour of .
. *positive* .	. independence .	. *negative* .
. auto- .	. .	. auto- .
. correlation .	. .	. correlation .

$$0 \qquad d_L \qquad d_U \qquad 2 \quad (4 - d_U) \quad (4 - d_L) \qquad 4$$

The values of d_L and d_U are tabulated on p. 333 for various values of n, the sample size, and k', the number of explanatory variables exclusive of a constant. As one might expect, the size of the inconclusive region increases as k' increases and decreases as n increases.

Testing for autocorrelation in the presence of a lagged dependent variable

The Durbin-Watson test is designed for use with regression equations in which all the explanatory variables are exogenous. In the presence of a lagged dependent variable the d statistic is biased towards 2 and hence may indicate serial independence when autocorrelation is in fact present. Thus an alternative test is required in this situation. Notice however that the Durbin-Watson test is not completely useless here: if, despite being biased towards acceptance of the null hypothesis, it indicates the presence of autocorrelation this decision can clearly stand.

Consider the equation

$$Y_t = \alpha_1 Y_{t-1} + \ldots + \alpha_r Y_{t-r} + \beta_1 X_{1t} + \ldots + \beta_k X_{kt} + u_t$$

An alternative test for first-order autocorrelation in such an equation is provided by Durbin's h-statistic:

$$h = \hat{\rho} \sqrt{\left(\frac{n}{1 - n \cdot \hat{V}(\hat{\alpha}_1)} \right)}$$

where $\hat{\rho}$ is the least squares estimate of ρ based on the OLS residuals from the fitted regression

$$\hat{\rho} = \frac{\sum\limits_{t=2}^{n} e_t e_{t-1}}{\sum\limits_{t=2}^{n} e_{t-1}^2}$$

and $\hat{V}(\hat{\alpha}_1)$ is the estimated variance of the OLS estimate of α_1.

Under the null hypothesis of serial independence, h has a standard normal distribution (for large n). Thus the calculated value of h can simply be compared with the appropriate critical point from the standard normal tables.

Notice that h is not defined if $n\hat{V}(\hat{\alpha}_1) \geqslant 1$. However, Durbin showed that an asymptotically equivalent test is given by regressing e_t on $e_{t-1}, Y_{t-1}, \ldots, Y_{t-r}, X_{1t}, \ldots, X_{kt}$ and then testing the significance of the coefficient of e_{t-1} in the usual way. Hence this can be used when the h-statistic is not defined.

Testing for higher-order autocorrelation

The Durbin-Watson statistic tests only for first-order auto-correlation, the hope being that even if autocorrelation of some higher order were present the first order autocorrelation would show up significant. Although this need not be the case it is likely when using annual data. However, particularly when using quarterly data, we may wish to test for higher order autocorrelation. We consider first the case of testing against an alternative hypothesis that specifies the auto-correlation to be of a particular order. When using quarterly data the most commonly considered case is

$$u_t = \rho_4 u_{t-4} + \epsilon_t$$

i.e. that the current error term is correlated with that of the same quarter last year, rather than that of the previous quarter.

Note that this is not a general AR(4) process, but rather one with $\phi_1 = \phi_2 = \phi_3 = 0$. The Durbin-Watson test procedure extends quite straightforwardly to this case. The appropriate test statistic is given by

$$d_4 = \frac{\sum_{t=5}^{n} (e_t - e_{t-4})^2}{\sum_{t=1}^{n} e_t^2}.$$

The tables* give d_L and d_U in the same way as the Durbin-Watson tables and the decision process is the same as with the original Durbin-Watson statistic.

We might also wish to examine the possibility that autocorrelation of other orders is present, without necessarily having a very clear idea of what orders to expect. One possibility might be to extend the Durbin-Watson statistic, as was done for d_4, to test for each order of autocorrelation in turn. However, performance of these tests would require construction of tables for each one. This would be exceedingly tedious. Instead a rough-and-ready approach can be taken by examining the *estimated residual correlogram*. Recall that the autocorrelation function was given by

$$\rho_k = \frac{E(u_t u_{t-k})}{E(u_t^2)}.$$

The sample equivalent, called the *sample autocorrelation function*, is defined by

$$r_k = \frac{\sum_{t=k+1}^{n} u_t u_{t-k}}{\sum_{t=1}^{n} u_t^2}.$$

---

* See K. F. Wallis – "Testing for fourth order autocorrelation in quarterly regression equations", *Econometrica*, July 1972.

Consider the null hypothesis of no autocorrelation:

$$H_0 : \rho_k = 0 \text{ for all } k \neq 0.$$

It can be shown that under H_0 the r_k are asymptotically normally distributed with

$$E(r_k) \cong -\frac{1}{n} \quad \text{and} \quad \text{var}\,(r_k) \cong \frac{1}{n}.$$

So if we could observe the u_t we could plot the sample correlogram for u (i.e. the r_k), draw in approximate 95% confidence limits at

$$-\frac{1}{n} \pm \frac{2}{\sqrt{n}}$$

and look for autocorrelations that fell outside these limits. Of course, in practice, we cannot observe the u_t and hence must instead examine the estimated *residual autocorrelation function*

$$\hat{r}_k = \frac{\displaystyle\sum_{t=k+1}^{n} e_t e_{t-k}}{\displaystyle\sum_{t=1}^{n} e_t^{\,2}}.$$

For low values of k, the confidence intervals for $\hat{r}_k$ are somewhat narrower than those for r_k. How much narrower depends on the explanatory variables in the equation – this is where the bounds to the critical point of the Durbin-Watson statistic come in. (The Durbin-Watson statistic and its extensions are of course closely related to these statistics: $d \cong 2(1 - \hat{r}_1)$, $d_4 \cong 2(1 - \hat{r}_4)$ and similarly for the possible extensions for any other order autocorrelation.) For large values of k, however, $-1/n \pm 2/\sqrt{n}$ is still a reasonable approximation to the 95% confidence interval, and is in fact often further approximated to

$$\pm \frac{2}{\sqrt{n}}.$$

The following procedure is therefore sometimes adopted. Calculate the residual correlogram (i.e. the $\hat{r}_k$) in the usual way. Values of $\hat{r}_k$ which lie outside the range $\pm 2/\sqrt{n}$ are taken to be significantly different from zero and indicative of autocorrelation of order k, while for low values of k an $\hat{r}_k$ inside this range but close to the boundary is treated as requiring further investigation.

It should be remembered when examining a correlogram that even if the u_t are serially independent the probability of obtaining an $\hat{r}_k$-value outside this range increases with the number plotted. For example, if we plot $\hat{r}_k$, $k = 1, \ldots, 20$ we should expect to get one "significant" value (at the 5% significance level) if the underlying process were random.

Comparison of the shape of the residual correlogram with the theoretical correlograms of section 8.3 can also provide useful information about the process generating the disturbances.

The Box-Pierce portmanteau statistic

Instead of looking at the $\hat{r}_k$ separately we can look at them together by calculating the Box-Pierce portmanteau statistic defined as

$$Q_m = n \sum_{k=1}^{m} \hat{r}_k^2 .$$

Under the null hypothesis of no autocorrelation, Q_m has a χ^2 distribution (approximately). If the residuals from which the $\hat{r}_k$ are calculated are from the OLS estimation of an equation that contains no lagged dependent variables then this χ^2 distribution will have m degrees of freedom. If the test is applied to an equation that contains only lagged dependent variables, then Q_m is calculated in exactly the same way but now has a χ^2 distribution with $m - l$ degrees of freedom where l is the length of the longest lag among the lagged dependent variables. Unfortunately if the list of explanatory variables contains *both* exogenous variables and lags of the dependent variable, the approximation on which the test is based is no longer valid and the test is inappropriate. (See below for an alternative test.)

One problem with the test concerns the choice of m. On the one hand the distribution of Q_m being approximately χ^2 depends on n being large relative to m. On the other hand the statistic can only indicate autocorrelation up to order m. Therefore if m is chosen too small the test can miss higher order autocorrelation, while if m is chosen too large the statistic no longer has the distribution on which the test is based. As a rough indication, if $n = 60$, a choice of m of about 12 is probably appropriate.

A further problem with the test is that it does not reject the null hypothesis often enough. Hence it fails to pick up autocorrelation more often than it should. Thus insignificant values of Q_m should be treated with caution and not taken as necessarily indicating serial independence (much the same as when examining the lower end of the full correlogram).

An extension of Durbin's alternative test

Finally we consider a test that is asymptotically equivalent to the Box-Pierce test, but is also valid when the list of explanatory variables includes both exogenous and lagged endogenous variables. It is an extension of Durbin's alternative to his h statistic (see p. 228).

Consider again the equation

$$Y_t = \alpha_1 Y_{t-1} + \ldots + \alpha_r Y_{t-r} + \beta_1 X_{1t} + \ldots + \beta_k X_{kt} + u_t, \qquad t = 1, \ldots, n$$

and suppose now that the errors are generated by a pth-order autoregressive process

$$u_t = \phi_1 u_{t-1} + \phi_2 u_{t-2} + \ldots + \phi_p u_{t-p} + \epsilon_t.$$

Then we wish to test the null hypothesis that $\phi_1 = \phi_2 = \ldots = \phi_p = 0$. This can be done by regressing the OLS residual e_t on its first p lags $e_{t-1}, \ldots, e_{t-p}$ and the original explanatory variables $Y_{t-1}, \ldots, Y_{t-r}, X_{1t}, \ldots, X_{kt}$. If the null hypothesis of serially independent errors is correct, then nR^2 (i.e. the product of the size of the sample used in the original regression and the R^2 calculated from this regression using the residuals) has asymptotically a χ^2 distribution with p degrees of freedom. Hence we will reject the null hypothesis of serial independence if nR^2 is greater than the selected critical point of the $\chi^2(p)$ distribution. This test is also known as the *Lagrange Multiplier test* for pth order autocorrelation.

8.5 ESTIMATION IN THE PRESENCE OF AUTOCORRELATION

We now consider what to do if our testing indicates the presence of autocorrelation. We will examine in this section various techniques for the estimation of a simple regression equation with a single explanatory variable

$$Y_t = \alpha + \beta X_t + u_t$$

where the u_t are generated by a first-order autoregressive process

$$u_t = \rho u_{t-1} + \epsilon_t.$$

The extension of the techniques to equations containing more than one explanatory variable and to higher order autoregressive processes is straightforward.

The various techniques are all based on transforming the equation into one with serially independent errors. This is achieved by first lagging the equation and multiplying through by ρ, to give

$$\rho Y_{t-1} = \alpha\rho + \beta\rho X_{t-1} + \rho u_{t-1},$$

and then subtracting this from the original to give

$$Y_t - \rho Y_{t-1} = \alpha(1 - \rho) + \beta(X_t - \rho X_{t-1}) + \epsilon_t.$$

If ρ were known, since the equation satisfies the classical assumptions, we could simply regress $(Y_t - \rho Y_{t-1})$ on $(X_t - \rho X_{t-1})$ using OLS to produce best (i.e. minimum variance) linear unbiased estimates again. However, ρ is in general not known and must be estimated. The following methods are all based on this approach. The most commonly used is discussed first.

(1) *The Cochrane-Orcutt Iterative Method*

This method involves using the OLS residuals to provide an estimate of ρ. This estimate is then used to generate transformed variables and the equation re-estimated. The residuals from this re-estimation can then be used to get an improved estimate of ρ and so on iteratively. The full procedure is as follows:

(i)　Estimate the equation

$$Y_t = \alpha + \beta X_t + u_t$$

by OLS and calculate the residuals $e_1, e_2, \ldots, e_n$. Use these to estimate, by OLS, the first order autoregressive process $u_t = \rho u_{t-1} + \epsilon_t$ with the unobservable u_t replaced by their estimates, the e_t. This gives

$$\hat{\rho} = \frac{\displaystyle\sum_{t=2}^{n} e_t e_{t-1}}{\displaystyle\sum_{t=2}^{n} e_{t-1}^2}$$

(ii)　Construct transformed variables for $t = 2, \ldots, n$

$$Y_t^* = Y_t - \hat{\rho} Y_{t-1}; \quad X_t^* = X_t - \hat{\rho} X_{t-1}$$

and estimate, by OLS, the equation

$$Y_t^* = \alpha^* + \beta X_t^* + u_t^*,$$

where $\alpha^* = \alpha(1 - \hat{\rho})$, and hence $\hat{\alpha} = \hat{\alpha}^*/(1 - \hat{\rho})$. From the revised estimates calculate the new residuals $e_1^*, \ldots, e_n^*$ by substitution into the original equation:

$$e_t^* = Y_t - \hat{\alpha} - \hat{\beta}X_t.$$

Use these to obtain a new estimate of ρ:

$$\hat{\hat{\rho}} = \frac{\displaystyle\sum_{t=2}^{n} e_t^* e_{t-1}^*}{\displaystyle\sum_{t=2}^{n} e_{t-1}^{*\,2}}.$$

(iii) Construct new transformed variables $(Y_t - \hat{\hat{\rho}}Y_{t-1})$ and $(X_t - \hat{\hat{\rho}}X_{t-1})$ and repeat step (ii). Continue iterations until the estimate of ρ converges (i.e. until the estimate of ρ changes by less than some specified small number in successive iterations).

A simplified version of this method is sometimes used.

(2) *The Cochrane-Orcutt Two-Step Method*

This consists merely of stopping the Cochrane-Orcutt iterative method after the estimates of α^* and β have been obtained at the start of the second stage. Thus ρ is estimated only once and the data transformed only once. Most computer regression packages contain a routine for estimation by the Cochrane-Orcutt iterative method, but when such a routine is not available this two-step method can be carried out very simply. In fact it can be simplified even further by noticing that an estimate of ρ can be obtained direct from the Durbin-Watson statistic since $d \simeq 2(1 - \hat{\rho})$. Another simple two-step procedure is considered next.

(3) *Durbin's Two-Step Method*

This differs from the preceding method only in the initial estimation of ρ. The transformed equation can be written as

$$Y_t = \alpha(1 - \rho) + \rho Y_{t-1} + \beta X_t - \beta \rho X_{t-1} + \epsilon_t.$$

The four coefficients here are functions of only three parameters. Hence this equation involves a (non-linear) restriction and so cannot be estimated by OLS. Durbin's method consists of estimating it by OLS ignoring the non-linear restriction simply to provide an estimate of ρ and then using this to transform the data as in the Cochrane-Orcutt method. Thus the procedure is as follows:

(i) Regress Y_t on Y_{t-1}, X_t and X_{t-1} using OLS and take the coefficient on Y_{t-1} as the estimate of ρ.

(ii) Construct transformed variables $Y_t^* = Y_t - \hat{\rho} Y_{t-1}$ and $X_t^* = X_t - \hat{\rho} X_{t-1}$ and estimate by OLS, the equation

$$Y_t^* = \alpha^* + \beta X_t^* + u_t^*.$$

The methods so far described have the drawback, which may be important in small samples, of having to drop the initial observation when estimating the transformed equations. This can be overcome, if so desired, in the following way.

(4) *The Prais-Winsten Modification*

This is a modification to the Cochrane-Orcutt method. $\hat{\rho}$ is estimated as before. The transformed variables are defined as before for $t = 2, \ldots, n$ and we define in addition

$$Y_1^* = \sqrt{1 - \rho^2} \cdot Y_1; \quad X_1^* = \sqrt{1 - \rho^2} \cdot X_1.$$

The remainder of the procedure is then carried out using the full sample.

Notice that this transformation is such as to make the variance of the transformed error for $t = 1$ equal to that of all the other transformed errors.

The transformed error for $t = 1$ is given by

$$u_1^* = \sqrt{1 - \rho^2} \cdot u_1.$$

Thus

$$\operatorname{var}(u_1^*) = (1 - \rho^2)\operatorname{var}(u_1) = (1 - \rho^2)\sigma_u^2.$$

The other transformed errors are $u_t^* = \epsilon_t \ (t = 2, \ldots, n)$ since

$$u_t = \rho u_{t-1} + \epsilon_t.$$

Thus since u_{t-1} is independent of ϵ_t

$$E(u_t^2) = \rho^2 E(u_{t-1}^2) + E(\epsilon_t^2).$$

So we also have

$$\operatorname{var}(\epsilon_t) = (1 - \rho^2)\sigma_u^2.$$

(5) *The Hildreth-Lu Search Method*

This method consists of specifying a grid of values for ρ. That is a set of values for ρ at regular intervals between a minimum and maximum. Then for *each* value on the grid the data are transformed using that value of ρ to construct

$$Y_t^* = Y_t - \rho Y_{t-1}; \quad X_t^* = X_t - \rho X_{t-1}$$

and OLS used to estimate the equation

$$Y_t^* = \alpha^* + \beta X_t^* + u_t^*.$$

The regression that gives the lowest residual sum of squares is selected: the value of ρ that gave rise to it is taken as the estimate $\hat{\rho}$, and its coefficients as the estimates of α and β. Notice that it is important, if the method is to work, that the true value of ρ (which is of course unknown) should lie between the minimum and maximum values chosen. In practice we will probably have previously estimated the equation by OLS and found a Durbin-Watson statistic that indicated the presence of autocorrelation. Thus we have a "first round" approximation to $\hat{\rho}$ before we start: $\hat{\rho} \cong 1 - \frac{1}{2}d$. So we should ensure that our specified interval encompasses this point. The method can be refined slightly as follows. Having found the value of ρ on the grid that gives the smallest residual sum of squares we can then set up a narrower and finer grid and repeat the procedure. For example, if we start with a grid from 0.2 to 0.8 at intervals of 0.1 and $\rho = 0.6$ gives the smallest *RSS* we might then take a grid from 0.5 to 0.7 at intervals of 0.01.

(6) *Direct estimation of the transformed equation by non-linear least squares or maximum likelihood*

The Hildreth-Lu search method if repeated with increasingly fine grids is equivalent to minimisation of the residual sum of squares

$$\sum_{t=2}^{n} (Y_t - \rho Y_{t-1} - \alpha(1 - \rho) - \beta(X_t - \rho X_{t-1}))^2$$

with respect to α, β *and* ρ. But this is equivalent to direct estimation of the transformed equation

$$Y_t = \alpha(1 - \rho) + \rho Y_{t-1} + \beta X_t - \beta \rho X_{t-1} + \epsilon_t$$

by Least Squares taking account of the non-linear restriction between the parameters, i.e. to the Least Squares estimation of

$$Y_t = \gamma_1 + \gamma_2 Y_{t-1} + \gamma_3 X_t + \gamma_4 X_{t-1} + \epsilon_t$$

subject to

$$\gamma_4 = -\gamma_2\gamma_3.$$

Direct minimisation of the residual sum of squares with respect to α, β and ρ gives the *Non-Linear Least Squares* estimates. In previous least squares regression problems we have minimised the residual sum of squares by setting the first derivatives with respect to the coefficients equal to zero. The resultant "normal" equations have been linear in the coefficients, and so easily solved to give formulae for the least squares estimates. In this case, however, the parameters enter non-linearly (note the product $\beta\rho$) and so the first-order conditions for a minimum will not lead to convenient expressions for $\hat{\alpha}, \hat{\beta}$ and $\hat{\rho}$. Some form of non-linear minimisation technique is required to find the estimates and it is not possible to write down an analytic form for them.

If we assume that the ϵ_t are normally distributed then Maximum Likelihood estimation of α, β and ρ directly is also possible. This method also requires some form of non-linear optimisation technique.

When the ϵ_t are normally distributed all the previously considered methods are asymptotically equivalent to Maximum Likelihood, which provides consistent estimators. Hence all the methods examined here give consistent estimators themselves.

The use of first differences

One way that researchers have sometimes attempted to deal with the problem of autocorrelation is by the use of first differences. The method consists of transforming the original data on Y and X into first differences $\Delta Y_t = (Y_t - Y_{t-1})$ and $\Delta X_t = (X_t - X_{t-1})$ and then regressing ΔY_t on ΔX_t. The rationale behind the method is the belief that for annual data the true value of ρ may be close to 1. Consider the equation

$$Y_t = \alpha + \beta X_t + u_t.$$

This also holds at time $t-1$,

$$Y_{t-1} = \alpha + \beta X_{t-1} + u_{t-1},$$

and on subtracting from the previous equation we obtain

$$\Delta Y_t = \beta \Delta X_t + \Delta u_t.$$

If ρ is close to 1, Δu_t will be close to ϵ_t. Note that the constant term drops out. If the transformed equation is estimated with a constant, this is equivalent to the inclusion of a linear time trend in the original equation:

$$Y_t = \alpha + \beta X_t + \delta t + u_t.$$

Again, lagging the equation gives

$$Y_{t-1} = \alpha + \beta X_{t-1} + \delta(t-1) + u_{t-1},$$

and on subtracting we have

$$\Delta Y_t = \beta \Delta X_t + \delta + \Delta u_t,$$

so the estimate of the constant in the transformed equation would be the estimate of the coefficient on the time trend in the original equation; in either case α is not estimated.

If the assumption that $\rho = 1$ is badly wrong this method, far from improving on the OLS estimates, may give *less* efficient estimates with more seriously miscalculated standard errors. This is because if $\rho < 1$ then Δu_t will have negative autocorrelation. In a sense OLS is based on the assumption that $\rho = 0$ whilst this method is based on the assumption that $\rho = 1$ and if $\rho = 1$ is a worse assumption to make than $\rho = 0$ then the method of first differences will give "worse" estimates than OLS.

8.6 PREDICTION IN THE PRESENCE OF AUTOCORRELATION

We will again illustrate with the case of a single explanatory variable

$$Y_t = \alpha + \beta X_t + u_t$$

and suppose that the u_t are generated by a first-order autoregressive process

$$u_t = \rho u_{t-1} + \epsilon_t$$

where $-1 < \rho < 1$ and the ϵ_t satisfy the classical assumptions including that of serial independence. The prediction procedure outlined previously (sections 5.5 and 6.4) takes as our forecast

$$\hat{Y}_f = \hat{\alpha} + \hat{\beta} X_f.$$

This is implicitly obtained by setting the unknown error u_f equal to zero. Whilst this may be a reasonable procedure when the errors are serially independent (since they have zero mean), in the presence of autocorrelation we have additional information that should be taken into account to obtain the best forecast.

Prediction of Y_{n+1}

Suppose initially that we wish to predict Y_{n+1}. Rather than setting u_{n+1} to zero to give the prediction, we note that the AR(1) scheme gives the best forecast of u_{n+1} as ρu_n, and we substitute estimates $\hat{\rho}$ and e_n respectively to obtain the forecast $\hat{\rho} e_n$. Thus we take as our forecast of Y_{n+1} the following expression:

$$\begin{aligned}\hat{Y}_{n+1} &= \hat{\alpha} + \hat{\beta} X_{n+1} + \hat{\rho} e_n \\ &= \hat{\alpha} + \hat{\beta} X_{n+1} + \hat{\rho}(Y_n - \hat{\alpha} - \hat{\beta} X_n) \\ &= \hat{\rho} Y_n + \hat{\alpha}(1 - \hat{\rho}) + \hat{\beta}(X_{n+1} - \hat{\rho} X_n).\end{aligned}$$

This suggests how we could alternatively have obtained our forecast from the transformed model:

$$Y_t^* = \alpha^* + \beta X_t^* + u_t^*,$$

where

$$Y_t^* = Y_t - \hat{\rho} Y_{t-1}$$

$$X_t^* = X_t - \hat{\rho} X_{t-1}$$

$$\alpha^* = \alpha(1 - \hat{\rho}).$$

Then prediction of Y_{n+1}^* in the usual way gives

$$\hat{Y}_{n+1}^* = \hat{\alpha}^* + \hat{\beta} X_{n+1}^*$$

therefore

$$\hat{Y}_{n+1} - \hat{\rho} Y_n = \hat{\alpha}(1 - \hat{\rho}) + \hat{\beta}(X_{n+1} - \hat{\rho} X_n)$$

and so

$$\hat{Y}_{n+1} = \hat{\rho} Y_n + \hat{\alpha}(1 - \hat{\rho}) + \hat{\beta}(X_{n+1} - \hat{\rho} X_n)$$

which is the same as above.

So prediction is in fact done in the usual way, but on the transformed equation.

Prediction of Y_{n+2}, etc.

Suppose now that we wish to predict more than just one period ahead. We start with prediction of Y_{n+2}. Advancing our previous prediction equation one period gives

$$\hat{Y}_{n+2} = \hat{\rho} Y_{n+1} + \hat{\alpha}(1 - \hat{\rho}) + \hat{\beta}(X_{n+2} - \hat{\rho} X_{n+1}).$$

However, Y_{n+1} will in general not be observed and hence will itself need to be forecast, giving

$$\hat{Y}_{n+2} = \hat{\rho} \hat{Y}_{n+1} + \hat{\alpha}(1 - \hat{\rho}) + \hat{\beta}(X_{n+2} - \hat{\rho} X_{n+1}).$$

If we use the prediction for Y_{n+1} already obtained, then

$$
\begin{aligned}
\hat{Y}_{n+2} &= \hat{\rho}\{\hat{\rho}Y_n + \hat{\alpha}(1 - \hat{\rho}) + \hat{\beta}(X_{n+1} - \hat{\rho}X_n)\} \\
&\quad + \hat{\alpha}(1 - \hat{\rho}) + \hat{\beta}(X_{n+2} - \hat{\rho}X_{n+1}) \\
&= \hat{\rho}^2 Y_n + \hat{\alpha}(1 - \hat{\rho}^2) + \hat{\beta}(X_{n+2} - \hat{\rho}^2 X_n).
\end{aligned}
$$

Notice that knowledge of X_{n+1} is not required to predict Y_{n+2}, despite the autocorrelation. Prediction of Y_{n+3} can be undertaken in a similar manner.

$$
\begin{aligned}
\hat{Y}_{n+3} &= \hat{\rho}\hat{Y}_{n+2} + \hat{\alpha}(1 - \hat{\rho}) + \hat{\beta}(X_{n+3} - \hat{\rho}X_{n+2}) \\
&= \hat{\rho}\{\hat{\rho}^2 Y_n + \hat{\alpha}(1 - \hat{\rho}^2) + \hat{\beta}(X_{n+2} - \hat{\rho}^2 X_n)\} \\
&\quad + \hat{\alpha}(1 - \hat{\rho}) + \hat{\beta}(X_{n+3} - \hat{\rho}X_{n+2}) \\
&= \hat{\rho}^3 Y_n + \hat{\alpha}(1 - \hat{\rho}^3) + \hat{\beta}(X_{n+3} - \hat{\rho}^3 X_n).
\end{aligned}
$$

We can see that repeated substitution of forecasts gives the prediction of Y, s periods ahead, as

$$
\hat{Y}_{n+s} = \hat{\rho}^s Y_n + \hat{\alpha}(1 - \hat{\rho}^s) + \hat{\beta}(X_{n+s} - \hat{\rho}^s X_n)
$$

which requires knowledge of X_{n+s} but not of the values of X in the periods between n and $n + s$.

8.7 THE IMPLICATIONS OF AUTOCORRELATION FOR DYNAMIC SPECIFICATION

What conclusions should we draw from obtaining a significant value of one of the test-statistics discussed above and what should we do next? The traditional view, and the one expressed so far in this chapter, is that since all our t-ratios will be miscalculated we should re-estimate the equation taking account of autocorrelation by one of the methods discussed in section 8.5. Thus autocorrelation is viewed as a nuisance for which allowance must be made when estimation and significance testing is carried out.

In this section a slightly different interpretation of autocorrelation is considered. It will be presented in the context of the simple two-variable model with an error generated by a first order autoregressive process:

$$Y_t = \alpha + \beta X_t + u_t$$

$$u_t = \rho u_{t-1} + \epsilon_t.$$

Recall from section 8.5 that we can transform the equation into one with a serially independent error term, ϵ_t:

$$Y_t = \alpha(1 - \rho) + \rho Y_{t-1} + \beta X_t - \beta \rho X_{t-1} + \epsilon_t.$$

This can be stated as a dynamic linear regression equation with a non-linear restriction on its parameters:

$$Y_t = \gamma_1 + \gamma_2 Y_{t-1} + \gamma_3 X_t + \gamma_4 X_{t-1} + \epsilon_t$$

subject to

$$\gamma_2 \gamma_3 + \gamma_4 = 0.$$

Suppose to begin with that this restriction is true. Then, given that most computer packages contain a routine for the Cochrane-Orcutt technique, the simple two-variable model with an autoregressive error can be regarded as a convenient simplification of the more general dynamic model in the sense that it reduces the number of parameters to be estimated from four to three and hence improves the efficiency of the estimates. Thus an autoregressive error process can sometimes be used to simplify the dynamic specification of an equation.

However, suppose now that the above restriction is not true. In other words suppose that the correct specification of the equation is

$$Y_t = \gamma_1 + \gamma_2 Y_{t-1} + \gamma_3 X_t + \gamma_4 X_{t-1} + \epsilon_t$$

without any restrictions on the parameters. Then if we estimate the simple two-variable model without any lags

$$Y_t = \alpha + \beta X_t + u_t$$

we will probably obtain a significant value of the Durbin-Watson statistic since this equation with the u's generated by an AR(1) process is a better approximation to the "correct" specification than this equation with the assumption that the u's are purely random. Informally, u is picking up the effect of the omitted lagged Y and X. Since Y is obviously autocorrelated and X probably so, u will be also. The actual problem with this equation, however, is one of misspecification, in particular the omission of X_{t-1} and Y_{t-1}. Thus in this instance, a significant Durbin-Watson statistic is in fact indicating dynamic misspecification. It is only in the case of the restriction discussed above being true that the simplification of an autoregressive error process is appropriate. The more general implication to be drawn is that of dynamic misspecification.

EXERCISES

8.1 Consider the simple equation

$$Y_t = \alpha + \beta X_t + u_t$$

where u_t is generated by a second order autoregressive process

$$u_t = \phi_1 u_{t-1} + \phi_2 u_{t-2} + \epsilon_t.$$

Explain how you would extend the Cochrane-Orcutt iterative procedure described in the text to estimate the parameters of this model.

8.2 Derive the equation that you would estimate to obtain the non-linear least squares estimates of the parameters in exercise 8.1. How many restrictions are there on the coefficients of this equation?

8.3 Calculate the Durbin-Watson statistic for the equation estimated in exercise 5.1.

8.4 Show that the ARMA(1, 1) process

$$u_t = \phi u_{t-1} + \epsilon_t - \theta \epsilon_{t-1}$$

has an autocorrelation function which satisfies

$$\rho_k = \phi \rho_{k-1} \text{ for } k > 1.$$

8.5 Discuss how you could test jointly for first- and fourth-order autocorrelation in a simple linear regression model.

8.6 Consider the model

$$Y_t = \beta Y_{t-1} + u_t \qquad -1 < \beta < 1$$
$$u_t = \rho u_{t-1} + \epsilon_t \qquad -1 < \rho < 1$$

where the ϵ_t are serially independent.

(a) Show that

$$E(u_t Y_{t-1}) = \frac{\rho \sigma_u^2}{1 - \rho \beta}.$$

What are the consequences of this for the OLS estimate of β?

(b) Let $\hat{\beta}$ be the OLS estimator of β, $\hat{\rho}$ the estimator of ρ based on the OLS residuals and d the Durbin-Watson statistic for first-order autocorrelation based on the OLS residuals. Then show that

$$\text{plim} (\hat{\beta} + \hat{\rho}) = \beta + \rho$$

and

$$\text{plim } d = 2\left[1 - \frac{\rho\beta(\beta + \rho)}{1 + \beta\rho}\right].$$

What are the practical implications of these results?

8.7 Consider the equation

$$Y_t = \beta Y_{t-1} + u_t$$

where u_t is given by

$$u_t = \phi u_{t-2} + \epsilon_t$$

the periods representing seasons, say summer and winter. Evaluate the covariance between u_t and Y_{t-1}.

IX

HETEROSCEDASTICITY

9.1 THE CAUSES OF HETEROSCEDASTICITY

One of the assumptions of the classical model is that

$$\text{var}(u_i) = E(u_i^2) = \sigma_u^2, \text{ a constant}$$

i.e. that the error terms all have the same variance. The failure of this assumption is known as *heteroscedasticity*.

To illustrate, consider the relationship between consumption and disposable income across a cross-section of families. Those with higher incomes have more flexibility over the choice of consumption level than those on lower incomes. Hence we may find that the variance in consumption for a given level of disposable income rises with income. This would give rise to a scatter diagram of the data with the appearance of Figure 9.1.

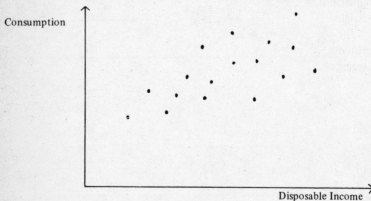

Figure 9.1

Along the same line of argument, the variation in investment among large firms may be greater than among small firms, and other illustrations of a similar nature abound. Another possibility is that the marginal propensity to consume may not be constant across the sample. In this case the variation in the mpc will be subsumed in the error term and cause the error variance to vary with income. This will be seen formally in section 9.6.

Heteroscedasticity can also be a sign of the misspecification of an equation. The omission of a relevant explanatory variable will cause the errors to be heteroscedastic if that variable exhibits non-constant variance, as for example would a trended time-series (this also will be seen formally in section 9.6). The indicated course of action in this case would be a respecification of the equation rather than estimation to take account of the heteroscedasticity using procedures that will be discussed below.

9.2. THE CONSEQUENCES FOR OLS

The consequences of heteroscedasticity are essentially the same as those of autocorrelation – they are both violations of the assumption that the variance-covariance matrix of the errors can be written as $\sigma_u^2 \mathbf{I}$. The OLS coefficient estimates are still both unbiased and consistent (the assumption of a constant error variance was not used in the proof of either). However, they are inefficient. That is, they no longer have the property of minimum variance, so that it is possible to obtain more reliable estimates (we will see how later). Finally, the OLS estimates of the variances of the coefficients will be biased. So the t-ratios which make use of these expressions will also be biased. Consider the simple case of a single explanatory variable:

$$Y_i = \beta_1 + \beta_2 X_i + u_i$$

where $E(u_i^2) = \sigma_i^2$. The direction of the bias in the OLS estimate of the variance of $\hat{\beta}_2$ depends on the direction of the association between $(X_i - \bar{X})^2$ and σ_i^2. If $(X_i - \bar{X})^2$ and σ_i^2 are positively related, then the calculated variance of $\hat{\beta}_2$ underestimates the true one. Hence the calculated t-ratio will be an overestimate and we may take as significant a variable which in fact is not. If, on the other hand, $(X_i - \bar{X})^2$ and σ_i^2 are negatively related, the opposite is the case and we may obtain an insignificant t-ratio for a variable which is in fact significant.

9.3 REPRESENTATIONS OF HETEROSCEDASTICITY

In what follows it will be necessary to assume some *form* for the variation in σ_i^2 in order to consider efficient estimates, tests against particular alternatives, etc. This is analogous for example to assuming that the errors are generated by an AR(1) or some other process when considering autocorrelation.

One possible simple form is to take

$$\sigma_i^2 = \sigma^2 Z_i^h$$

where Z is a known variable, which may or may not be one of the explanatory variables in the equation under consideration, and h is a known (i.e. pre-specified) power. This form, sometimes referred to as "classical" heteroscedasticity, suffers from the disadvantage that a null hypothesis of homoscedastic errors cannot be specified in terms of a parametric restriction on the general model. Alternative forms, known as "mixed" heteroscedasticity, that do not suffer from this drawback have also been suggested. These include for example

$$\sigma_i^2 = \alpha_1 + \alpha_2 Z_i$$

and

$$\sigma_i = \gamma_1 + \gamma_2 Z_i$$

where the α's and γ's are unknown parameters. The hypothesis of homoscedasticity can in these cases be specified as $\alpha_2 = 0$ in the first and $\gamma_2 = 0$ in the second.

9.4 TESTING FOR HETEROSCEDASTICITY

There are several tests available for examination of the possibility of heteroscedastic errors, distinguished in large part by the form of alternative hypothesis specified. The most commonly used is considered first.

(1) *The Goldfeld-Quandt test*

This test specifies an alternative hypothesis in which σ_i^2 is monotonically related to the value of one of the explanatory variables, Z. It will also be assumed here that they are positively related. (Modification of the test statistic in the case where they are negatively related is straightforward). In this case we would expect larger (in absolute value) residuals to correspond to the larger values of Z. This suggests the following test procedure:

 (i)   Order the observations according to the value of Z.

 (ii) Omit p central observations. (We will return to the choice of p below).

 (iii) Fit separate regressions by OLS to the first $(n - p)/2$ observations and to the last $(n - p)/2$ observations, (providing p has been chosen so that $(n - p)/2 > k$).

 (iv) Letting RSS_1 denote the sum of squared residuals from the regression corresponding to the smaller values of Z and RSS_2 that from the sub-sample with larger values of Z, construct the test statistic

$$G = \frac{RSS_2}{RSS_1}.$$

Under the null hypothesis of homoscedasticity and assuming the errors to be normally distributed, G will have a Fisher's F-distribution with $\{\frac{1}{2}(n - p - 2k), \frac{1}{2}(n - p - 2k)\}$ degrees of freedom. However, under the alternative hypothesis of heteroscedasticity, G will tend to be large since the values of Z are larger for the second set of residuals than the first and hence the corresponding sum of squared residuals will tend to be larger as well. Thus we simply compare G with the critical point from the tables for the F-distribution in the usual way.

Unfortunately both how powerful the test is and its outcome depend on the choice of p. The power of the test is impaired if p is either too large or too small. A rough guide is that it should be slightly less than $n/3$. Experimental calculations by Goldfeld and Quandt for the case of a single explanatory variable suggest, for example, that the best choice for p is about 8 when $n = 30$ and about 16 when $n = 60$. The calculations also seem to indicate that choosing p too low is less serious than choosing it too high.

In practice we may be unsure which of the explanatory variables to use for the reordering of the observations (i.e. which variable to take as Z). In this case we can repeat the test for several of the explanatory variables in turn. Note, however, that multicollinearity between the explanatory variables may well mean that the outcome of the test does not vary much with the choice of Z.

(2) *The Glejser test*

This test is based on the OLS residuals, e_i, from a single regression on the full sample. We use these to run a second regression of the form

$$|e_i| = \gamma_0 + \gamma_1 Z_i{}^h$$

where h is chosen to be one of -1, $-\frac{1}{2}$, $\frac{1}{2}$, 1 and Z is one of the explanatory variables. The hypothesis $\gamma_1 = 0$ is then tested using the usual t-test. Glejser found that the power of the test is not seriously impaired if the wrong value of h is chosen.

One possible problem with the test is that the error in this second-stage equation is likely to itself be heteroscedastic. However, this test is extremely easy to carry out and as we shall see below leads on to a convenient method of estimation.

(3) *The Breusch-Pagan test*

The final test to be considered formulates the possible heteroscedasticity as

$$\sigma_i{}^2 = f(\alpha_1 + \alpha_2 Z_{2i} + \alpha_3 Z_{3i} + \ldots + \alpha_m Z_{mi})$$

where the function f does not need to be specified but is assumed independent of i. The null hypothesis of homoscedasticity can be written as

$$H_0 : \alpha_2 = \alpha_3 = \ldots = \alpha_m = 0$$

since in this case $\sigma_i^2 = f(\alpha_1)$ which is constant. The Z_j are assumed to be exogenous, along with all the explanatory variables in the equation itself, any of which can appear as Z's also. The test procedure is as follows:

(i) Estimate the original equation by OLS and calculate the residuals $e_1, e_2, \ldots, e_n$.

(ii) Construct the variable g defined by

$$g_i = \frac{1}{\tilde{\sigma}^2} e_i^2 \qquad i = 1, 2, \ldots, n$$

where

$$\tilde{\sigma}^2 = \frac{1}{n} \sum_{i=1}^{n} e_i^2 .$$

(Note that $\tilde{\sigma}^2$ is the M.L. but not the OLS estimate of the error variance).

(iii) Regress g on the Z variables (including a constant).

(iv) Construct the test-statistic:

$B = \frac{1}{2}$ (the explained sum of squares from this regression).

Under the null hypothesis of homoscedastic errors, B has (asymptotically) a χ^2 distribution with $(m - 1)$ degrees of freedom. Hence we simply compare B with the appropriate critical point from the χ^2 table. The test has a very general alternative hypothesis and is quite easy to carry out.

9.5 ESTIMATION UNDER HETEROSCEDASTICITY

There are two parallel approaches to the problem of estimation under heteroscedasticity. Firstly we can transform the equation into one with a constant error variance. If the resultant equation is linear in its parameters we can then estimate it by least squares. This method is known as *Weighted Least Squares*. If the resultant equation is not linear in the coefficients some form of two-step approximation can generally be used. Alternatively we can estimate the equation directly by Maximum Likelihood.

(1) *Simple Weighted Least Squares*

The simplest form of Weighted Least Squares (WLS) can be derived as follows. Suppose the heteroscedasticity is given by

$$E(u_i^2) = \sigma^2 Z_i^2$$

where Z is a known variable, possibly one of the explanatory variables in the equation. Such a specification might be assumed, for example, after finding a significant Goldfeld-Quandt statistic based on ordering the observations according to the value of the variable Z. The modified estimation procedure in this case is quite straight-forward. Suppose that our equation is

$$Y_i = \beta_1 + \beta_2 X_{2i} + \beta_3 X_{3i} + \ldots + \beta_k X_{ki} + u_i.$$

Division of the equation by Z_i gives

$$\frac{Y_i}{Z_i} = \beta_1 \frac{1}{Z_i} + \beta_2 \frac{X_{2i}}{Z_i} + \ldots + \beta_k \frac{X_{ki}}{Z_i} + \epsilon_i$$

where

$$\epsilon_i = \frac{u_i}{Z_i}.$$

Hence

$$E(\epsilon_i^2) = E\left(\frac{u_i^2}{Z_i^2}\right) = \frac{1}{Z_i^2}\, E(u_i^2)$$

providing Z is exogenous, and so

$$E(\epsilon_i^2) = \frac{1}{Z_i^2} \cdot \sigma^2 Z_i^2$$

$$= \sigma^2, \text{constant.}$$

The method of Weighted Least Squares consists of applying OLS to this equation in the usual way and will produce efficient estimates if the assumed form of heteroscedasticity is correct. Notice that only if the variable Z is in fact one of the X's will there be a constant term in the equation, and the intercept term of the original equation is estimated as the coefficient of the reciprocal of the weighting variable, Z. The method can be modified to other "classical" forms of heteroscedasticity, i.e. forms of the type

$$E(u_i^2) = \sigma^2 Z_i^h$$

for any given value of h. For example if we took $h = -1$, WLS would involving multiplying the equation through by $\sqrt{Z_i}$. A particular illustration of when this is appropriate is given by the following common situation (which also indicates the origin of the name).

Using grouped data

Use of data that has been aggregated over groups of different sizes (e.g. industry-level data) may give rise to heteroscedasticity of this form. Suppose that our economic model is a micro-relationship such as

$$Y_{ij} = \beta_1 + \beta_2 X_{ij} + u_{ij}$$

where the subscripts refer to the ith individual (or firm) in the jth industry. We then wish to estimate the relationship using industry-level data. Let $Y_{.j}$ and $X_{.j}$ be the means of the variables in the jth industry and n_j be the number of individuals (or firms) in the jth industry. Then the aggregate relationship is given by

$$Y_{.j} = \beta_1 + \beta_2 X_{.j} + u_{.j}$$

where

$$u_{.j} = \frac{1}{n_j} \sum_{i=1}^{n_j} u_{ij}.$$

If $\text{var}(u_{ij}) = \sigma^2$ (constant), then $\text{var}(u_{.j}) = \sigma^2/n_j$. Hence the aggregate equation will be subject to heteroscedasticity. The WLS estimators are given by estimating

$$\sqrt{n_j}Y_{.j} = \beta_1\sqrt{n_j} + \beta_2(\sqrt{n_j}X_{.j}) + \epsilon_j,$$

thus the cross-products in the numerators and denominators of the estimators will all be *weighted* by n_j, the number of individual (or firm) observations in the group.

(2) *Two-step WLS for more general formulations*

The models considered so far have assumed the "classical" form of heteroscedasticity. The error variance is proportional to a known power of a known variable. We now turn to models which assume forms of "mixed" heteroscedasticity. For example, we might assume

$$E(u_i^2) = \alpha_1 + \alpha_2 Z_i$$

where Z may or may not be one of the explanatory variables in the equation, but must be exogenous. The main advantage of this form, as we have already seen, is that the hypothesis of homoscedasticity can be written simply as $H_0 : \alpha_2 = 0$. Given such a form for the mean of u_i^2 we might reasonably take

$$u_i^2 = \alpha_1 + \alpha_2 Z_i + v_i$$

where v_i is a random variable with mean zero. If we replace the unobserved u_i by the residuals e_i we can then estimate α_1 and α_2 by OLS. Hence we can get estimates of the σ_i^2 and thus re-estimate the original equation taking account of the heteroscedasticity. This produces the two-step WLS estimates. Again if the assumed form of heteroscedasticity is correct they are efficient. The full procedure is as follows:

(i)   Estimate the original equation by OLS and calculate the residuals.

(ii)   Regress e_i^2 on Z_i to obtain OLS estimates of α_1 and α_2 and from these calculate

$$\hat{\sigma}_i = \sqrt{(\hat{\alpha}_1 + \hat{\alpha}_2 Z_i)} \qquad i = 1, 2, \ldots, n$$

(iii)   Divide through the original equation by $\hat{\sigma}_i$ and estimate the transformed equation by OLS:

$$\frac{Y_i}{\hat{\sigma}_i} = \beta_1\left(\frac{1}{\hat{\sigma}_i}\right) + \beta_2\left(\frac{X_{2i}}{\hat{\sigma}_i}\right) + \ldots + \beta_k\left(\frac{X_{ki}}{\hat{\sigma}_i}\right) + \epsilon_i.$$

Notice that the method can straightforwardly be extended to an iterative procedure. However, there is a potentially serious problem with this method: it is possible that for some observations $\hat{\alpha}_1 + \hat{\alpha}_2 Z_i$ could be negative, in which case the method is not applicable in this form.

An alternative procedure which does not suffer from this last drawback assumes another form of "mixed" heteroscedasticity:

$$E(u_i^2) = (\gamma_1 + \gamma_2 Z_i)^2$$

and then uses the absolute value rather than the square of the residual in estimating γ_1 and γ_2. It thus incorporates the Glejser test and so provides a convenient combined estimation and test approach. The full procedure in this case will be as follows:

(i)   Estimate the original equation by OLS and calculate the residuals.

(ii)   Regress $|e_i|$ on Z_i to obtain OLS estimates of γ_1 and γ_2 and from these calculate

$$\hat{\sigma}_i = \hat{\gamma}_1 + \hat{\gamma}_2 Z_i \qquad i = 1, 2, \ldots, n$$

(Note that the fact that some of the $\hat{\sigma}_i$ may be negative does not matter, since when the moments are formed in the OLS estimation in (iii) below the negative signs will cancel out for any particular observation. Thus we can take either $\hat{\sigma}_i = \hat{\gamma}_1 + \hat{\gamma}_2 Z_i$ or $\hat{\sigma}_i = |\hat{\gamma}_1 + \hat{\gamma}_2 Z_i|$ and the resultant estimates in (iii) will be the same. It is the estimation of $\sigma_i{}^2$ that is important rather than the estimation of σ_i.)

(iii) Divide through the original equation by $\hat{\sigma}_i$ and estimate the transformed equation by OLS:

$$\frac{Y_i}{\hat{\sigma}_i} = \beta_1 \left(\frac{1}{\hat{\sigma}_i}\right) + \beta_2 \left(\frac{X_{2i}}{\hat{\sigma}_i}\right) + \ldots + \beta_k \left(\frac{X_{ki}}{\hat{\sigma}_i}\right) + \epsilon_i$$

This method also can be extended to an iterative procedure.

(3) *Maximum Likelihood*

If we assume that the u_i are normally distributed then we can use the maximum likelihood method to estimate the coefficients of the equation and the parameters in the expression for $E(u_i{}^2)$ at the same time. If the u_i are normally distributed, then so are the Y_i and

$$E(Y_i) = \sum_{j=1}^{k} \beta_j X_{ji}$$

$$\text{var}\,(Y_i) = \sigma_i{}^2$$

Hence the log of the likelihood function is given by

$$\log L = -\frac{n}{2}\log 2\pi - \frac{1}{2}\sum_{i=1}^{n} \log \sigma_i{}^2 - \frac{1}{2}\sum_{i=1}^{n} \left(\frac{Y_i - \sum_{j=1}^{k} \beta_j X_{ji}}{\sigma_i}\right)^2.$$

Suppose we then specify the form of the σ_i as above

$$\sigma_i = \gamma_1 + \gamma_2 Z_i$$

where recall Z can be (and usually is) one of the X's. The log likelihood is then given by

$$\log L = -\frac{n}{2}\log 2\pi - \frac{1}{2}\sum_{i=1}^{n}(\gamma_1 + \gamma_2 Z_i)^2 - \frac{1}{2}\sum_{i=1}^{n}\left(\frac{Y_i - \sum_{j=1}^{k}\beta_j X_{ji}}{\gamma_1 + \gamma_2 Z_i}\right)^2$$

which must then be maximised with respect to $\beta_1, \ldots, \beta_k, \gamma_1$, and γ_2, by some form of numerical optimization routine.

9.6 THE INTERPRETATION OF HETEROSCEDASTICITY

It was pointed out at the start of this section that observed heteroscedasticity in the calculated residuals can be the result of misspecification of the equation and/or variation in the coefficients, as well as of heteroscedasticity in the unobservable disturbance term of the "true" equation. We will now look a little more closely at this.

Consider first the possibility that the equation is misspecified to the extent that a relevant explanatory variable has been left out. Call it W_t. Thus the "true" relationship might be given by

$$Y_t = \beta_1 + \beta_2 X_{2t} + \ldots + \beta_k X_{kt} + \gamma W_t + u_t$$

whilst we are estimating the equation

$$Y_t = \beta_1 + \beta_2 X_{2t} + \ldots + \beta_k X_{kt} + u_t^*.$$

Thus $\mathrm{var}\,(u_t^{*2}) = \gamma^2\,\mathrm{var}\,(W_t) + \sigma_u^{2}$ (assuming W_t to be exogenous) which will in general not be constant. Thus for example if one of the relevant Z's in the Breusch-Pagan test is from outside the equation, one possible interpretation of a significant test statistic is that the variable should have been *in* the equation. (The consequences of omitting a relevant variable from the equation were considered in section 6.6.)

Consider next the possibility that one of the coefficients in the equation is not constant. Suppose, for example, that the "true" relationship is given by

$$Y_t = \beta_1 + \beta_2 X_{2t} + \ldots + \beta_{kt} X_{kt} + u_t$$

where β_{kt} varies with t (the other β's are still assumed constant). We will suppose that this variation is random and hence that β_{kt} is given by

$$\beta_{kt} = \bar{\beta}_k + v_t$$

where v_t is a random disturbance with mean zero. Then in the estimating equation under a constant coefficient assumption, namely

$$Y_t = \beta_1 + \beta_2 X_{2t} + \ldots + \bar{\beta}_k X_{kt} + u_t^*,$$

the error variance is given by

$$E(u_t^{*2}) = X_{kt}^2 \sigma_v^2 + \sigma_u^2,$$

assuming that X_{kt} is exogenous and that u and v are independent. This will clearly in general not be constant. Hence when significant heteroscedasticity is discovered in any of the above tests based on one of the explanatory variables, one possible explanation is that there is variation in the corresponding coefficient. It may be noted in passing that variation in the coefficients of an equation can be the result of misspecification of the functional form, i.e. of the "true" relationship not being linear.

EXERCISES

9.1 Show for the simple regression equation

$$Y_i = \beta_1 + \beta_2 X_i + u_i$$

where $E(u_i^2) = \sigma_i^2$, that if $(X_i - \bar{X})^2$ and σ_i^2 are positively related, then the usual OLS formula for the variance of $\hat{\beta}_2$ is biased downwards.

9.2 Consider the single regression equation without a constant

$$Y_i = \beta X_i + u_i.$$

Under what assumptions would

(a) $\dfrac{1}{n} \Sigma \dfrac{Y_i}{X_i}$

(b) $\dfrac{\Sigma Y_i}{\Sigma X_i}$

be the best linear unbiased estimator of β?

9.3 Give an intuitive explanation of why WLS estimation of an equation whose error term is known to be heteroscedastic is more efficient than OLS estimation.

9.4 Show, for the two-variable regression case, that OLS regression on individual data is more efficient than WLS estimation using grouped data.

X

THE ESTIMATION OF STRUCTURAL EQUATIONS

10.1 OLS AND SIMULTANEOUS EQUATION BIAS

In chapters 5 to 9 we have been concerned exclusively with the estimation of reduced form equations, i.e. equations in which the dependent variable is the only current endogenous variable in the equation. In this chapter we turn our attention to the estimation of structural equations. In this first section we will see that application of OLS to a structural equation generally results in biased and inconsistent estimates, a problem known as *simultaneous equation bias*. In section 10.2 we examine a particular situation in which OLS avoids this bias and then in the remaining sections of the chapter we consider some of the alternative methods of estimation that are available to overcome simultaneous equation bias.

Consider the case of the following simple structural equation

$$Y_{1t} = \alpha + \beta Y_{2t} + u_t$$

where Y_1 and Y_2 are both current endogenous variables. The OLS estimate of β is calculated as

$$\hat{\beta} = \frac{\Sigma (Y_{2t} - \bar{Y}_2)(Y_{1t} - \bar{Y}_1)}{\Sigma (Y_{2t} - \bar{Y}_2)^2}$$

and on substituting from the equation the sampling error is obtained as

$$\hat{\beta} - \beta = \frac{\Sigma (Y_{2t} - \bar{Y}_2)(u_t - \bar{u})}{\Sigma (Y_{2t} - \bar{Y}_2)^2}.$$

Since Y_2 is an endogenous variable, it will in most situations be correlated with u just as Y_1 is. Thus in general the second term here has neither zero expected value nor zero probability limit. Therefore $\hat{\beta}$ is both biased and inconsistent.

We now examine briefly the direction and magnitude of this inconsistency by means of two examples. Consider first a simple consumption function

$$C_t = \alpha + \beta Y_t + u_t.$$

Elementary macroeconomics tells us that the variable Y is not exogenous.

The model being considered contains at least one other equation, namely an income identity such as

$$Y_t = C_t + I_t,$$

where I is the level of investment, assumed to be exogenous. This income identity is obviously an over-simplification ignoring as it does both government and the balance of payments. However, the conclusions are not altered by the inclusion of other exogenous expenditures. The problem of simultaneous equation bias arises because Y is not independent of u. This can be seen clearly by considering the reduced form of the model:

$$C_t = \frac{\alpha}{1-\beta} + \frac{\beta}{1-\beta} I_t + \frac{1}{1-\beta} u_t$$

$$Y_t = \frac{\alpha}{1-\beta} + \frac{1}{1-\beta} I_t + \frac{1}{1-\beta} u_t.$$

The second equation indicates that Y is related to u; recall from chapter 2 that in general each endogenous variable of a model is related to all structural disturbances via the reduced form. To examine the direction of the inconsistency induced, consider the OLS estimate of β. We can use the simplifying notation of chapter 5 for second-order moments to write it as

$$\hat{\beta} = \frac{m_{YC}}{m_{YY}}$$

and on substituting from the equation we get

$$\hat{\beta} = \beta + \frac{m_{Yu}}{m_{YY}}.$$

Converting the reduced form equation for Y into deviations about means gives

$$(Y_t - \bar{Y}) = \frac{1}{1-\beta} \{(I_t - \bar{I}) + (u_t - \bar{u})\}$$

which we can use to express m_{Yu} and m_{YY} in terms of the exogenous variable and the error term.

$$m_{Yu} = \frac{1}{n} \sum (Y_t - \bar{Y})(u_t - \bar{u})$$

$$= \frac{1}{n} \cdot \frac{1}{1-\beta} \sum \{(I_t - \bar{I}) + (u_t - \bar{u})\}(u_t - \bar{u})$$

$$= \frac{1}{1-\beta} \left\{ \frac{1}{n} \sum (I_t - \bar{I})(u_t - \bar{u}) + \frac{1}{n} \sum (u_t - \bar{u})^2 \right\}$$

$$= \frac{1}{1-\beta} \{m_{Iu} + m_{uu}\}$$

$$m_{YY} = \frac{1}{n} \sum (Y_t - \bar{Y})^2$$

$$= \frac{1}{n} \cdot \left(\frac{1}{1-\beta}\right)^2 \sum \{(I_t - \bar{I}) + (u_t - \bar{u})\}^2$$

$$= \left(\frac{1}{1-\beta}\right)^2 \left\{ \frac{1}{n} \sum (I_t - \bar{I})^2 + \frac{1}{n} \sum (u_t - \bar{u})^2 + \frac{2}{n} \sum (I_t - \bar{I})(u_t - \bar{u}) \right\}$$

$$= \left(\frac{1}{1-\beta}\right)^2 \{m_{II} + m_{uu} + 2m_{Iu}\}$$

Thus

$$\hat{\beta} - \beta = \frac{(1 - \beta)(m_{Iu} + m_{uu})}{(m_{II} + m_{uu} + 2m_{Iu})}.$$

Whilst $\hat{\beta}$ is clearly biased, we have difficulty taking the expected value to evaluate the bias because a random variable appears in both numerator and denominator. However, the asymptotic situation (as $n \to \infty$) is quite straightforward: $\plim_{n \to \infty}(m_{Iu})$ is the population covariance between I and u, which is zero since I is exogenous; $\plim_{n \to \infty}(m_{uu}) = \text{var}(u)$ and $\plim_{n \to \infty}(m_{II}) = \text{var}(I)$, the population variances. Therefore

$$\plim_{n \to \infty}(\hat{\beta} - \beta) = \frac{(1 - \beta)\,\text{var}(u)}{\text{var}(I) + \text{var}(u)}$$

Under the conventional assumption that the marginal propensity to consume is less than one, this expression is positive. Hence $\hat{\beta}$ is (asymptotically) biased upwards. Note also that the above expression is less than $(1 - \beta)$. Thus

$$\beta < \plim_{n \to \infty}\hat{\beta} < 1.$$

Finally, an additional insight can be given into the interpretation of the inconsistency in $\hat{\beta}$ as follows.

$$\plim_{n \to \infty}\hat{\beta} = \beta + \frac{(1 - \beta)\,\text{var}(u)}{\text{var}(I) + \text{var}(u)}$$

$$= \frac{\beta\,\text{var}(I) + \text{var}(u)}{\text{var}(I) + \text{var}(u)}$$

$$= \lambda\beta + (1 - \lambda)\,1$$

where

$$\lambda = \frac{\text{var}(I)}{\text{var}(I) + \text{var}(u)}$$

Thus the probability limit of $\hat{\beta}$ is a weighted average of β (the effect of Y on C in the consumption function) and 1 (the effect in the identity), the weights being given by the relative magnitudes of the variances of the exogenous variable and the error term.

As our second illustration we take the demand and supply model considered as Case 3 in section 4.2 and add disturbance terms to give

$$D : Q_t = \alpha_0 + \alpha_1 P_t + u_{1t}$$

$$S : Q_t = \beta_0 + \beta_1 P_t + \beta_3 W_t + u_{2t}$$

We examine the inconsistency in the OLS estimate of α_1 in the demand equation, which is given by

$$\hat{\alpha}_1 = \frac{\Sigma(P_t - \bar{P})(Q_t - \bar{Q})}{\Sigma(P_t - \bar{P})^2}$$

$$= \frac{m_{PQ}}{m_{PP}} \, .$$

Substitution from the demand equation gives

$$\hat{\alpha}_1 = \alpha_1 + \frac{m_{Pu_1}}{m_{PP}} \, .$$

We now wish to express this in terms of the exogenous variable, W, and the error terms u_1 and u_2. The reduced form equation for P is given by

$$P_t = \frac{1}{\alpha_1 - \beta_1} \{(\beta_0 - \alpha_0) + \beta_3 W_t + (u_{2t} - u_{1t})\}$$

which in terms of deviations about means gives

$$(P_t - \bar{P}) = \frac{1}{\alpha_1 - \beta_1} \{\beta_3(W_t - \bar{W}) + (u_{2t} - \bar{u}_2) - (u_{1t} - \bar{u}_1)\}$$

and thus

$$m_{Pu_1} = \frac{1}{\alpha_1 - \beta_1} \{\beta_3 m_{Wu_1} + m_{u_2 u_1} - m_{u_1 u_1}\}$$

$$m_{PP} = \left(\frac{1}{\alpha_1 - \beta_1}\right)^2 \{\beta_3{}^2 m_{WW} + m_{u_2 u_2}$$

$$+ m_{u_1 u_1} - 2\beta_3 m_{Wu_1} + 2\beta_3 m_{Wu_2} - 2m_{u_1 u_2}\}.$$

In the case where u_1 and u_2 are assumed to be independent,

$$\operatorname*{plim}_{n \to \infty} (m_{Pu_1}) = \frac{-1}{\alpha_1 - \beta_1} \operatorname{var}(u_1)$$

$$\operatorname*{plim}_{n \to \infty} (m_{PP}) = \left(\frac{1}{\alpha_1 - \beta_1}\right)^2 \{\beta_3{}^2 \operatorname{var}(W) + \operatorname{var}(u_2) + \operatorname{var}(u_1)\}.$$

Hence

$$\operatorname*{plim}_{n \to \infty} (\hat{\alpha}_1 - \alpha_1) = \frac{-(\alpha_1 - \beta_1) \operatorname{var}(u_1)}{\beta_3{}^2 \operatorname{var}(W) + \operatorname{var}(u_2) + \operatorname{var}(u_1)}.$$

Under the assumption that $\alpha_1 < 0$ and $\beta_1 > 0$, this expression is positive and thus $\hat{\alpha}_1$ will be (asymptotically) biased upwards (i.e. towards zero). We can also see that

$$\operatorname*{plim}_{n \to \infty} \hat{\alpha}_1 = \alpha_1 - (\alpha_1 - \beta_1)\lambda = (1 - \lambda)\alpha_1 + \lambda\beta_1$$

where

$$\lambda = \frac{\operatorname{var}(u_1)}{\beta_3{}^2 \operatorname{var}(W) + \operatorname{var}(u_2) + \operatorname{var}(u_1)}.$$

Thus the probability limit of $\hat{\alpha}_1$ is a weighted average of α_1 (the effect of P on Q in the demand equation) and β_1 (the effect of P on Q in the supply equation).

In the case where u_1 and u_2 are correlated, the direction of the bias is uncertain: plim $\hat{\alpha}_1$ is still a weighted average of α_1 and β_1, but now the weights do not necessarily lie between zero and one.

These examples illustrate a general situation in which estimation of an equation that is not in reduced form by OLS results in estimates that are biased and inconsistent. This emphasises the need to think carefully about whether the equation that we are estimating is a structural or reduced-form equation. This entails considering for each of the explanatory variables in our equation whether it can be regarded as predetermined with respect to the dependent variable in the equation or whether they are in fact jointly determined.

10.2 RECURSIVE SYSTEMS

Before looking at some of the alternatives to OLS for the estimation of simultaneous systems we consider a special case in which OLS estimates of a structural equation *are* consistent. This is the case where the model we are considering is recursive. A *recursive system* is one which satisfies two conditions:

(i) The matrix of coefficients of the endogenous variables is triangular (possibly after the equations have been re-ordered).

(ii) Each equation's error term is independent of all the other error terms in all time periods.

Note that this second requirement is stronger than it may seem at first sight. An error term represents (amongst other things) the influence of omitted variables and it seems likely that some of these may be common to a number of the equations in a model.

If the two conditions are satisfied, then the structural equations form a causal chain and there are no feedbacks between current endogenous variables. The system can be set out as follows

$$Y_{1t} \qquad\qquad\qquad + \sum_{k=1}^{K} \gamma_{1k} X_{kt} = u_{1t}$$

$$\beta_{21} Y_{1t} + Y_{2t} \qquad\qquad + \sum_{k=1}^{K} \gamma_{2k} X_{kt} = u_{2t}$$

$$\beta_{31} Y_{1t} + \beta_{32} Y_{2t} + Y_{3t} \qquad + \sum_{k=1}^{K} \gamma_{3k} X_{kt} = u_{3t}$$

$$\vdots \qquad\qquad\qquad\qquad\qquad \vdots$$

$$\beta_{G1} Y_{1t} + \beta_{G2} Y_{2t} + \beta_{G3} Y_{3t} + \ldots + Y_{Gt} + \sum_{k=1}^{K} \gamma_{Gk} X_{kt} = u_{Gt}$$

with each error term independent of all the others. (G is the number of endogenous variables in the model and K the number of predetermined variables, as in earlier chapters.)

At first sight it may seem that only the first equation is identified; the others appear not to satisfy the order condition. However, it turns out that the restriction of independent errors (a restriction of a kind not considered in chapter 4) is sufficient to identify the system.

Consider the first two equations. The first is identified, excluding $G - 1$ variables. The second appears to be unidentified, for adding any multiple of the first to the second produces a new equation containing exactly the same variables. However, the requirement that the first and second structural equations have independent errors is now crucial, for no linear combination of the first and second equations will have an error term independent of u_1, (the linear combination will itself contain u_1). So such a linear combination would not pass as the second equation, which is thereby identified. And so on.

Given that all the equations are identified, we now turn to their estimation. The first equation is straightforward: it contains only one current endogenous variable. Hence OLS regression of Y_1 on the X's will give consistent estimates of the γ_{1k}'s. Consider now estimating the second equation. The "explanatory" endogenous variable Y_1 and the error term u_2 have covariance given by

$$E(Y_{1t}u_{2t}) = E\{(u_{1t} - \Sigma\gamma_{1k}X_{kt})u_{2t}\}$$
$$= E(u_{1t}u_{2t}) - \Sigma\gamma_{1k}E(X_{kt}u_{2t})$$
$$= 0$$

since u_1 and u_2 are assumed independent and the X's are all predetermined. This means that Y_1 can be regarded as predetermined with respect to this equation. Thus an OLS regression of Y_2 on Y_1 and the X's will provide consistent estimates of β_{21} and the γ_{2k}'s. Likewise, in the third equation Y_1 and Y_2 are independent of u_3 and so can be treated as predetermined: they can be thought of as having been determined earlier in the causal chain. Hence OLS will produce consistent estimates. In general, when we come to estimate the gth equation, the independent error assumption allows us to regard the endogenous variables Y_1, Y_2, ..., Y_{g-1} determined in the preceding equations as predetermined with respect to that equation — they are independent of the error term in that equation. In conclusion, the two special requirements of no feedback from higher-numbered to lower-numbered endogenous variables and independent errors eliminate the problem of simultaneous equation bias and allow consistent estimation of structural equations by OLS.

A simple example is provided by the cobweb model, previously used as an example of a dynamic model (exercise 3.4). The quantity supplied of a commodity produced in an annual crop depends on the previous year's price; the current price is determined by the demand equation. After re-ordering and re-normalizing we can write the model in triangular form as follows:

$$Q_t \qquad + \gamma P_{t-1} = u_{1t}$$
$$\beta Q_t + P_t \qquad = u_{2t}.$$

The first equation, already being in its reduced form, can be consistently estimated by OLS (we assume the errors to be non-autocorrelated).

However, this is only true for the second equation if u_1 and u_2 are independent, whereupon the model becomes recursive. Then Q is independent of u_2, and a simple regression of P on Q consistently estimates β. If u_1 and u_2 are correlated, we no longer have a recursive system, and OLS is inapplicable. Which case is appropriate depends mainly on our view as to whether or not it is reasonable to assume that none of the variables omitted from the supply equation and hence appearing in u_1 also appear in u_2 as variables omitted from the demand equation.

10.3 INDIRECT LEAST SQUARES

Given that in general OLS produces inconsistent estimates of the parameters in structural equations, we now turn to the problem of finding another method of estimation that will provide consistent estimates in this situation. The difficulty arose as a result of the error term being correlated with the explanatory variable. The reduced form equations, however, are free from this problem. This suggests that we might estimate the reduced form equations by OLS and then, attempt to deduce estimates of the structural parameters from the reduced form parameter estimates. To illustrate the approach we return to our consumption function example. Recall that the reduced form equations of the model are:

$$C_t = \frac{\alpha}{1-\beta} + \frac{\beta}{1-\beta} I_t + \frac{1}{1-\beta} u_t$$

$$Y_t = \frac{\alpha}{1-\beta} + \frac{1}{1-\beta} I_t + \frac{1}{1-\beta} u_t.$$

Given the OLS estimate of the slope of the first reduced form equation, $\hat{\pi}_{12}$, we can obtain an estimate of β from

$$\frac{\hat{\beta}}{1-\hat{\beta}} = \hat{\pi}_{12}.$$

Solving for $\hat{\beta}$ gives

$$\hat{\beta} = \frac{\hat{\pi}_{12}}{1 + \hat{\pi}_{12}}.$$

Alternatively we can derive an estimate of β from $\hat{\pi}_{22}$, the OLS estimate of the slope of the second reduced form equation. They are related by

$$\frac{1}{1 - \hat{\beta}} = \hat{\pi}_{22},$$

which can be solved for $\hat{\beta}$ to give

$$\hat{\beta} = \frac{\hat{\pi}_{22} - 1}{\hat{\pi}_{22}}.$$

For these two estimates of β to be identical we require the reduced form estimates to satisfy

$$\hat{\pi}_{22} - \hat{\pi}_{12} = 1.$$

The two reduced form slope estimates are given by

$$\hat{\pi}_{12} = \frac{m_{CI}}{m_{II}} \quad \text{and} \quad \hat{\pi}_{22} = \frac{m_{YI}}{m_{II}}.$$

Thus the two estimates of β will be identical if

$$m_{YI} - m_{CI} = m_{II}.$$

The key to this is provided by the income identity. Writing it in mean deviation form gives

$$(Y_t - \bar{Y}) = (C_t - \bar{C}) + (I_t - \bar{I})$$

which multiplied through by $(I_t - \bar{I})$, summed over t and divided through by n gives

$$m_{YI} = m_{CI} + m_{II}.$$

So whichever route we use to obtain the estimate of β, we arrive at the same result. This is precisely what we would expect from the fact that the consumption function in this model is just-identified and hence the structural parameter values can be deduced uniquely from the reduced form coefficient values. This method of estimation is known as *Indirect Least Squares* (ILS). It only produces unique parameter estimates when applied to a just-identified equation.

In this case we can write the resulting estimate of β in a slightly simpler form. The OLS estimate of the slope of the first reduced form equation is given by

$$\hat{\pi}_{12} = \frac{m_{CI}}{m_{II}}$$

and the ILS estimate of β is given in terms of it as

$$\hat{\beta} = \frac{\hat{\pi}_{12}}{1 + \hat{\pi}_{12}}.$$

Thus combining the two we have

$$\hat{\beta} = \frac{m_{CI}}{m_{II} + m_{CI}} = \frac{m_{CI}}{m_{YI}}$$

and so the indirect least squares estimate of β can be calculated directly as this ratio of sample moments.

An empirical illustration

We now illustrate the method of indirect least squares on the same data that were used for the empirical illustration presented in section 5.6. Recall that the data consist of 72 quarterly observations for the period 1960 quarter 1 to 1977 quarter 4 inclusive on two variables:

$$C = \text{Real consumers' expenditure}$$

$$DI = \text{Real personal disposable income}$$

(both in £million at 1975 prices).

The OLS estimate of the simple linear consumption function given in section 5.6 was

$$C = 2571 + 0.7331 \, DI.$$

The OLS estimates, using these data, of the two reduced form equations of the model are given by

$$C = 11677 + 1.4776 \, IN$$

$$DI = 11677 + 2.4776 \, IN$$

where the variable IN is constructed as $IN = DI - C$. Note first that the two intercepts in the reduced form equations are the same (as indicated on p. 269) and that the two slope estimates differ by 1 (as shown on p. 270).

From either slope coefficient the ILS estimate of the marginal propensity to consume is given by

$$\hat{\beta} = \frac{1.4776}{2.4776} = 0.5964.$$

Note that this is considerably less than the OLS estimate, which was biased upwards towards 1 (see section 10.1). From the estimated reduced form intercepts we can calculate the ILS estimate of the intercept of the consumption function as

$$\hat{\alpha} = \frac{11677}{2.4776} = 4713.$$

Thus the ILS estimate of our simple linear consumption function is

$$C = 4713 + 0.5964 \, DI.$$

We saw above that the ILS estimate of β can be calculated directly from the sample moments (see p. 271). The sample moments for these data (all divided by a factor of 10^6) are given by:

	C	Y	I
C	2.79622	3.57155	0.77534
Y		4.87162	1.30007
I			0.52473

Thus by direct calculation, the ILS estimate of β is given by

$$\frac{m_{CI}}{m_{YI}} = \frac{0.77534}{1.30007} = 0.5964$$

as compared with the OLS estimate given by

$$\frac{m_{CY}}{m_{YY}} = \frac{3.57155}{4.87162} = 0.7331.$$

Consistency

We now turn to the question of consistency. Does the Indirect Least Squares estimate have the property of consistency that the direct least squares estimate lacked? To answer this we express $\hat{\beta}$ in terms of error terms and exogenous variables, and then use our assumptions about these variables. Multiplying the reduced form equations at time t through by $(I_t - \bar{I})$, summing over t from 1 to n and dividing through by n gives

$$m_{CI} = \frac{\beta}{1 - \beta} \, m_{II} + \frac{1}{1 - \beta} \, m_{uI}$$

$$m_{YI} = \frac{1}{1 - \beta} \, m_{II} + \frac{1}{1 - \beta} \, m_{uI}.$$

Substituting these in the expression gained above for the indirect least squares estimator gives

$$\hat{\beta} = \frac{\beta m_{II} + m_{uI}}{m_{II} + m_{uI}} \; .$$

Once again we cannot evaluate $E(\hat{\beta})$ in a finite sample case, for a random variable appears in both numerator and denominator. However, the asymptotic situation (as $n \to \infty$) is quite straightforward: plim (m_{uI}) is the population covariance between u and I, which is zero since I is exogenous, and plim (m_{II}) = var (I), the population variance. Therefore

$$\plim_{n \to \infty} \hat{\beta} = \frac{\beta \text{var} (I)}{\text{var} (I)} = \beta.$$

Thus $\hat{\beta}$ is a consistent estimate of β.

Before considering the general case we first look at another method of estimation that can be used to estimate a just-identified structural equation. In fact we will see that the resultant estimates are the same as the ILS estimates obtained in this section. After considering that method in the context of our consumption function illustration, we examine the application of *both* methods to a general structural equation.

10.4 THE METHOD OF INSTRUMENTAL VARIABLES

Before examining the method in the context of a general structural equation, we illustrate the approach by returning to our consumption function example. Writing it in mean deviation form gives

$$C_t - \overline{C} = \beta(Y_t - \overline{Y}) + (u_t - \overline{u}).$$

We have seen, in section 10.1, that the OLS estimate of β is biased and inconsistent. We can think of this OLS estimate as having been obtained by forming moments with the "explanatory" variable, Y_t, to give

$$m_{CY} = \beta m_{YY} + m_{uY}$$

and then setting m_{uY} to zero to give the least squares normal equation

$$m_{CY} = \hat{\beta} m_{YY}.$$

This method fails to give an unbiased or consistent estimate of β because m_{uY} has non-zero expected value. We have also seen such a situation arise in the context of measurement error in the explanatory variable, and in a reduced form equation containing a lagged dependent variable and an autocorrelated error term. For an equation satisfying all the classical assumptions the normal equations, obtained by setting the moment between the error term and each explanatory variable equal to its expected value of zero, provide consistent estimates.

This suggests that we might form moments with a variable that *is* independent of the error term, i.e. a predetermined variable. The only one in our present model is I_t, and so we have

$$\frac{1}{n}\Sigma(C_t - \bar{C})\,(I_t - \bar{I}) = \beta\frac{1}{n}\Sigma(Y_t - \bar{Y})\,(I_t - \bar{I}) + \frac{1}{n}\Sigma(u_t - \bar{u})\,(I_t - \bar{I})$$

or

$$m_{CI} = \beta m_{YI} + m_{uI}.$$

Now u_t and I_t are independent, so $E(m_{uI}) = 0$, and so setting m_{uI} equal to its expected value gives the "quasi-normal" equation

$$m_{CI} = \check{\beta} m_{YI},$$

which results in the estimator

$$\check{\beta} = \frac{m_{CI}}{m_{YI}}.$$

We call I_t an instrumental variable (or an instrument) and the resulting estimate is the *instrumental variable* (IV) estimate.

We notice immediately that the IV estimate is identical to the ILS estimate $\hat{\beta}$ derived in the previous section (p. 271). Hence the IV estimate in this case will have the same properties as the ILS estimate. In particular the IV estimate will be consistent but not necessarily unbiased.

The general procedure for obtaining IV estimates which we have followed is to form moments with the instrumental variables (here the predetermined variables in the model) and derive estimating equations for the coefficients (quasi-normal equations: similar to the "normal" equations of OLS) by setting the moments between the instrumental variables and the error term equal to their expected values of zero. In the consumption function example I_t was the instrumental variable. It is a variable in the model and so correlated with all the endogenous variables (via the reduced form equations). In particular

$$E(m_{YI}) \neq 0.$$

But it is independent of the error term:

$$E(m_{uI}) = 0.$$

These are both necessary requirements for any instrumental variable, which is why the predetermined variables in the model are ideal. There was no problem of choosing an appropriate instrumental variable: we required one such variable in order to form one quasi-normal equation which would give an estimate of the single parameter β, and there was just one predetermined variable available. This is a consequence of the just-identified nature of the equation. The order condition (see p. 90) for just-identifiability guarantees that there will be the right number of instrumental variables. In the case of an over-identified equation there will not be unique IV estimates. We will return to this point below. We now turn our attention to the case of a general structural equation. To do so we need to introduce some matrix notation for such an equation.

Matrix notation for a general structural equation

Suppose, without loss of generality, that the structural equation we wish to estimate is the first in the model. We can write it as

$$Y_{1t} = \beta_2 Y_{2t} + \ldots + \beta_H Y_{Ht} + \gamma_1 X_{1t} + \ldots + \gamma_J X_{Jt} + u_{1t}$$

$$(t = 1, \ldots, n)$$

Notice that we have written the equation in the familiar form with the "dependent" variable on the left-hand side and the "explanatory" variables and error term on the right. This means that compared with the representation of a general equation in chapter 2 (see p. 21) all coefficients other than that of the variable "normalised" on, Y_1, have the opposite sign. We write the equation in matrix notation as

$$\mathbf{y}_1 = \mathbf{Y}\beta + \mathbf{X}^*\gamma + \mathbf{u}$$

where $\mathbf{y}_1$ is the $n \times 1$ vector of observations on the "dependent" variable (i.e. the endogenous variable on which the equation has been normalised); $\mathbf{Y} = (\mathbf{y}_2, \mathbf{y}_3, \ldots, \mathbf{y}_H)$ is the matrix of observations on the "right-hand side" endogenous variables and is $n \times (H-1)$, H being the number of included endogenous variables; β is the $(H-1) \times 1$ vector of coefficients on $\mathbf{y}_2, \ldots, \mathbf{y}_H$; $\mathbf{X}^*$ is the matrix of observations on the predetermined variables *included* in the equation and is $n \times J$; γ is the $J \times 1$ vector of coefficients on them and $\mathbf{u}$ is the $n \times 1$ vector of disturbances. Let $\mathbf{X}$ denote the matrix of observations on *all* the predetermined variables in the model, of which there are K. It is $n \times K$ and can be partitioned as

$$\mathbf{X} = (\mathbf{X}^* : \mathbf{X}^\circ)$$

where $\mathbf{X}^\circ$ is the matrix of observations on those predetermined variables that are *excluded* from this equation and is $n \times (K-J)$. Finally the matrix of observations on all the right-hand-side variables will be denoted by $\mathbf{Z}$. So

$$\mathbf{Z} = (\mathbf{Y} : \mathbf{X}^*)$$

and is $n \times (H - 1 + J)$. Thus the equation we are considering can also be written as

$$y_1 = Z\binom{\beta}{\gamma} + u.$$

The general case of instrumental variables

Having established the notation of the general structural equation we return to consideration of the method of Instrumental Variables. In order to estimate the $H - 1$ β's and the J γ's we need $H - 1 + J$ quasi-normal equations. Clearly, it is alright to construct such equations by forming moments with $X_1, \ldots, X_J$ in turn, for these are predetermined and independent of u (contemporaneously at any rate), so these variables can be their own instruments. Endogenous variables, however, cannot be used, so we need some other variables to form moments with in place of $Y_2, \ldots, Y_H$. The remaining candidates in the model which meet the requirements are $X_{J+1}, \ldots, X_K$. To be able to write down an expression for the estimates we now utilise our matrix notation. Instead of putting the equation in mean deviation form to eliminate the constant and then multiplying through by each of the instruments also in mean deviation form we will keep all the variables in their original form and utilise the matrices as established in the previous paragraph. (This is exactly parallel to the way we proceeded to derive the OLS estimates. See pp. 109 and 146.) Multiplying the equation through by X', the matrix of instruments, and setting $X'u$ equal to its expected value of 0 gives the IV quasi-normal equations as

$$X'y_1 = X'Z\binom{\hat{\beta}}{\hat{\gamma}}.$$

So the IV estimates will be given by

$$\binom{\hat{\beta}}{\hat{\gamma}} = (X'Z)^{-1}X'y_1$$

provided that $X'Z$ is non-singular. This requires at least that $X'Z$ be square, which is only the case if **X** and **Z** have the same dimensions, i.e. if $K = H - 1 + J$. Thus we require that the equation be just-identified. To see this another way recall from above that we require $H - 1 + J$ quasi-normal equations to solve for the estimates of the β's and γ's. Hence we require **X'** to be $(H - 1 + J) \times n$, that is, we need $K = H - 1 + J$.

Since the X variables are all predetermined they will be independent of the errors, yet correlated with all the endogenous variables in the model. That is, they naturally satisfy the necessary requirements for intruments mentioned in the simple case considered earlier. Formally, consistency requires that the **X** matrix satisfy

(i) $\operatorname{plim}\left(\dfrac{1}{n} \mathbf{X'Z}\right)$ is non-singular,

(ii) $\operatorname{plim}\left(\dfrac{1}{n} \mathbf{X'u}\right) = \mathbf{0}$.

The first of these conditions requires that each of the X variables be correlated (in the limit) with at least one of the Z's and that each of the Z's be correlated with at least one of the X's. The second requires that each of the X's be uncorrelated with the errors. To see that these conditions are necessary for consistency we substitute the equation into the above expression for the estimator to give

$$\begin{pmatrix} \hat{\beta} \\ \hat{\gamma} \end{pmatrix} = \begin{pmatrix} \beta \\ \gamma \end{pmatrix} + (\mathbf{X'Z})^{-1} \mathbf{X'u}.$$

Taking probability limits then gives

$$\operatorname{plim} \begin{pmatrix} \hat{\beta} \\ \hat{\gamma} \end{pmatrix} = \begin{pmatrix} \beta \\ \gamma \end{pmatrix} + \left[\operatorname{plim}\left(\frac{1}{n} \mathbf{X'Z}\right)\right]^{-1} \left[\operatorname{plim}\left(\frac{1}{n} \mathbf{X'u}\right)\right]$$

$$= \begin{pmatrix} \beta \\ \gamma \end{pmatrix}.$$

Thus, given the above conditions, the IV estimates are consistent.

Equivalence of IV and ILS

We saw earlier that in our consumption function illustration the IV and ILS estimates were identical. We will now see that this holds true for any just-identified structural equation. Consider estimation of our general structural equation by ILS. The reduced form equations of the model are given by

$$\mathbf{y}_1 = \mathbf{X}\boldsymbol{\pi}_1 + \mathbf{v}_1$$

$$\vdots$$

$$\mathbf{y}_H = \mathbf{X}\boldsymbol{\pi}_H + \mathbf{v}_H$$

where $\boldsymbol{\pi}_i$, $i = 1, \ldots, H$ are all $K \times 1$. Forming these column vectors into a matrix, we can write the complete set of reduced form equations together as

$$(\mathbf{y}_1 : \mathbf{Y}) = \mathbf{X}\boldsymbol{\Pi}' + \text{a matrix of errors},$$

where $\boldsymbol{\Pi}' = (\boldsymbol{\pi}_1, \boldsymbol{\pi}_2, \ldots, \boldsymbol{\pi}_H)$ is the transpose of the reduced form coefficient matrix defined in chapter 2 (see p. 24). The structural equation that we are estimating can be written as

$$\mathbf{y}_1 - \mathbf{Y}\boldsymbol{\beta} = \mathbf{X}^*\boldsymbol{\gamma} + \mathbf{X}^\circ \mathbf{0} + \mathbf{u}$$

and thus, putting it into the same form as the reduced form equations above, as

$$(\mathbf{y}_1 : \mathbf{Y})\begin{pmatrix} 1 \\ -\boldsymbol{\beta} \end{pmatrix} = \mathbf{X}\begin{pmatrix} \boldsymbol{\gamma} \\ \mathbf{0} \end{pmatrix} + \mathbf{u}$$

Hence the ILS estimates will be given by the solution to

$$\hat{\boldsymbol{\Pi}}'\begin{pmatrix} 1 \\ -\hat{\boldsymbol{\beta}} \end{pmatrix} = \begin{pmatrix} \hat{\boldsymbol{\gamma}} \\ \mathbf{0} \end{pmatrix}$$

where $\hat{\Pi}'$ is the matrix of OLS estimates of the reduced form coefficients. Its columns will be given by

$$\hat{\pi}_1 = (\mathbf{X}'\mathbf{X})^{-1}\mathbf{X}'\mathbf{y}_1$$

$$\vdots$$

$$\hat{\pi}_H = (\mathbf{X}'\mathbf{X})^{-1}\mathbf{X}'\mathbf{y}_H.$$

Combining them together gives

$$\hat{\Pi}' = (\mathbf{X}'\mathbf{X})^{-1}\mathbf{X}'(\mathbf{y}_1 : \mathbf{Y}).$$

Thus by substitution

$$(\mathbf{X}'\mathbf{X})^{-1}\mathbf{X}'(\mathbf{y}_1 : \mathbf{Y})\begin{pmatrix} 1 \\ -\hat{\beta} \end{pmatrix} = \begin{pmatrix} \hat{\gamma} \\ 0 \end{pmatrix}$$

and so

$$(\mathbf{X}'\mathbf{X})^{-1}\mathbf{X}'\mathbf{y}_1 - (\mathbf{X}'\mathbf{X})^{-1}\mathbf{X}'\mathbf{Y}\hat{\beta} = \begin{pmatrix} \hat{\gamma} \\ 0 \end{pmatrix}.$$

Multiplying through by $\mathbf{X}'\mathbf{X}$ gives

$$\mathbf{X}'\mathbf{y}_1 - \mathbf{X}'\mathbf{Y}\hat{\beta} = \mathbf{X}'\mathbf{X}\begin{pmatrix} \hat{\gamma} \\ 0 \end{pmatrix}.$$

But $\mathbf{X} = (\mathbf{X}^* : \mathbf{X}^\circ)$ and the compatibility of the partitioning means that

$$\mathbf{X}\begin{pmatrix} \hat{\gamma} \\ 0 \end{pmatrix} = (\mathbf{X}^* : \mathbf{X}^\circ)\begin{pmatrix} \hat{\gamma} \\ 0 \end{pmatrix} = \mathbf{X}^*\hat{\gamma}.$$

Hence

$$\mathbf{X}'\mathbf{y}_1 - \mathbf{X}'\mathbf{Y}\beta = \mathbf{X}'\mathbf{X}^*\hat{\gamma}$$

giving

$$X'y_1 = X'Y\beta + X'X^*\hat{\gamma}$$

$$= X'Z\begin{pmatrix} \hat{\beta} \\ \hat{\gamma} \end{pmatrix}.$$

Since the equation being estimated is just-identified $X'Z$ is square. If it is also non-singular then

$$\begin{pmatrix} \hat{\beta} \\ \hat{\gamma} \end{pmatrix} = (X'Z)^{-1}X'y_1$$

which is identical to the IV estimates derived above.

Over-identified equations

If the equation is over-identified, then $K - J > H - 1$, and there are more excluded predetermined variables to act as instruments than we require. This presents us with the problem of how to choose $H - 1$ instrumental variables for the endogenous explanatory variables from the $K - J$ available. Equivalently, writing the condition as $K > H - 1 + J$, we have more quasi-normal equations than coefficients, and there is not a unique solution for the β's and γs. Any set of $H - 1 + J$ equations out of the K will provide consistent estimates and there will be as many estimates of each structural parameter as there are ways of choosing $H - 1 + J$ from K. The method of Two-Stage Least Squares discussed in the next section constructs the "optimal" set of instruments in such a situation.

10.5   ESTIMATION OF AN OVER-IDENTIFIED EQUATION: TWO-STAGE LEAST SQUARES

If the equation we wish to estimate is over-identified, the method of Indirect Least Squares presents us with multiple solutions for the structural parameter estimates in terms of the reduced form estimates, and no way of choosing between them. Similarly the method of Instrumental Variables in the simple form discussed so far has more predetermined variables avilable to act as instruments than are required, and the problem is how to choose between them. Equivalently, if we form the quasi-normal equations for the complete set of instruments there is not a unique solution for the structural parameters. Discarding some of the instruments is clearly arbitrary. The method to be considered in this section constructs the optimal set of instruments, not by discarding some, but by taking linear combinations. The resultant estimates will be weighted averages of the multiple solutions to the quasi-normal equations. The method is known as *Two-Stage Least Squares* (2SLS), for reasons that will become clear from its derivation. We start by examining a simple case with a small number of explanatory variables, only one right-hand-side endogenous variable and only one over-identifying restriction. The general case will be examined later. Consider the equation

$$Y_{1t} = \alpha + \beta Y_{2t} + \gamma X_{1t} + u_t$$

and suppose that there are just two other predetermined variables in the model, X_2 and X_3. (As usual Y's denote endogenous variables and X's predetermined variables). A feature of the method of Two-Stage Least Squares is that one does not need to specify the whole of the rest of the model, only the list of predetermined variables.

Recall that the problem with direct OLS estimation in this case is due to the fact that the right-hand-side endogenous variable, Y_2, is correlated with the error term, u. The method of Two-Stage Least Squares tackles this problem by using a variable that behaves like Y_2 but is independent of u: the reduced form predictions of Y_2. If the reduced form parameters were known, $E(Y_2)$ would simply be a linear combination of X_1, X_2 and X_3 (all predetermined variables) and therefore independent of u. Hence we could simply use this in place of Y_2. In practice of course the reduced form parameters are not known. However, we can get consistent estimates of them using OLS and this is exactly what 2SLS does. Thus the method of Two-Stage Least Squares involves the following two stages.

(i)   Estimate the reduced form equation for Y_2 by OLS and from these estimates calculate the predicted values of Y_2, say $\hat{Y}_2$.

(ii)   Replace Y_2 in the structural equation to be estimated by $\hat{Y}_2$ and estimate this modified equation by OLS.

Let us now examine more formally how the method operates.

Stage 1

The reduced form equation for Y_2 can be written

$$Y_{2t} = \pi_0 + \pi_1 X_{1t} + \pi_2 X_{2t} + \pi_3 X_{3t} + v_t.$$

Denoting the OLS estimate of π_i by $\hat{\pi}_i$ $(i = 0, 1, 2, 3)$, the predicted values of Y_2 will be given by

$$\hat{Y}_{2t} = \hat{\pi}_0 + \hat{\pi}_1 X_{1t} + \hat{\pi}_2 X_{2t} + \hat{\pi}_3 X_{3t}, \qquad t = 1, \ldots, n.$$

Stage 2

Replacing Y_2 in the original structural equation by $\hat{Y}_2$ gives

$$Y_{1t} = \alpha + \beta \hat{Y}_{2t} + \gamma X_{1t} + u_t^*$$

where $u_t^* = u_t + \beta \hat{v}_t$ and $\hat{v}_t = Y_{2t} - \hat{Y}_{2t}$ is the residual from the reduced form equation. Estimation of this equation by OLS gives the normal equations

$$\Sigma Y_{1t} = n\hat{\alpha} + \hat{\beta}\Sigma \hat{Y}_{2t} + \hat{\gamma}\Sigma X_{1t}$$

$$\Sigma Y_{1t}\hat{Y}_{2t} = \hat{\alpha}\Sigma \hat{Y}_{2t} + \hat{\beta}\Sigma \hat{Y}_{2t}^2 + \hat{\gamma}\Sigma X_{1t}\hat{Y}_{2t}$$

$$\Sigma Y_{1t}X_{1t} = \hat{\alpha}\Sigma X_{1t} + \hat{\beta}\Sigma \hat{Y}_{2t}X_{1t} + \hat{\gamma}\Sigma X_{1t}^2.$$

Solution of these equations for $\hat{\alpha}$, $\hat{\beta}$ and $\hat{\gamma}$ gives the 2SLS estimates. It can be shown that these estimates are consistent, but this will be left to the general case, (see p. 291).

As mentioned at the start of the section, the 2SLS estimator is in fact an Instrumental Variable estimator. This can be demonstrated as follows. To define Instrumental Variable estimates for the equation in question we need to form moments with *two* instruments. There are *three* predetermined variables as candidates and the problem is how to choose. Rather than simply discarding one of them, 2SLS takes a linear combination, namely the linear combination given by the reduced form estimator for Y_2:

$$\hat{Y}_{2t} = \hat{\pi}_0 + \hat{\pi}_1 X_{1t} + \hat{\pi}_2 X_{2t} + \hat{\pi}_3 X_{3t}.$$

To see this, suppose we have estimated the reduced form equation for Y_2 and consider the Instrumental Variable estimates defined by forming moments from the original equation with X_{1t} and $\hat{Y}_{2t}$. Multiplication of these quasi-normal equations through by n gives

$$\Sigma(Y_{1t} - \bar{Y}_1)(\hat{Y}_{2t} - \bar{Y}_2) = \tilde{\beta}\Sigma(Y_{2t} - \bar{Y}_2)(\hat{Y}_{2t} - \bar{Y}_2)$$
$$+ \tilde{\gamma}\Sigma(X_{1t} - \bar{X}_1)(\hat{Y}_{2t} - \bar{Y}_2)$$
$$\Sigma(Y_{1t} - \bar{Y}_1)(X_{1t} - \bar{X}_1) = \tilde{\beta}\Sigma(Y_{2t} - \bar{Y}_2)(X_{1t} - \bar{X}_1) + \tilde{\gamma}\Sigma(X_{1t} - \bar{X}_1)^2.$$

(Note that $\Sigma\hat{v}_t = 0$, so $\bar{\hat{Y}}_2 = \bar{Y}_2$.)

How do these compare with the OLS normal equations in the second stage given above? The first of the OLS normal equations gives

$$\hat{\alpha} = \bar{Y}_1 - \hat{\beta}\bar{Y}_2 - \hat{\gamma}\bar{X}_1$$

which when substituted into the other two equations gives

$$\Sigma(Y_{1t} - \bar{Y}_1)(\hat{Y}_{2t} - \bar{Y}_2) = \hat{\beta}\Sigma(\hat{Y}_{2t} - \bar{Y}_2)^2 + \hat{\gamma}\Sigma(X_{1t} - \bar{X}_1)(\hat{Y}_{2t} - \bar{Y}_2)$$
$$\Sigma(Y_{1t} - \bar{Y}_1)(X_{1t} - \bar{X}_1) = \hat{\beta}\Sigma(\hat{Y}_{2t} - \bar{Y}_2)(X_{1t} - \bar{X}_1) + \hat{\gamma}\Sigma(X_{1t} - \bar{X}_1)^2.$$

The two sets of equations appear to differ in two respects. However, taking the expression multiplying $\tilde{\beta}$ in the first equation of the first pair, we have

$$\Sigma(Y_{2t} - \bar{Y}_2)(\hat{Y}_{2t} - \bar{Y}_2) = \Sigma(\hat{Y}_{2t} + \hat{v}_t - \bar{Y}_2)(\hat{Y}_{2t} - \bar{Y}_2)$$
$$= \Sigma(\hat{Y}_{2t} - \bar{Y}_2)^2 + \Sigma\hat{v}_t(\hat{Y}_{2t} - \bar{Y}_2)$$
$$= \Sigma(\hat{Y}_{2t} - \bar{Y}_2)^2,$$

(since OLS residuals are uncorrelated with regression estimates and hence

$$\Sigma \hat{v}_t (\hat{Y}_{2t} - \bar{Y}_2) = \hat{\pi}_1 \Sigma \hat{v}_t (X_{1t} - \bar{X}_1)$$

$$+ \hat{\pi}_2 \Sigma \hat{v}_t (X_{2t} - \bar{X}_2) + \hat{\pi}_3 \Sigma \hat{v}_t (X_{3t} - \bar{X}_3) = 0),$$

which is the relevant expression in the first equation of the second pair. Similarly, from the second equation of the first pair we consider

$$\Sigma (Y_{2t} - \bar{Y}_2)(X_{1t} - \bar{X}_1) = \Sigma (\hat{Y}_{2t} - \hat{v}_t - \bar{Y}_2)(X_{1t} - \bar{X}_1)$$

$$= \Sigma (\hat{Y}_{2t} - \bar{Y}_2)(X_{1t} - \bar{X}_1)$$

since $\Sigma \hat{v}_t (X_{1t} - \bar{X}_1) = 0$.

Thus the two sets of equations can be seen to be identical. Hence $\tilde{\beta} = \hat{\beta}$ and $\tilde{\gamma} = \hat{\gamma}$ and the 2SLS estimates can be regarded as Instrumental Variable estimates using the *included* predetermined variables and the appropriate reduced form predictions as instruments.

Before moving on to the general case, a cautionary note concerning standard errors and *t*-ratios. These require an estimate of the error variance, σ_u^2. (The derivation of the variance-covariance matrix of the coefficients is left to the general case – see p. 293). The estimated error variance is calculated exactly as in the OLS regression case (see section 6.2) by dividing the residual sum of squares by the degrees of freedom. However, note that these residuals are given by substituting the 2SLS estimates back into the original structural equation:

$$e_t = Y_{1t} - \hat{\alpha} - \hat{\beta} Y_{2t} - \hat{\gamma} X_{1t}.$$

They are not the same as the residuals from the second stage OLS regression, as those have $\hat{Y}_{2t}$ substituted for Y_{2t}:

$$\hat{u}_t^* = Y_{1t} - \hat{\alpha} - \hat{\beta} \hat{Y}_{2t} - \hat{\gamma} X_{1t}$$

$$= e_t + \hat{\beta}(Y_{2t} - \hat{Y}_{2t})$$

$$= e_t + \hat{\beta} v_t.$$

Thus the standard errors and t-ratios given by the second stage OLS regression are *not* the correct ones. It is necessary to return to the original equation and plug in the coefficient estimates $\hat{\alpha}$, $\hat{\beta}$ and $\hat{\gamma}$ to calculate the correct standard errors and t-ratios.

The general case

We now turn our attention to the estimation of a general structural equation given in matrix notation by

$$y_1 = Y\beta + X^*\gamma + u.$$

(see p. 277 for an explanation of the notation). The method of Two-Stage Least Squares extends naturally from the simple illustrative case considered above. The two stages involved are as follows.

Stage 1

The first stage involves OLS estimation of the reduced form equations for $y_2, \ldots, y_H$ which are given by

$$y_2 = X\pi_2 + v_2$$

$$\vdots$$

$$y_H = X\pi_H + v_H$$

($\pi_i, i = 2, \ldots, H$ are all $K \times 1$ vectors).

The OLS estimates of the parameters are given by

$$\hat{\pi}_2 = (X'X)^{-1}X'y_2$$

$$\vdots$$

$$\hat{\pi}_H = (X'X)^{-1}X'y_H$$

and thus the predicted values of the y_i are given by

$$\hat{y}_2 = X\hat{\pi}_2 = X(X'X)^{-1}X'y_2$$

$$\vdots$$

$$\hat{y}_H = X\hat{\pi}_H = X(X'X)^{-1}X'y_H.$$

If we define a $n \times (H-1)$ matrix $\hat{Y}$ out of these vectors

$$\hat{Y} = (\hat{y}_2, \hat{y}_3, \ldots, \hat{y}_H),$$

then combining together these expressions, $\hat{Y}$ will be given by

$$\hat{Y} = X(X'X)^{-1}X'Y.$$

Stage 2

The second stage involves replacing Y in the original structural equation by $\hat{Y}$ and estimating the modified equation by OLS. Replacing Y by $\hat{Y}$ gives

$$y_1 = \hat{Y}\beta + X^*\gamma + u^*$$

$$= (\hat{Y} : X^*)\begin{pmatrix}\beta \\ \gamma\end{pmatrix} + u^*.$$

Estimating this by OLS gives

$$\begin{pmatrix}\hat{\beta} \\ \hat{\gamma}\end{pmatrix} = [(\hat{Y} : X^*)'(\hat{Y} : X^*)]^{-1} (\hat{Y} : X^*)'y_1$$

$$= \begin{bmatrix}\hat{Y}'\hat{Y} & \hat{Y}'X^* \\ X^{*'}\hat{Y} & X^{*'}X^*\end{bmatrix}^{-1}\begin{bmatrix}\hat{Y}'y_1 \\ X^{*'}y_1\end{bmatrix}.$$

To express these estimates in terms of the original data matrices, we make use of two simplifications:

(i) $\hat{Y}'\hat{Y} = \{Y'X(X'X)^{-1}X'\}\{X(X'X)^{-1}X'Y\}$

$\qquad = Y'X(X'X)^{-1}X'Y.$

(ii) $X^{*'}\hat{Y} = X^{*'}(Y - \hat{V})$

where $\hat{V} = (\hat{v}_2, \hat{v}_3, \ldots, \hat{v}_H)$ and $\hat{v}_i$ is the residual vector from the reduced form equation for y_i (for $i = 2, \ldots, H$). Hence $X^{*'}\hat{V} = 0$, a $J \times (H-1)$ matrix with all elements zero. Therefore

$$X^{*'}\hat{Y} = X^{*'}Y.$$

Given these two simplifications, we can express the vector of 2SLS estimates directly in terms of the original data matrices:

$$\binom{\hat{\beta}}{\hat{\gamma}} = \begin{bmatrix} Y'X(X'X)^{-1}X'Y & Y'X^* \\ X^{*'}Y & X^{*'}X^* \end{bmatrix}^{-1} \begin{bmatrix} Y'X(X'X)^{-1}X'y_1 \\ X^{*'}y_1 \end{bmatrix}$$

As in the simple case discussed earlier, 2SLS is an Instrumental Variables estimator using $\hat{Y}$ as instruments. Taking the expression for the Instrumental Variables estimator on p. 278, partitioning and replacing X° by $\hat{Y}$ gives

$$\binom{\hat{\beta}}{\hat{\gamma}} = \begin{bmatrix} \hat{Y}'Y & \hat{Y}'X^* \\ X^{*'}Y & X^{*'}X^* \end{bmatrix}^{-1} \begin{bmatrix} \hat{Y}'y_1 \\ X^{*'}y_1 \end{bmatrix}.$$

Substituting $\hat{Y} = X(X'X)^{-1}X'Y$ and $\hat{Y}'X^* = Y'X^*$ gives the 2SLS estimator as presented in the previous paragraph. The problem of selecting appropriate instruments has therefore been solved not by throwing some variables away, but by taking $H-1$ linear combinations of all K predetermined variables. The linear combinations used have been obtained by ordinary least squares estimation of the reduced form, and it is possible to show that this is the "best" way to select instruments. If 2SLS is applied to a just-identified equation, then the resulting estimates are the same as those given by instrumental variables and indirect least squares. The equivalence in this case can be seen quite clearly if we first consider an alternative formulation of the 2SLS estimates, not in terms of partitioned matrices. Define an $n \times (H - 1 + J)$ matrix $\hat{Z}$ by

$$\hat{Z} = (\hat{Y} : X^*)$$

corresponding to the definition of Z on p. 277. Then the second stage of 2SLS defines the estimates as

$$\begin{pmatrix} \hat{\beta} \\ \hat{\gamma} \end{pmatrix} = (\hat{Z}'\hat{Z})^{-1}\hat{Z}'y_1.$$

We next put $\hat{Z}$ in terms of directly observable data matrices. From p. 288 we have

$$\hat{Y} = X(X'X)^{-1}X'Y.$$

For compatibility we will now look at

$$X(X'X)^{-1}X'X^*.$$

The $n \times J$ matrix X^* can be written as

$$X^* = (X^* : X^\circ)\begin{pmatrix} I \\ 0 \end{pmatrix} = X\begin{pmatrix} I \\ 0 \end{pmatrix}$$

where I is the $J \times J$ identity matrix and 0 is a $(K - J) \times J$ matrix with all elements zero. Then

$$X(X'X)^{-1}X'X^* = X(X'X)^{-1}X'X\begin{pmatrix} I \\ 0 \end{pmatrix}$$

$$= X\begin{pmatrix} I \\ 0 \end{pmatrix}$$

$$= X^*.$$

Therefore

$$\hat{Z} = (\hat{Y} : X^*) = X(X'X)^{-1}X'(Y : X^*) = X(X'X)^{-1}X'Z.$$

Substituting this in the above expression for the 2SLS estimates gives

$$\begin{pmatrix} \hat{\beta} \\ \hat{\gamma} \end{pmatrix} = (\hat{Z}'\hat{Z})^{-1}\hat{Z}'y_1$$

$$= \{Z'X(X'X)^{-1}X'X(X'X)^{-1}X'Z\}^{-1}Z'X(X'X)^{-1}X'y_1$$

$$= \{Z'X(X'X)^{-1}X'Z\}^{-1}Z'X(X'X)^{-1}X'y_1.$$

(Recall that Z is the matrix of observations on the "right-hand-side" variables in the original equation and X is the matrix of observations on *all* the predetermined variables in the model.)

We can now easily see the equivalence of 2SLS to other estimators when the equation is just-identified. If the equation is just-identified then $K = J + H - 1$ and the matrix $Z'X$ is square and by assumption invertible. Thus each moment matrix appearing in the curly brackets above can be inverted separately, giving

$$\begin{pmatrix} \hat{\beta} \\ \hat{\gamma} \end{pmatrix} = (X'Z)^{-1}X'X(Z'X)^{-1}Z'X(X'X)^{-1}X'y_1$$

$$= (X'Z)^{-1}X'y_1,$$

the Instrumental Variable estimator using all the predetermined variables in the model as instruments.

We now move on to consider the consistency of the 2SLS estimator. The second stage equation is given by

$$y_1 = \hat{Y}\beta + X^*\gamma + u^*$$

$$= \hat{Y}\beta + X^*\gamma + (u + \hat{V}\beta)$$

and the OLS estimator of this equation is given by

$$\begin{pmatrix} \hat{\beta} \\ \hat{\gamma} \end{pmatrix} = (\hat{Z}'\hat{Z})^{-1}\hat{Z}'y_1$$

$$= \begin{pmatrix} \beta \\ \gamma \end{pmatrix} + (\hat{Z}'\hat{Z})^{-1}\hat{Z}'(u + \hat{V}\beta).$$

Now

$$\hat{Z}'\hat{V} = \begin{pmatrix} \hat{Y}'\hat{V} \\ X^{*'}\hat{V} \end{pmatrix} = \begin{pmatrix} Y'X(X'X)^{-1}X'\hat{V} \\ (I:0)\,X'\hat{V} \end{pmatrix} = 0$$

since $\hat{V}$ is the matrix of least squares residuals from the reduced form regressions on X. Thus

$$\begin{pmatrix} \hat{\beta} \\ \hat{\gamma} \end{pmatrix} = \begin{pmatrix} \beta \\ \gamma \end{pmatrix} + (\hat{Z}'\hat{Z})^{-1}\hat{Z}'u.$$

Therefore, taking probability limits, we have

$$\plim_{n\to\infty} \begin{pmatrix} \hat{\beta} \\ \hat{\gamma} \end{pmatrix} = \begin{pmatrix} \beta \\ \gamma \end{pmatrix} + \plim_{n\to\infty} \left(\frac{1}{n}\hat{Z}'\hat{Z}\right)^{-1} \cdot \plim_{n\to\infty} \left(\frac{1}{n}\hat{Z}'u\right)$$

and we must consider the last factor, which has two components:

$$\plim\left(\frac{1}{n}\hat{Z}'u\right) = \begin{bmatrix} \plim\dfrac{1}{n}\hat{Y}'u \\[2ex] \plim\dfrac{1}{n}X^{*'}u \end{bmatrix}$$

In the second component X^* contains only predetermined variables, and so

$$\plim\left(\frac{1}{n}X^{*'}u\right) = 0.$$

In the first component $\hat{Y}$ is given as $X\hat{\Pi}^*$ where $\hat{\Pi}^* = (\hat{\pi}_2, \ldots, \hat{\pi}_H)$, the OLS estimates of the coefficients in the reduced form equations for $y_2, \ldots, y_H$ only. Hence

$$\plim\left(\frac{1}{n}\hat{Y}'u\right) = \plim\left(\frac{1}{n}\hat{\Pi}^{*'}X'u\right)$$

$$= \plim\hat{\Pi}^{*'}\,\plim\left(\frac{1}{n}X'u\right)$$

$$= \Pi^{*'}\,\plim\left(\frac{1}{n}X'u\right)$$

since the OLS estimates of the reduced form parameters are consistent. Therefore

$$\text{plim}\left(\frac{1}{n}\hat{\mathbf{Y}}'\mathbf{u}\right) = \Pi^{*\prime}\mathbf{0} = \mathbf{0}$$

since $\mathbf{X}$ contains only predetermined variables. Thus the 2SLS estimates are consistent. As usual in structural equation estimation, one cannot prove unbiasedness and once again the consistency fails if any of the predetermined variables are lagged endogenous and the error term is autocorrelated.

We can compute an approximate covariance matrix of the coefficient estimates in order to calculate standard errors and carry out tests of hypotheses. The estimated error variance, $\hat{\sigma}_u^{\,2}$, is given by the residual sum of squares divided by the degrees of freedom $(n - (H - 1 + J))$ and the cautionary note mentioned in the illustrative case above, about getting the residuals by substituting the coefficient estimates back into the original structural equation rather than from the second stage OLS regression, is equally important here too. The asymptotic covariance matrix is then estimated by

$$\hat{\sigma}_u^{\,2}(\hat{\mathbf{Z}}'\hat{\mathbf{Z}})^{-1}$$

which substituting for $\hat{\mathbf{Z}}$ gives

$$\hat{\sigma}_u^{\,2}\{\mathbf{Z}'\mathbf{X}(\mathbf{X}'\mathbf{X})^{-1}\mathbf{X}'\mathbf{Z}\}^{-1}$$

and standard errors of the coefficients are obtained by taking square roots of diagonal elements as usual.

Earlier, we used R^2 to measure the proportion of the original variance in the dependent variable explained by the regression as a whole. Now, however, we have more than one (jointly) dependent variable in our equation and the meaning becomes none too clear. Further the total sum of squares cannot be partitioned into explained and unexplained sums of squares for 2SLS estimates, since the residuals are not orthogonal to all the explanatory variables. Thus for example, the residual sum of squares can exceed the total sum of squares. Hence, if calculated via the residual sum of squares, R^2 can be negative.

An aside on the terminology of IV estimators

The method of instrumental variables was introduced in the context of a just-identified structural equation, in which case the estimates were given by

$$\begin{pmatrix} \hat{\beta} \\ \hat{\gamma} \end{pmatrix} = (\mathbf{X}'\mathbf{Z})^{-1}\mathbf{X}'\mathbf{y}_1.$$

We have now seen that the 2SLS estimator, even when applied to an overidentified equation, can be interpreted as an IV estimator. In general any estimator of this type is referred to as an IV estimator even if the number of "instruments" exceeds the number of right-hand-side variables.

Formally, any estimator of the form

$$\begin{pmatrix} \hat{\beta} \\ \hat{\gamma} \end{pmatrix} = (\hat{\mathbf{Z}}'\mathbf{Z})^{-1}\hat{\mathbf{Z}}'\mathbf{y}_1$$

where $\hat{\mathbf{Z}} = \mathbf{W}(\mathbf{W}'\mathbf{W})^{-1}\mathbf{W}'\mathbf{Z}$ is an IV estimator of our structural equation. $\mathbf{W}$ is the matrix of instruments and may have any number of columns $\geqslant H - 1 + J$. If $\mathbf{W} = \mathbf{X}$ then the estimator is the 2SLS estimator and if the number of instrument equals $H - 1 + J$ then we are back with the IV estimator of section 10.4.

All the estimation techniques examined in this chapter (OLS, ILS, IV, 2SLS and A2SLS below) are referred to as "single equation" methods because they estimate the structural equations of a model singly. Methods which estimate all the parameters of a model simultaneously, known as "systems" methods, are not considered in this book. The two types of method are also known, respectively, as "limited information" and "full information" because the latter type make use of all the available information in the model, whereas the former type only utilize the information on the single equation being estimated at the time.

10.6 ESTIMATION IN THE PRESENCE OF AUTOCORRELATION

In this final section we consider the estimation of a structural equation whose error is autocorrelated. We look first at a method of estimation that is asymptotically efficient among single equation methods, *Autoregressive Two-Stage Least Squares* (A2SLS), and then at some possible modifications to avoid a problem that may arise when it is applied to large models. We start by considering an illustrative two equation model, although the method will be expounded for a general structural equation as well. Suppose initially that we wish to estimate the first equation of the following model

$$Y_{1t} = \alpha_1 + \beta_1 Y_{2t} + \gamma_{11} X_{1t} + \gamma_{14} Y_{1t-1} + u_{1t}$$

$$Y_{2t} = \alpha_2 + \beta_2 Y_{1t} + \gamma_{22} X_{2t} + \gamma_{23} X_{3t} + u_{2t}$$

(the X's are all exogenous variables) and that the error term in that equation is generated by a first-order autoregressive process

$$u_{1t} = \rho u_{1t-1} + \epsilon_{1t}.$$

Thus we have a combination of the problems of simultaneity, lagged endogenous variables and autocorrelation. We can transform the first equation (as in section 8.5) to one with a serially independent error term by lagging, multiplying through by ρ and subtracting from the original to give

$$Y_{1t} - \rho Y_{1t-1} = \alpha_1(1 - \rho) + \beta_1 Y_{2t} - \beta_1 \rho Y_{2t-1} + \gamma_{11} X_{1t} - \gamma_{11} \rho X_{1t-1}$$
$$+ \gamma_{14} Y_{1t-1} - \gamma_{14} \rho Y_{1t-2} + \epsilon_{1t}.$$

If we transform the second equation in a similar way and then solve the two for the current endogenous variables Y_{1t} and Y_{2t} in terms of the other variables we obtain what are known as the "augmented reduced form equations". They will give Y_{1t} and Y_{2t} as functions of $\{Y_{1t-1}, Y_{2t-1}, X_{1t}, X_{2t}, X_{3t}, X_{1t-1}, X_{2t-1}, X_{3t-1}, Y_{1t-2}\}$. This set of variables will provide the instruments for the A2SLS method of estimation. The method will consist of estimating alternately the transformed equation (by IV (in the general sense of p. 294) using this set as instruments) and ρ in an iterative fashion. Before we can transform the equation in the estimation procedure we must have an estimate of ρ. This initial estimate of ρ must therefore come from the original equation. However, estimation of the original equation by 2SLS will not provide consistent estimates since Y_{1t-1} is correlated with u_{1t} (through u_{1t-1}). Hence its residuals will not provide a consistent estimate of ρ to start us off. A modified estimator is needed which does not use lagged endogenous variables as instruments but rather treats them in the same way as current endogenous variables. The set of instruments for these initial estimates must consist only of strictly exogenous variables out of the above set. Notice that we could have formed the predictions for Y_{2t} by regressing it on $\{X_{1t}, X_{2t}, X_{3t}\}$ and formed the predictions for Y_{1t-1} by regressing it on $\{X_{1t-1}, X_{2t-1}, X_{3t-1}\}$. However, if separate sets of instruments are used to form the predictions of Y_{2t} and Y_{1t-1}, the independence of these predictions from the structural equation error term is not assured. Hence we must use the same set of instruments for both.

The procedure for the estimation of our illustrative structural equation (the first equation in the above model) by A2SLS is as follows:

(i) Construction of consistent initial estimates: Treat the lagged endogenous variable Y_{1t-1} as if it were current endogenous and estimate the equation by IV ignoring the autocorrelation. Use only the strictly exogenous variables in the model and their lags as instruments. The two-stage method of constructing these estimates would therefore involve first obtaining predictions of Y_{2t} and Y_{1t-1} by regressing them on $\{X_{1t}, X_{2t}, X_{3t}, X_{1t-1}, X_{2t-1}, X_{3t-1}\}$ and then in the second stage estimating

$$Y_{1t} = \alpha_1 + \beta_1 \hat{Y}_{2t} + \gamma_{11} X_{1t} + \gamma_{14} \hat{Y}_{1t-1} + u^*_{1t}$$

by OLS again.

(ii)   Given consistent estimates of $\alpha_1, \beta_1, \gamma_{11}, \gamma_{14}$ estimate ρ by

$$\hat{\rho} = \frac{\displaystyle\sum_{t=2}^{n} e_t e_{t-1}}{\displaystyle\sum_{t=2}^{n} e_{t-1}^2}$$

where $e_t = Y_{1t} - \hat{\alpha}_1 - \hat{\beta}_1 Y_{2t} - \hat{\gamma}_{11} X_{1t} - \hat{\gamma}_{14} Y_{1t-1}$ (and not the residual from the second stage OLS).

(iii) Transform the variables in the equation using this estimate, e.g. $Y_{1t} - \hat{\rho} Y_{1t-1}$, and estimate the transformed equation by IV using the full set of instruments discussed above. The two-stage method would therefore involve first obtaining predictions of $Y_{2t} - \hat{\rho} Y_{2t-1}$ by regressing it on $\{Y_{1t-1}, Y_{2t-1}, X_{1t}, X_{2t}, X_{3t}, X_{1t-1}, X_{2t-1}, X_{3t-1}, Y_{1t-2}\}$. Call them $\hat{Y}_{2t}^*$. (Note that it can be shown that this will be identical to regressing Y_{2t} on this set of variables and taking $\hat{Y}_{2t} - \hat{\rho} Y_{2t-1}$.) The second stage involves using OLS to estimate the transformed equation with $Y_{2t} - \hat{\rho} Y_{2t-1}$ replaced by its predictions, i.e. estimating

$$Y_{1t} - \hat{\rho} Y_{1t-1} = \alpha_1(1 - \hat{\rho}) + \beta_1 \hat{Y}_{2t}^* + \gamma_{11}(X_{1t} - \hat{\rho} X_{1t-1})$$

$$+ \gamma_{14}(Y_{1t-1} - \hat{\rho} Y_{1t-2}) + \text{error term}$$

by OLS.

(iv)   Re-estimate ρ using the new estimates of $\alpha_1, \beta_1, \gamma_{11}$, and γ_{14} as in (ii) above and iterate until convergence.

Standard errors of all the parameters can be obtained from (iii) in the final iteration in the same way as for 2SLS, remembering that the residuals require substitution back and are not the same as those in the second stage OLS.

This procedure generalises to the estimation of any structural equation in an extremely straightforward manner. We can write a general structural equation in matrix notation as

$$y_1 = Y\beta + X^*\gamma + u = Z \begin{pmatrix} \beta \\ \gamma \end{pmatrix} + u$$

and the full set of predetermined variables in the model is given by $X = (X^* : X^\circ)$ which may include both exogenous and lagged endogenous variables (see back to p. 277 for an explanation of the notation). A subscript -1 on a matrix will be used to indicate the corresponding matrix containing the first lags of the variables. The A2SLS procedure for this general equation will involve the following steps:

(i)   Treat any lagged endogenous variables in X^* as if they were current endogenous and estimate the equation, ignoring the autocorrelation, by IV using the strictly exogenous variables in X and X_{-1} as instruments.

(ii)   Estimate ρ from the residuals in the usual way.

(iii) Transform the equation using this estimate and estimate the transformed equation by IV using $\{y_{1,-1}, Y_{-1}, X, X_{-1}\}$ as instruments for $Y - \hat{\rho}Y_{-1}$. (Note that variables common to X and $y_{1,-1}$ or Y_{-1} should appear only once in the matrix of instruments.)

(iv)   Repeat (ii) and (iii) until convergence.

Given the initial consistent estimates, the method involves iteratively solving the following for $\begin{pmatrix} \hat{\beta} \\ \hat{\gamma} \end{pmatrix}$ and $\hat{\rho}$:

$$\begin{pmatrix} \hat{\beta} \\ \hat{\gamma} \end{pmatrix} = [(\hat{Z} - \hat{\rho}Z_{-1})'(\hat{Z} - \hat{\rho}Z_{-1})]^{-1}[(\hat{Z} - \hat{\rho}Z_{-1})'(y_1 - \hat{\rho}y_{1,-1})]$$

where

$$\hat{Z} = (\hat{Y} : X^*)$$
$$\hat{Y} = .W(W'W)^{-1}W'Y$$
$$W = (y_{1,-1} : Y_{-1} : X : X_{-1}).$$

excluding any variables common to $\mathbf{X}$ and $\mathbf{y}_{1,-1}$ or $\mathbf{Y}_{-1}$, and

$$\hat{\rho} = \frac{\mathbf{e}'\mathbf{e}_{-1}}{\mathbf{e}'_{-1}\mathbf{e}_{-1}}$$

where

$$\mathbf{e} = \mathbf{y}_1 - \mathbf{Y}\hat{\beta} - \mathbf{X}^*\hat{\gamma}.$$

The A2SLS estimates are consistent and asymptotically efficient among "limited information" estimators. This consistency is not dependent on the consistency of the initial estimates. Hence 2SLS or even OLS could be used to provide the initial estimate of ρ. However, it is likely that convergence will take longer from an inconsistent initial estimate than from a consistent one.

In a large model, or even a moderately sized one, the number of exogenous variables may be such as to make step (iii) infeasible or at best very short on degrees of freedom. In such a case modification of the list of instruments used in step (iii) is necessary. It can be shown that to preserve the consistency of the estimates, the list of instruments must at least include $\{\mathbf{y}_{1,-1}, \mathbf{Y}_{-1}, \mathbf{X}^*, \mathbf{X}^*_{-1}\}$. That is to say any modification to the list of instruments must be to the excluded predetermined variables and their lags. Any set of instruments that contains these will provide consistent estimates, but reduction of the list of instruments will in general involve an efficiency loss. One way to reduce the list that can sometimes be employed without too great a fall in efficiency is to use $\{\mathbf{y}_{1,-1}, \mathbf{Y}_{-1}, \mathbf{X}^*, \mathbf{X}^*_{-1}, \mathbf{X}^\circ - \hat{\rho}\mathbf{X}^\circ_{-1}\}$.

EXERCISES

10.1 Use the data presented in exercise 5.1 to calculate ILS and IV estimates of the simple consumption function. Check that they are the same.

10.2 Explain how you would estimate the parameters in each equation of the following model.

$$\begin{aligned}
Y_{1t} + \beta_{12}Y_{2t} \quad & + \gamma_{11} + \gamma_{12}X_{2t} & = u_{1t} \\
Y_{2t} \quad & + \gamma_{21} \quad + \gamma_{23}X_{3t} &= u_{2t} \\
\beta_{32}Y_{2t} + Y_{3t} + \gamma_{31} \quad & + \gamma_{33}X_{3t} &= u_{3t}
\end{aligned}$$

10.3 Consider the model

$$C_t = \alpha_0 + \alpha_1 Y_t + u_t$$

$$I_t = \beta_0 + \beta_1 Y_t + \beta_2 R_t + w_t$$

$$Y_t = C_t + I_t$$

endogenous variables: C_t, I_t, Y_t; exogenous variable: R_t.

Suppose that observations on the variables are available for $t = 1, \ldots, n$. Express the indirect least squares estimator and the instrumental variable estimator of the consumption equation in terms of these data. Show whether the two methods give the same answer and comment on the result.

10.4 For the model

$$Y_{1t} + \beta_{12} Y_{2t} + \gamma_{11} X_{1t} \qquad\qquad\qquad = u_{1t}$$

$$\beta_{21} Y_{1t} + \quad Y_{2t} \qquad\qquad + \gamma_{22} X_{2t} + \gamma_{23} X_{3t} = u_{2t}$$

the matrix of sums of products of observed values is as follows

	Y_1	Y_2	X_1	X_2	X_3
Y_1	100	200	30	20	40
Y_2	200	900	0	50	160
X_1	30	0	100	0	0
X_2	20	50	0	50	0
X_3	40	160	0	0	40

(a) Find indirect least squares and instrumental variable estimates of the parameters of the second equation: check that they are identical.

(b) Compare the OLS and 2SLS estimates of β_{12} and γ_{11}.

10.5 For the model

$$C_t = \alpha + \beta Y_t + u_t$$
$$Y_t = C_t + I_t$$

endogenous variables: C_t, Y_t; exogenous variable: I_t,

compare the variances of the OLS and ILS estimates of β.

10.6 For the model

$$Y_{1t} = \beta_{12} Y_{2t} + \gamma_{11} X_{1t} + u_{1t}$$
$$Y_{2t} = \beta_{21} Y_{1t} + \gamma_{22} X_{2t} + \gamma_{23} X_{3t} + u_{2t}$$

the sample moment matrices $\mathbf{X'X}$ and $\mathbf{X'y}$ are

$$\begin{bmatrix} 1 & 0 & 0 \\ 0 & 20 & 0 \\ 0 & 0 & 10 \end{bmatrix} \quad \text{and} \quad \begin{bmatrix} 5 & 10 \\ 40 & 20 \\ 20 & 30 \end{bmatrix} \quad \text{respectively.}$$

Obtain estimates of the reduced form equations, (a) by ordinary least squares and (b) from estimates of the structural equations obtained using two-stage least squares or indirect least squares as appropriate. Why do the two estimates differ? Would you change your estimation procedure if it were specified that $\beta_{12} = 0$ and u_1, u_2 are independent?

10.7 Compare the following methods of estimating the equation

$$Y_t = \gamma_1 X_t + \gamma_2 Y_{t-1} + u_t.$$

(a) Solve the equations

$$\Sigma Y_t X_t = \hat{\gamma}_1 \Sigma X_t^2 + \hat{\gamma}_2 \Sigma Y_{t-1} X_t$$
$$\Sigma Y_t X_{t-1} = \hat{\gamma}_1 \Sigma X_t X_{t-1} + \hat{\gamma}_2 \Sigma Y_{t-1} X_{t-1}.$$

(b) Regress Y_{t-1} on X_{t-1} to obtain $\hat{Y}_{t-1}$ and then regress Y_t on X_t and $\hat{Y}_{t-1}$ to estimate γ_1 and γ_2.

(c) Regress Y_{t-1} on X_t and X_{t-1} to obtain $\hat{Y}_{t-1}$ and then regress Y_t on X_t and $\hat{Y}_{t-1}$ to estimate γ_1 and γ_2.

(d) Regress Y_{t-1} on X_t, X_{t-1} and Y_{t-2} to obtain $\hat{Y}_{t-1}$ and then regress Y_t on X_t and $\hat{Y}_{t-1}$ to estimate γ_1 and γ_2.

REVIEW PROBLEMS

R1   Consider the following model

consumption function: $C_t = \alpha_1 C_{t-1} + \alpha_2 Y_t + u_t$

income definition: $Y_t = C_t + I_t + G_t$

investment function: $I_t = \beta Y_t + v_t$

endogenous variables: C_t, I_t, Y_t; exogenous variables: G_t.

(a) Obtain the reduced form equation for Y_t, and hence the final equation for Y_t.

(b) Assuming that $u_t = v_t = 0$ for all t (i.e. the model is exact), and that $G_t = \bar{G}$ for all t, obtain the equilibrium value of income. Under what conditions on the parameters is this equilibrium stable?

(c) Suppose that, given time series of observations on Y_t and G_t, we wish to estimate the coefficients of the final equation in order to use the equation to predict future values of income. What statistical problems might arise in estimating these coefficients?

R2   In exercise 3.4, on the cobweb model, two alternative supply functions are specified. Given time series data on observed price and quantity, how would you determine whether quantity supplied depended on the previous year's price or on a forecast of the current year's price? State carefully any assumptions that you make.

R3   Compare and contrast the "partial adjustment" and "adaptive expectations" arguments for the presence of the lagged dependent variable in a regression equation by considering the following two models.

(a) $y_t^* = \beta_1 x_t + \beta_2 z_t$

$y_t - y_{t-1} = (1 - \gamma)(y_t^* - y_{t-1}) + u_t$

(b) $y_t = \beta_1 \hat{x}_{t+1} + \beta_2 z_t + u_t$

$\hat{x}_{t+1} = \gamma \hat{x}_t + (1 - \gamma) x_t$

For each model derive an equation which could be estimated given time-series data on y, x and z. What problems of estimation and interpretation, if any, might arise? How would you discriminate between the two models? How is your answer affected if $\beta_2 = 0$?

R4   The following hypotheses are postulated to describe the demand for raw material inventories (stocks) by a small firm:

(i) The firm chooses its inventory level so as to minimise the associated costs.

(ii) The costs depend on the squared deviation of actual from desired inventory level (disequilibrium costs) and the square of the difference between the current and previous period's inventory level (adjustment costs).

(iii) The desired inventory level depends on the firm's level of output and the price of raw materials.

Derive an equation which may be estimated from time series data on inventory level, price and output. What problems of estimation and interpretation, if any, might arise?

As an alternative to (iii), consider the following hypothesis:

(iv) The desired inventory level depends on the firm's level of output and the anticipated price of raw materials, where

anticipated price is formed from observed price by an
adaptive expectations hypothesis.

Derive an equation which may be estimated from time series
data on inventory level, price and output. What problems of
estimation and interpretation, if any, might arise?

Given the time series data, how might you discriminate
between hypotheses (iii) and (iv)?

R5 (a) Assess the identification of the parameters of the following
five-equation system:

$$y_{1t} + \beta_{12}y_{2t} \qquad + \beta_{14}y_{4t} \qquad + \gamma_{11}x_{1t} \qquad\qquad\qquad + \gamma_{14}x_{4t} = u_{1t}$$

$$y_{2t} + \beta_{23}y_{3t} \qquad + \beta_{25}y_{5t} \qquad + \gamma_{22}x_{2t} \qquad\qquad\qquad = u_{2t}$$

$$y_{3t} \qquad\qquad + \gamma_{31}x_{1t} \qquad + \gamma_{33}x_{3t} \qquad = u_{3t}$$

$$y_{1t} \quad + \beta_{43}y_{3t} + \quad y_{4t} \qquad\qquad + \gamma_{42}x_{2t} \qquad + \gamma_{44}x_{4t} = u_{4t}$$

$$y_{3t} \qquad + \quad y_{5t} \qquad - \quad x_{2t} \qquad\qquad = 0$$

(b) How are your conclusions altered if $\gamma_{33} = 0$?

(c) How would you estimate the third equation, in order to test
the hypothesis that $\gamma_{33} = 0$?

(d) What information about the values of the parameters of the
second equation could be obtained from data on the variables
of the model?

R6 Consider the following model

consumption function: $\quad C_t = \alpha + \beta Y_{t-1} + u_{1t}$

investment function: $\qquad I_t = \gamma(Y_t - Y_{t-1}) + u_{2t}$

income definition: $\qquad\quad Y_t = C_t + I_t + G_t$

endogenous variables: C_t, I_t, Y_t; exogenous variable: G_t.

(a) Obtain the final equation for Y_t. For what combinations of parameter values is the system stable?

(b) For a case in which $0 < \beta < 1$ and $\gamma > 1$, the following rule to determine G_t is introduced:

$$G_t = \delta_0 + \delta_1 Y_{t-1}.$$

What value of δ_1 is required in order to stabilize the system?

(c) Given time-series data on the variables of the model, briefly explain how you would obtain consistent estimates of the parameters of the model under the original specification.

R7 Consider the following model:

consumption function: $C_t = \alpha_0 + \alpha_1 Y'_{t-1} + u_{1t}$

investment function: $I_t = \beta_0 + \beta_1 Y_t + u_{2t}$

income definition: $Y_t = C_t + I_t + G_t$

disposable income: $Y'_t = Y_t - T_t$

endogenous variables: C_t, I_t, Y_t, Y'_t; exogenous variables: G_t, T_t.

(a) Obtain the final equation for Y_t. Under what conditions on the parameters is the system stable?

(b) Show that extending the model by adding a tax function

$$T_t = \gamma_0 + \gamma_1 Y_t$$

enlarges the range of values of the parameters α_1 and β_1 for which the system is stable, so that the proportionate tax might be considered a stabilizing infuence. How is this changed if a balanced budget

$$G_t = T_t$$

is additionally imposed?

(c) Given time series data on the variables of the model, briefly explain how you would estimate the consumption and investment functions

    (i) under the original specification

    (ii) under the specification of part (b).

State carefully any assumptions that you make.

R8 (a) Assess the identifiability of the equations of the following models:

(1)
$$C_t = \alpha_1 Y_t + \alpha_2 r_{t-1} + u_{1t}$$
$$I_t = \beta_1 Y_t + \beta_2 r_{t-1} + u_{2t}$$
$$Y_t = C_t + I_t$$

endogenous variables: Y_t, C_t, I_t; exogenous variables: r_t.

(2)
$$M_t = \gamma_1 r_t + \gamma_2 M_{t-1} + v_{1t}$$
$$r_t = \delta_1 M_t + \delta_2 M_{t-1} + \delta_3 Y_t + v_{2t}$$

endogenous variables: M_t, r_t; exogenous variables: Y_t.

(b) Obtain the reduced form equation for Y_t in model (1), and the reduced form equation for r_t in model (2).

(c) Assess the identifiability of a two-equation model comprising the reduced form equation for Y_t in model (1) (an "I–S curve") and the reduced form equation for r_t in model (2) (an "L–M curve"). Given time series data on Y, r, and M, how would you estimate this model? How is the estimation of the second equation of this model changed if it is assumed that the u's and v's are mutually uncorrelated?

R9 The following hypotheses are postulated to describe the market for a perishable product supplied by a monopolist.

(i) The desired demand for the product depends on its price and consumers' income, but in a single period actual demand is only partially adjusted to the desired level.

(ii) The price of the product is determined by its cost and the demand in the previous period.

(iii) The monopolist supplies whatever quantity is demanded at the price ruling.

(a) Set up a two-equation structural form to represent this market (obtaining a formulation which only involves observable variables, namely current and/or lagged values of quantity, price, cost and income).

(b) Discuss the problems, if any, which might be encountered if you attempted to estimate the model given the required time series data.

(c) How are these problems changed if cost becomes an endogenous variable, depending on current output? Outline the steps to be taken in any estimation procedure you propose to use.

R10 The following equation was estimated by Ordinary Least Squares on quarterly data for 1963 to 1972 inclusive

$$Y_t = 2.417 + 0.724X_t$$
$$(0.702)\ (0.081)$$

$R^2 = 0.678.$ Residual sum of squares = 137.21.

(a) The investigator felt that the effect of X on Y was not constant over time and so estimated the following equation:

$$Y_t = 1.932 - 0.044X_t + 0.024(X_t . T)$$
$$(0.719)\ (0.028)\quad (0.017)$$

where T is a time trend with the first quarter of 1960 as zero. Interpret the results and compare with the original estimates.

What evidence is there that the effect of X on Y has changed over time?

(b) Two further regressions using the original specification were run separately for the periods 1963 quarter 1 to 1966 quarter 3 and 1966 quarter 4 to 1972 quarter 4:

1963(Q1) − 1966(Q3) : Residual sum of squares = 33.04

1966(Q4) − 1972(Q4) : Residual sum of squares = 68.19

Test the assertion that a "structural break" occurred between quarters 3 and 4 of 1966.
    Compare with part (a). What should we conclude about the effect of X on Y?

R11 It is postulated that, since the probability of an unemployed person finding a job for which he is suited is proportional to the number of vacancies, then the median duration of unemployment, Y, depends on the number of vacancies, X_1. The following relationship was estimated (by Ordinary Least Squares) using annual data for the period 1949–72 inclusive.

$$Y_t = 15.08 - 2.15X_{1t}$$
$$(8.97)(-3.86)$$

Numbers in parentheses are t-ratios.

Explained sum of squares = 52.198

Residual sum of squares = 77.262

Durbin-Watson statistic = 0.64

Two further regressions using the same specifications were run separately for the periods 1949–65 and 1966–72.

1949–65 Residual sum of squares = 43.11

1966–72 Residual sum of squares = 5.987

The researcher then noticed that the National Insurance Act of 1966 provides for earnings related benefits. He felt that this might make unemployed people less willing to accept a particular job offer and therefore would increase the average duration of unemployment. Further consideration of economic theory suggested that rises in permanent income might have the same effect. Accordingly the following equation was run for 1949–72:

$$Y_t = 1.10 - 0.0096X_{1t} - 4.56X_{2t} + 0.034X_{3t}$$
$$\quad (0.52) \quad (-2.81) \quad (-1.36) \quad (4.60)$$

where Y_t and X_{1t} are as before, X_{2t} is the ratio of net income when unemployed to average net income when employed and X_{3t} is a measure of permanent income.

Explained sum of squares = 109.24

Residual sum of squares = 20.22

Durbin-Watson statistic =   1.29

Again separate regressions were run for 1949–65 and 1966–72.

1949–65 Residual sum of squares = 16.04

1966–72 Residual sum of squares = 2.05

(a) For both specifications test the assertion that a "structural break" occurred between 1965 and 1966 and comment briefly on the implications of your tests.

(b) What problems are present in the above estimation? What are the implications of these problems for the results given above and for the tests conducted in part (a).

(c) Discuss briefly any conclusions that can be drawn from this analysis.

OUTLINE SOLUTIONS TO
EVEN-NUMBERED EXERCISES

2.2 The value of G required to achieve the target value Y^* is

$$G = (1 - \beta)Y^* - (\alpha + I - \beta T).$$

This exercise does not change the classification of variables.

3.2 Applying the Koyck transformation, the final equation is obtained as

$$y_t = \alpha(1 - \lambda) + \beta_1 x_t + (\beta_2 - \lambda\beta_1)x_{t-1} + \lambda y_{t-1}.$$

The partial adjustment hypothesis

$$y_t - y_{t-1} = (1 - \gamma)(y_t^* - y_{t-1})$$

in conjunction with the hypothesis that

$$y_t^* = \alpha + \delta_1 x_t + \delta_2 x_{t-1}$$

yields the final equation

$$y_t = \alpha(1 - \gamma) + \delta_1(1 - \gamma)x_t + \delta_2(1 - \gamma)x_{t-1} + \gamma y_{t-1}.$$

3.4   This is the "cobweb" model. The final equation for price is

$$P_t = \frac{\beta_0 - \alpha_0}{\alpha_1} + \frac{\beta_1}{\alpha_1} P_{t-1},$$

so the stability condition is

$$-1 < \frac{\beta_1}{\alpha_1} < 1.$$

Thus in the usual situation with $\alpha_1 < 0$ and $\beta_1 > 0$ we require $(1/\beta_1) > -1/\alpha_1$, that is, in the conventional P–Q diagram, S must be steeper than D.

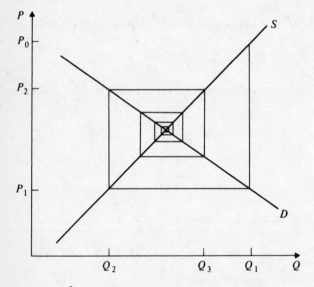

Substituting $\hat{P}_t$ for P_{t-1} in the supply equation, where

$$\hat{P}_t = (1 - \theta)P_{t-1} + \theta\hat{P}_{t-1} = (1 - \theta) \sum_{j=0}^{\infty} \theta^j P_{t-1-j},$$

equating the right-hand sides of the demand and supply equations, and applying the Koyck transformation leads to the following final equation for price:

$$P_t = \frac{(1-\theta)(\beta_0 - \alpha_0)}{\alpha_1} + \left\{ \frac{\beta_1}{\alpha_1}(1-\theta) + \theta \right\} P_{t-1}.$$

Assuming that $\alpha_1 < 0$, $\beta_1 > 0$ as usual, but that $|\beta_1/\alpha_1| > 1$ so that the previous system is unstable, the new stability condition is satisfied if

$$-\alpha_1 - \beta_1 > \theta(\alpha_1 - \beta_1) > \alpha_1 - \beta_1.$$

Hence a previously unstable system is stabilized if θ is in the range

$$0 < \frac{\beta_1 + \alpha_1}{\beta_1 - \alpha_1} < \theta < 1.$$

Alternatively, since the original case obtains when $\theta = 0$, one could draw a stability diagram with axes α_1, β_1, and show that positive values of θ enlarge the shaded area.

3.6
$$Y_t = \frac{\alpha + G_t}{1 - \beta - \gamma} - \frac{\gamma}{1 - \beta - \gamma} Y_{t-1}.$$

Stable values of β and γ are indicated by the shaded area:

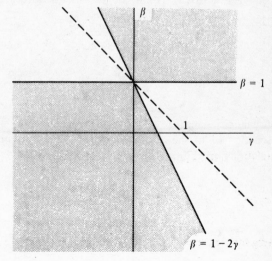

3.8   For the model of exercise 3.5:

$$C_t = \frac{\alpha + \beta I_t}{1 - \beta} + \frac{\gamma}{1 - \beta} C_{t-1} + \frac{u_t}{1 - \beta}$$

For the model of exercise 3.6:

$$C_t = \frac{\alpha + \beta G_t}{1 - \beta - \gamma} - \frac{\gamma}{1 - \beta - \gamma} C_{t-1} + \frac{(1 - \gamma)u_t + \gamma u_{t-1}}{1 - \beta - \gamma}.$$

If u_t is non-autocorrelated, C_{t-1} is independent of u_t, but in the second case C_{t-1} is not independent of the composite disturbance term in the final equation.

4.2   (a) (1) is not identified (rank condition fails), (2) is over-identi-fied, (3) is not identified, (4) is over-identified, and (5) is an identity, fully specified *a priori,* so no question of its identifiability arises.

       (b) According to the order condition, incorporating the homo-geneous linear restriction, (1) is just identified, (2) and (4) are over-identified, and (3) is not identified. In order to check whether the first equation satisfies the extended rank condi-tion, we examine the following array

$$\begin{bmatrix} 0 & 0 & 0 \\ 1 & 0 & \gamma_{32} \\ 1 & \beta_{42} & \gamma_{42} \end{bmatrix}.$$

The determinant is zero, and so the equation is not identified. Substitution of the identity does not change the conclusions about identifiability.

5.2 $\hat{Y} = -4 + 1.33X$

The t-statistic for testing $H_0 : \beta = 1$ has the value 1.0, hence H_0 cannot be rejected.

5.4 The correlation coefficient is

$$r = \frac{\Sigma(X_t - \bar{X})(Y_t - \bar{Y})}{\sqrt{\Sigma(X_t - \bar{X})^2 \cdot \Sigma(Y_t - \bar{Y})^2}},$$

and the required result follows by substitution.

5.6 The coefficient $\hat{\alpha}$ is calculated as $\hat{\alpha} = \bar{Y} - \hat{\beta}\bar{X}$. Since $\bar{Y} = \alpha + \beta\bar{X} + \bar{u}$ and $\hat{\beta} - \beta = \Sigma W_t u_t$ the sampling error in $\hat{\alpha}$ is

$$\hat{\alpha} - \alpha = \bar{u} - \bar{X}\sum_{t=1}^{n} W_t u_t = \sum_{t=1}^{n}\left(\frac{1}{n} - \bar{X}W_t\right)u_t.$$

Therefore $E(\hat{\alpha}) = \alpha$. To obtain $E(\hat{\alpha} - \alpha)^2$ we use assumptions A2 and A3, which lead to

$$\text{var}(\hat{\alpha}) = \sigma_u^2 \sum_{t=1}^{n}\left(\frac{1}{n} - \bar{X}W_t\right)^2,$$

and evaluation of the summation gives

$$\text{var}(\hat{\alpha}) = \sigma_u^2\left(\frac{1}{n} + \frac{\bar{X}^2}{\Sigma(X_t - \bar{X})^2}\right) = \frac{\sigma_u^2 \Sigma X_t^2}{n\Sigma(X_t - \bar{X})^2}.$$

$$\text{cov}(\hat{\alpha}, \hat{\beta}) = E(\hat{\alpha} - \alpha)(\hat{\beta} - \beta) = E\left\{\sum\left(\frac{1}{n} - \bar{X}W_t\right)u_t \sum W_t u_t\right\}$$

$$= \sigma_u^2 \sum_{t=1}^{n}\left(\frac{1}{n} - \bar{X}W_t\right)W_t,$$

again using assumptions A2 and A3. Since $\Sigma W_t = 0$ this gives

$$\text{cov}(\hat{\alpha}, \hat{\beta}) = \frac{-\sigma_u^2 \bar{X}}{\Sigma(X_t - \bar{X})^2}.$$

Notice that this is negative (assuming $\bar{X}$ positive): an underestimate of α tends to be associated with an overestimate of β, and vice versa.

5.8   Substitution of the expressions for $\hat{\beta}$ and $\hat{\gamma}$ in terms of X_t, Y_t, $t = 1, \ldots, n$ verifies the relation $\hat{\beta}\hat{\gamma} = R^2$, from which the required result follows.

5.10 By substituting for $\hat{\alpha}$, the residuals can be written

$$e_t = (Y_t - \bar{Y}) - \hat{\beta}(X_t - \bar{X}).$$

The equation can be written in mean deviation form as

$$Y_t - \bar{Y} = \beta(X_t - \bar{X}) + (u_t - \bar{u}).$$

Substitution gives

$$e_t = (u_t - \bar{u}) - (\hat{\beta} - \beta)(X_t - \bar{X})$$

and thus

$$\Sigma e_t^2 = \Sigma(u_t - \bar{u})^2 + (\hat{\beta} - \beta)^2 \Sigma(X_t - \bar{X})^2$$
$$- 2(\hat{\beta} - \beta)\,\Sigma(X_t - \bar{X})(u_t - \bar{u}).$$

Consider the expected value of each term in turn.

$$E\{\Sigma(u_t - \bar{u})^2\} = E\left\{\Sigma u_t^2 - \frac{1}{n}(\Sigma u_t)^2\right\}$$

$$= \Sigma E(u_t^2) - \frac{1}{n}\,\Sigma\Sigma E(u_t u_s)$$

$$= n\sigma_u^2 - \frac{1}{n}n\sigma_u^2 \text{ (assuming serial independence)}$$

$$= (n - 1)\,\sigma_u^2$$

$$E\{(\hat{\beta} - \beta)^2 \ \Sigma(X_t - \bar{X})^2\} = \mathrm{var}\,(\hat{\beta})\ \Sigma(X_t - \bar{X})^2$$

$$= \sigma_u{}^2 \qquad \text{(from page 116)}$$

$$E\{(\hat{\beta} - \beta)\ \Sigma(X_t - \bar{X})\,(u_t - \bar{u})\} = E\{\Sigma W_t u_t\ \Sigma(X_t - \bar{X})\,(u_t - \bar{u})\}$$

$$\text{(from page 114)}$$

$$= E\{\Sigma W_t u_t\ \Sigma(X_t - \bar{X})\,u_t\}$$

$$= \Sigma W_t (X_t - \bar{X})\,E(u_t{}^2)$$

$$\text{(assuming serial independence)}$$

$$= \sigma_u{}^2\ \Sigma W_t (X_t - \bar{X})$$

$$= \sigma_u{}^2 .$$

Combining these together

$$E(\Sigma e_t{}^2) = (n-1)\sigma_u{}^2 + \sigma_u{}^2 - 2\sigma_u{}^2$$

$$= (n-2)\sigma_u{}^2.$$

Thus

$$E(\hat{\sigma}_u{}^2) = \sigma_u{}^2 .$$

6.2 $$\hat{C}_t = 115 + 0.40 DI_t + 0.53 C_{t-4}$$

Note that the equation is estimated on 16 observations only. The implied estimate of the (zero-growth) long-run m.p.c. is 0.85.

6.4 β_1 and β_5 can be estimated. β_2, β_3 and β_4 cannot themselves be estimated but $(\beta_2 + \beta_4)$ and $(\beta_3 - \beta_4)$ can.

6.6 The required interval is (14,080; 16,282).

7.2 $\quad \text{var}(\hat{\beta}_1) = \sigma_u^2/n_2$, $\text{var}(\hat{\beta}_2) = n\sigma_u^2/n_1 n_2$.

7.4 (a) $I_t = \gamma_0 + \gamma_1 r_t + \sum_{j=0}^{T} \beta_j S_{t-j} + u_t$

(b) $I_t = \gamma_0 + \gamma_1 r_t + \sum_{k=0}^{2} \alpha_k Z_{kt} + u_t$, $\qquad Z_{kt} = \sum_{j=0}^{T} j^k S_{t-j}$.

8.2 Subtract ϕ_1 times the equation lagged once plus ϕ_2 times the equation lagged twice from the original equation to give

$$Y_t = \alpha(1 - \phi_1 - \phi_2) + \phi_1 Y_{t-1} + \phi_2 Y_{t-2}$$
$$+ \beta X_t - \phi_1 \beta X_{t-1} - \phi_2 \beta X_{t-2} + \epsilon_t.$$

The 6 coefficients are a function of only 4 parameters. There are *two* non-linear restrictions.

Alternatively stated, we would want to estimate

$$Y_t = \gamma_1 + \gamma_2 Y_{t-1} + \gamma_3 Y_{t-2} + \gamma_4 X_t + \gamma_5 X_{t-1} + \gamma_6 X_{t-2} + \epsilon_t$$

subject to

$$\gamma_5 = -\gamma_2 \gamma_4 \text{ and } \gamma_6 = -\gamma_3 \gamma_4.$$

8.4 Multiplying through by u_{t-k} and taking expected values gives

$$E(u_t u_{t-k}) = \phi E(u_{t-1} u_{t-k}) + E(\epsilon_t u_{t-k}) - \theta E(\epsilon_{t-1} u_{t-k})$$
$$= \phi E(u_{t-1} u_{t-k}),$$

since u_{t-k} is independent of ϵ_t and ϵ_{t-1} for all $k > 1$. Dividing through by σ_u^2 gives

$$\rho_k = \phi \rho_{k-1} \text{ for } k > 1.$$

8.6   (a)   Repeated substitution for lagged Y in the equation for Y_t gives

$$Y_t = u_t + \beta u_{t-1} + \beta^2 u_{t-2} + \ldots$$

Lagging one period gives

$$Y_{t-1} = u_{t-1} + \beta u_{t-2} + \beta^2 u_{t-3} + \ldots$$

Multiplying through by u_t and taking expected values gives

$$E(u_t Y_{t-1}) = \sigma_u^2 \{ \rho + \beta \rho^2 + \beta^2 \rho^3 + \ldots \}$$

$$= \frac{\rho}{1 - \beta \rho} \, \sigma_u^2$$

Hence OLS estimates will be biased and inconsistent.

(b)

$$\hat{\beta} = \frac{\sum\limits_{t=2}^{n} Y_t Y_{t-1}}{\sum\limits_{t=2}^{n} Y_{t-1}^2}$$

Transforming the equation for Y in the usual way to produce an equation with serially independent error term gives

$$Y_t = (\beta + \rho) Y_{t-1} - \beta \rho Y_{t-2} + \epsilon_t.$$

Multiplying through by Y_{t-1} and summing gives

$$\Sigma Y_t Y_{t-1} = (\beta + \rho) \Sigma Y_{t-1}^2 - \beta \rho \Sigma Y_{t-1} Y_{t-2} + \Sigma \epsilon_t Y_{t-1}.$$

Dividing through by ΣY_{t-1}^2 gives

$$\hat{\beta} = (\beta + \rho) - \beta \rho \, \frac{\Sigma Y_{t-1} Y_{t-2}}{\Sigma Y_{t-1}^2} + \frac{\Sigma \epsilon_t Y_{t-1}}{\Sigma Y_{t-1}^2}.$$

We now consider taking probability limits. The first ratio has the same probability limit as $\hat{\beta}$ and the second ratio has probability limit zero since Y_{t-1} depends only on $\epsilon_{t-1}, \epsilon_{t-2}, \ldots$ Thus

$$\text{plim } \hat{\beta} = (\beta + \rho) - \beta\rho \text{ plim } \hat{\beta}$$

and so

$$\text{plim } \hat{\beta} = \frac{\beta + \rho}{1 + \beta\rho}$$

so the inconsistency is given by

$$\text{plim } \hat{\beta} - \beta = \frac{\rho(1 - \beta^2)}{1 + \beta\rho}.$$

We now turn our attention to $\hat{\rho}$. The OLS residuals are given by

$$e_t = Y_t - \hat{\beta} Y_{t-1}$$

and $\hat{\rho}$ is then given by

$$\hat{\rho} = \frac{\sum_{t=2}^{n} e_t e_{t-1}}{\sum_{t=2}^{n} e_{t-1}^2}.$$

Since Y_{t-1} and e_t are uncorrelated

$$\frac{1}{n}\Sigma e_t^2 = \frac{1}{n}\Sigma Y_t^2 - \hat{\beta}^2 \frac{1}{n}\Sigma Y_{t-1}^2.$$

Thus

$$\text{plim}\left(\frac{1}{n}\Sigma e_t^2\right) = \text{plim } (1 - \hat{\beta}^2) \text{ var } (Y).$$

Now considering the numerator,

$$\Sigma e_t e_{t-1} = \Sigma Y_t Y_{t-1} - \hat{\beta}\Sigma Y_{t-1}^2 - \hat{\beta}\Sigma Y_t Y_{t-2}$$
$$+ \hat{\beta}^2 \Sigma Y_{t-1} Y_{t-2} .$$

The first two terms on the right-hand side cancel by definition of $\hat{\beta}$. Thus

$$\Sigma e_t e_{t-1} = \hat{\beta}\{-\Sigma Y_t Y_{t-2} + \hat{\beta}\Sigma Y_{t-1} Y_{t-2}\} .$$

Multiplying the transformed equation for Y_t through by Y_{t-2} and summing gives

$$\Sigma Y_t Y_{t-2} = (\beta + \rho)\Sigma Y_{t-1} Y_{t-2} - \beta\rho\Sigma Y_{t-2}^2 + \Sigma \epsilon_t Y_{t-2}$$

Thus

$$\text{plim}\left(\frac{1}{n}\Sigma Y_t Y_{t-2}\right) = (\beta + \rho)\,\text{plim}\,\hat{\beta}\,\text{var}\,(Y) - \beta\rho\,\text{var}\,(Y).$$

Hence

$$\text{plim}\left(\frac{1}{n}\Sigma e_t e_{t-1}\right) = \text{plim}\,\hat{\beta}\,\{\beta\rho\,\text{var}\,(Y)$$

$$- (\beta + \rho)\,\text{plim}\,\hat{\beta}\,\text{var}\,(Y) + \text{plim}\,\hat{\beta}^2\,\text{var}\,(Y)\}$$

and so

$$\text{plim}\,\hat{\rho} = \text{plim}\left[\frac{\hat{\beta}\{\beta\rho - (\beta+\rho)\hat{\beta} + \hat{\beta}^2\}}{1 - \hat{\beta}^2}\right] = \frac{\rho\beta(\beta+\rho)}{1+\beta\rho} .$$

So the inconsistency is given by

$$\text{plim}\,\hat{\rho} - \rho = \frac{-\rho(1-\beta^2)}{1+\beta\rho} ,$$

equal but opposite sign to that in $\hat{\beta}$. Thus

$$\text{plim} \, (\hat{\beta} + \hat{\rho}) = \beta + \rho \, .$$

Considering now the Durbin-Watson statistic

$$\text{plim} \, d = 2 \, [1 - \text{plim} \, \hat{\rho}]$$

$$= 2 \left[1 - \frac{\rho\beta \, (\beta + \rho)}{1 + \beta\rho} \right].$$

Since $\hat{\rho}$ is inconsistent, d will be an inconsistent estimate of the "true" $D-W$ statistic based on the errors. If $\rho > 0$, $\hat{\rho}$ is inconsistent downwards and so d will be inconsistent upwards (but not past 2). Whilst if $\rho < 0$ $\hat{\rho}$ is inconsistent upwards and so d will be inconsistent downwards.

9.2   (a) If σ_i^2 was proportional to X_i^2.

(b) If σ_i^2 was proportional to X_i.

9.4   The micro-relationship is given by

$$Y_{ij} = \beta_1 + \beta_2 X_{ij} + u_{ij}$$

and if $\hat{\beta}_2$ is the OLS estimate of the slope coefficient

$$\text{var} \, (\hat{\beta}_2) = \frac{\sigma_u^2}{\sum_i \sum_j (X_{ij} - \bar{X})^2} \, .$$

The aggregate relationship is given by

$$Y_{.j} = \beta_1 + \beta_2 X_{.j} + u_{.j}$$

and if $\tilde{\beta}_2$ is the WLS estimate of the slope coefficient using grouped data,

$$\text{var}\,(\tilde{\beta}_2) = \frac{\sigma_u^{\,2}}{\sum\limits_j n_j\,(X_{.j} - \bar{X})^2}\,.$$

The inequality then follows from the fact that

$$\sum_i\sum_j (X_{ij} - \bar{X})^2 = \sum_i\sum_j (X_{ij} - X_{.j})^2 + \sum_j n_j\,(X_{.j} - \bar{X})^2.$$

10.2 *If u_{it} (i = 1, 2, 3) cannot be assumed independent*

The first equation is just identified. 2SLS, IV and ILS are all equivalent in this case and provide consistent estimates. X_3 is used as the intrument for Y_2.

The second equation contains no endogenous variables other than Y_2. Hence OLS regression of Y_2 on X_3 will provide unbiased and consistent estimates.

The third equation is not identified.

If u_{it} (i = 1, 2, 3) can be assumed independent

After reordering of equations and variables, the system is recursive. Hence OLS can be used on all three equations and will provide unbiased and consistent estimates.

10.4 (a) *Indirect Least Squares*

The reduced form coefficient estimates are given by:

$$\hat{\Pi}' = \begin{bmatrix} 100 & 0 & 0 \\ 0 & 50 & 0 \\ 0 & 0 & 40 \end{bmatrix}^{-1} \begin{bmatrix} 30 & 0 \\ 20 & 50 \\ 40 & 160 \end{bmatrix} = \begin{bmatrix} 0.3 & 0 \\ 0.4 & 1.0 \\ 1.0 & 4.0 \end{bmatrix}$$

(The first column gives the coefficient estimates of the reduced form equation for Y_1 and the second column those for Y_2). The ILS estimates of the second structural equation are then given by solving

$$
\begin{bmatrix} 0.3 & 0 \\ 0.4 & 1.0 \\ 1.0 & 4.0 \end{bmatrix} \begin{bmatrix} \hat{\beta}_{21} \\ 1 \end{bmatrix} + \begin{bmatrix} 0 \\ \hat{\gamma}_{22} \\ \hat{\gamma}_{23} \end{bmatrix} = \begin{bmatrix} 0 \\ 0 \\ 0 \end{bmatrix}
$$

Multiplying out and simplifying gives the ILS estimates as

$$\hat{\beta}_{21} = 0$$

$$\hat{\gamma}_{22} = -1$$

$$\hat{\gamma}_{23} = -4$$

Instrumental variables

Using the predetermined variables X_1, X_2, X_3 as instruments, the IV estimates are given by

$$
\begin{bmatrix} \hat{\beta}_{21} \\ \hat{\gamma}_{22} \\ \hat{\gamma}_{23} \end{bmatrix} = - \begin{bmatrix} \Sigma X_{1t} Y_{1t} & \Sigma X_{1t} X_{2t} & \Sigma X_{1t} X_{3t} \\ \Sigma X_{2t} Y_{1t} & \Sigma X_{2t}^2 & \Sigma X_{2t} X_{3t} \\ \Sigma X_{3t} Y_{1t} & \Sigma X_{3t} X_{2t} & \Sigma X_{3t}^2 \end{bmatrix}^{-1} \begin{bmatrix} \Sigma X_{1t} Y_{2t} \\ \Sigma X_{2t} Y_{2t} \\ \Sigma X_{3t} Y_{2t} \end{bmatrix}
$$

$$
= - \begin{bmatrix} 30 & 0 & 0 \\ 20 & 50 & 0 \\ 40 & 0 & 40 \end{bmatrix}^{-1} \begin{bmatrix} 0 \\ 50 \\ 160 \end{bmatrix} = \begin{bmatrix} 0 \\ -1 \\ -4 \end{bmatrix}
$$

(b) *Ordinary Least Squares*

OLS estimation of the first structural equation gives

$$\begin{bmatrix} \hat{\beta}_{12} \\ \hat{\gamma}_{11} \end{bmatrix} = - \begin{bmatrix} 900 & 0 \\ 0 & 100 \end{bmatrix}^{-1} \begin{bmatrix} 200 \\ 30 \end{bmatrix} = \begin{bmatrix} -2/9 \\ -3/10 \end{bmatrix}$$

Two Stage Least Squares

The 2SLS estimates of $(\beta_{12}, \gamma_{11})'$ are given by

$$-\left[(0 \quad 50 \quad 160) \begin{pmatrix} 100 & 0 & 0 \\ 0 & 50 & 0 \\ 0 & 0 & 40 \\ & 0 & \end{pmatrix}^{-1} \begin{pmatrix} 0 \\ 50 \\ 160 \\ 100 \end{pmatrix} \right]^{-1} \left[(0 \quad 50 \quad 160) \begin{pmatrix} 100 & 0 & 0 \\ 0 & 50 & 0 \\ 0 & 0 & 40 \\ & 30 & \end{pmatrix}^{-1} \begin{pmatrix} 30 \\ 20 \\ 40 \end{pmatrix} \right]$$

$$= - \begin{bmatrix} 50 + 640 & 0 \\ 0 & 100 \end{bmatrix}^{-1} \begin{bmatrix} 20 + 160 \\ 30 \end{bmatrix}$$

$$= - \begin{bmatrix} 1/690 & 0 \\ 0 & 1/100 \end{bmatrix} \begin{bmatrix} 180 \\ 30 \end{bmatrix}$$

$$= \begin{bmatrix} -6/23 \\ -3/10 \end{bmatrix}$$

10.6 (a) The transpose of the matrix of reduced form coefficient
. estimates is given, where $\mathbf{Y} = (\mathbf{y}_1 \ \mathbf{y}_2)$, by

$$\hat{\Pi}' = (\mathbf{X}'\mathbf{X})^{-1} \mathbf{X}'\mathbf{Y}$$

$$= \begin{bmatrix} 1 & 0 & 0 \\ 0 & 20 & 0 \\ 0 & 0 & 10 \end{bmatrix}^{-1} \begin{bmatrix} 5 & 10 \\ 40 & 20 \\ 20 & 30 \end{bmatrix} = \begin{bmatrix} 5 & 10 \\ 2 & 1 \\ 2 & 3 \end{bmatrix}$$

Hence the directly estimated reduced form equations are

$$\hat{Y}_1 = 5X_1 + 2X_2 + 2X_3$$
$$\hat{Y}_2 = 10X_1 + 1X_2 + 3X_3$$

(b) We consider first $\mathbf{Y'X(X'X)^{-1}X'Y}$ where $\mathbf{Y} = (\mathbf{y}_1\,\mathbf{y}_2)$.

$$\mathbf{Y'X(X'X)^{-1}X'Y} = \begin{bmatrix} 5 & 40 & 20 \\ 10 & 20 & 30 \end{bmatrix} \begin{bmatrix} 5 & 10 \\ 2 & 1 \\ 2 & 3 \end{bmatrix} = \begin{bmatrix} 145 & 150 \\ 150 & 210 \end{bmatrix}$$

The 2SLS estimates of the structural equations are then given by

$$\begin{bmatrix} \hat{\beta}_{12} \\ \hat{\gamma}_{11} \end{bmatrix} = \begin{bmatrix} 210 & 10 \\ 10 & 1 \end{bmatrix}^{-1} \begin{bmatrix} 150 \\ 5 \end{bmatrix} = \begin{bmatrix} 10/11 \\ -45/11 \end{bmatrix}$$

$$\begin{bmatrix} \hat{\beta}_{21} \\ \hat{\gamma}_{22} \\ \hat{\gamma}_{23} \end{bmatrix} = \begin{bmatrix} 145 & 40 & 20 \\ 40 & 20 & 0 \\ 20 & 0 & 10 \end{bmatrix}^{-1} \begin{bmatrix} 150 \\ 20 \\ 30 \end{bmatrix} = \begin{bmatrix} 2 \\ -3 \\ -1 \end{bmatrix}$$

Solving to obtain estimates of the reduced form equations gives

$$\hat{Y}_1 = 5X_1 + \frac{10}{3}X_2 + \frac{10}{9}X_3$$

$$\hat{Y}_2 = 10X_1 + \frac{11}{3}X_2 + \frac{11}{9}X_3.$$

These estimates satisfy the over-identifying restriction. Under the additional specification the model becomes recursive, and the structural equations can be consistently estimated by OLS.

R2 The alternative supply functions, including a disturbance term, are

(a) $Q_t = \beta_0 + \beta_1 P_{t-1} + u_t$

(b) $Q_t = \beta_0 + \beta_1 (1 - \theta) \sum\limits_{j=0}^{\infty} \theta^j P_{t-1-j} + u_t.$

There is no current endogenous variable on the right-hand side, and so OLS gives consistent estimates provided that u_t is non-autocorrelated. The infinite distributed lag in (b) cannot be estimated, however, but a choice between (a) and (b) might be made simply by adding P_{t-2} (or a few lagged values) to (a), estimating by OLS, and if any lagged P's are significant, (b) is preferred to (a). The obvious alternative is to avoid the infinite distributed lag by transforming to

(b') $Q_t = \beta_0 (1 - \theta) + \beta_1 (1 - \theta) P_{t-1} + \theta Q_{t-1} + (u_t - \theta u_{t-1})$

and choosing between (a) and (b) by testing the null hypothesis that $\theta = 0$. If this null hypothesis is correct, OLS estimates of (b') are consistent and the t-ratio of the coefficient of Q_{t-1} provides the usual test. If the null hypothesis is not correct, the disturbance term in (b') is autocorrelated, and OLS estimates are inconsistent: note that *both* P_{t-1} and Q_{t-1} are correlated with $(u_t - \theta u_{t-1})$. Consistent estimates can be obtained by IV, using P_{t-2} and Q_{t-2} as instruments.

R4 Choosing the current inventory level I_t to minimise the cost function

$$a_1 (I_t - I_t^*)^2 + a_2 (I_t - I_{t-1})^2$$

gives the decision rule (partial adjustment)

$$I_t = (1 - \gamma) I_t^* + \gamma I_{t-1}$$

where $\gamma = a_2/(a_1 + a_2)$. Hypothesis (iii) can be written

$$I_t^* = \beta_1 + \beta_2 X_t + \beta_3 P_t.$$

Adding disturbance terms u_{1t} and u_{2t}, and substituting for I_t^*, gives the estimating equation

$$I_t = \beta_1(1 - \gamma) + \beta_2(1 - \gamma)X_t + \beta_3(1 - \gamma)P_t$$
$$+ \gamma I_{t-1} + \{u_{1t} + (1 - \gamma)u_{2t}\}.$$

If the disturbances are non-autocorrelated, and X and P are predetermined, then an OLS regression yields consistent estimates of $\beta_1, \beta_2, \beta_3$ and γ. (If X or P are endogenous, then an IV estimator is required.)

Hypothesis (iv) implies that the previous equation becomes

$$I_t = \beta_1(1 - \gamma) + \beta_2(1 - \gamma)X_t + \beta_3(1 - \gamma)\hat{P}_{t+1} + \gamma I_{t-1} + v_t$$

where $v_t = u_{1t} + (1 - \gamma)u_{2t}$ and $\hat{P}_{t+1}$ is given by

$$\hat{P}_{t+1} = (1 - \theta)P_t + \theta\hat{P}_t.$$

Applying the Koyck transformation gives the estimating equation

$$I_t = \beta_1(1 - \gamma)(1 - \theta) + \beta_2(1 - \gamma)X_t - \theta\beta_2(1 - \gamma)X_{t-1}$$
$$+ \beta_3(1 - \gamma)(1 - \theta)P_t + (\gamma + \theta)I_{t-1} - \gamma\theta I_{t-2} + v_t - \theta v_{t-1}.$$

There are two difficulties in estimating this equation by OLS. First the six coefficients are functions of five parameters, so if one is interested in estimating the basic parameters, imposition of the implied restriction is necessary. Secondly the Koyck transformation induces an autocorrelated error term, if the u's are non-autocorrelated, moreover the autocorrelation itself depends on the parameter θ. Both problems can be overcome by a non-linear least squares estimator.

Discrimination between hypotheses (iii) and (iv), or between the corresponding estimating equations, amounts to testing the hypothesis that $\theta = 0$. A test could be based on the t-ratio of $\hat{\theta}$ obtained in non-linear least squares estimation. Alternatively, if the last equation is estimated without the coefficient restriction, one could test the joint significance of X_{t-1} and I_{t-2}. Some indication might also be obtained by estimating this equation by OLS and testing the residuals for negative autocorrelation using Durbin's h-test.

R6   (a)   The final equation is

$$Y_t = \frac{1}{1-\gamma} \{\alpha + (\beta - \gamma)Y_{t-1} + G_t + u_{1t} + u_{2t}\}.$$

Values of β and γ for which the system is stable are indicated by the shaded area in the diagram.

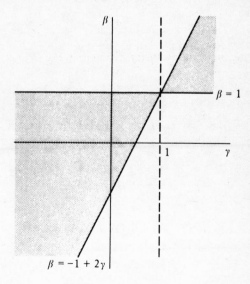

(b) With the additional equation for G_t, the final equation becomes

$$Y_t = \frac{1}{1 - \gamma} \{\alpha + \delta_0 + (\beta - \gamma + \delta_1) Y_{t-1} + u_{1t} + u_{2t}\} .$$

If $0 < \beta < 1$ and $\gamma > 1$, the stability condition is satisfied if $-\beta + 2\gamma - 1 > \delta_1 > 1 - \beta$

(c) The consumption function contains no current endogenous variable on the right-hand side, and so is already in reduced form. A least squares regression of C_t on Y_{t-1} will yield consistent estimates of α and β, provided that the disturbances are non-autocorrelated.

   The investment function contains a current endogenous variable on the right-hand side and is over-identified, so it can be consistently estimated by two-stage least squares. The first stage comprises OLS estimation of the reduced form equation for Y, which is the final equation given in (a) above, and calculation of the fitted values $\hat{Y}_t$, $t = 1, \ldots, n$. The second stage comprises OLS regression of I_t on $(\hat{Y}_t - Y_{t-1})$, without an intercept. The resulting estimate of γ is consistent provided again that the disturbances are non-autocorrelated.

R8 (a) (1) : neither equation is identified

   (2) : the first equation is identified provided that $\delta_3 \neq 0$, but the second equation is not identified.

(b)
$$Y_t = \frac{1}{1 - \alpha_1 - \beta_1} \{(\alpha_2 + \beta_2) r_{t-1} + u_{1t} + u_{2t}\}$$

$$r_t = \frac{1}{1 - \gamma_1 \delta_1} \{\delta_3 Y_t + (\gamma_2 \delta_1 + \delta_2) M_{t-1}$$

$$+ \delta_1 v_{1t} + v_{2t}\} .$$

(c) Writing the two-equation model as

$$Y_t = \theta_1 r_{t-1} + w_{1t}$$
$$r_t = \theta_2 Y_t + \theta_3 M_{t-1} + w_{2t},$$

both equations are identified provided that the θ's are non-zero. The first equation has only a lagged endogenous variable on the right-hand side, and can be consistently estimated by OLS, assuming that the disturbances are non-autocorrelated. The second equation can be consistently estimated by indirect least squares or IV (using r_{t-1} as an instrumental variable for Y_t). If the u's and v's are uncorrelated then w_1 and w_2 are uncorrelated and the model becomes recursive, whereupon the second equation can be consistently estimated by OLS.

R10 With $n = 40$, the first regression gives clear evidence of a significant effect of X on Y. The second regression allows the effect of X on Y to vary from a value of $(-0.044 + 0.024 \times 12) = 0.244$ in the first quarter of 1963 to a value of $(-0.044 + 0.024 \times 51) = 1.180$ in the last quarter of 1972, the average value of 0.712 being close to the original estimate under the assumption of constancy. Despite this wide variation, the second regression does not support the hypothesis of a linearly trending effect of X on Y, since the coefficient of the additional variable is not significantly different from zero. There is some evidence of multicollinearity problems, however, since neither coefficient is significantly different from zero yet the regression overall is significant: adding a variable cannot decrease R^2, so R^2 in the second regression must be at least 0.678, and such a value provides an F-statistic, with $(2,37)$ degrees of freedom, of 38.95, which clearly exceeds the relevant critical value. If X is itself a trending variable, then X and XT will be highly correlated.

On testing for a structural break, the value of the appropriate F-statistic is calculated to be 6.40, and since the 5% significance point with (2,36) degrees of freedom is 3.26, the data do not support the null hypothesis of parameter constancy.

The tests carried out at (a) and (b) give different answers to the question of whether the effect of X on Y has changed over time, but the alternative hypotheses differ between the two cases. The evidence suggests that the effect of X on Y has changed over time, but not in a smoothly trending manner.

TABLE
DURBIN-WATSON STATISTIC: 5% SIGNIFICANCE POINTS OF d_L AND d_U

n	$k'=1$ d_L	d_U	$k'=2$ d_L	d_U	$k'=3$ d_L	d_U	$k'=4$ d_L	d_U	$k'=5$ d_L	d_U	$k'=6$ d_L	d_U	$k'=7$ d_L	d_U	$k'=8$ d_L	d_U	$k'=9$ d_L	d_U	$k'=10$ d_L	d_U
15	1.077	1.361	0.946	1.543	0.814	1.750	0.685	1.977	0.562	2.220	0.447	2.471	0.343	2.727	0.251	2.979	0.175	3.216	0.111	3.438
16	1.106	1.371	0.982	1.539	0.857	1.728	0.734	1.935	0.615	2.157	0.502	2.388	0.398	2.624	0.304	2.860	0.222	3.090	0.155	3.304
17	1.133	1.381	1.015	1.536	0.897	1.710	0.779	1.900	0.664	2.104	0.554	2.318	0.451	2.537	0.356	2.757	0.272	2.975	0.198	3.184
18	1.158	1.391	1.046	1.535	0.933	1.696	0.820	1.872	0.710	2.060	0.603	2.258	0.502	2.461	0.407	2.668	0.321	2.873	0.244	3.073
19	1.180	1.401	1.074	1.536	0.967	1.685	0.859	1.848	0.752	2.023	0.649	2.206	0.549	2.396	0.456	2.589	0.369	2.783	0.290	2.974
20	1.201	1.411	1.100	1.537	0.998	1.676	0.894	1.828	0.792	1.991	0.691	2.162	0.595	2.339	0.502	2.521	0.416	2.704	0.336	2.885
21	1.221	1.420	1.125	1.538	1.026	1.669	0.927	1.812	0.829	1.964	0.731	2.124	0.637	2.290	0.546	2.461	0.461	2.633	0.380	2.806
22	1.239	1.429	1.147	1.541	1.053	1.664	0.958	1.797	0.863	1.940	0.769	2.090	0.677	2.246	0.588	2.407	0.504	2.571	0.424	2.735
23	1.257	1.437	1.168	1.543	1.078	1.660	0.986	1.785	0.895	1.920	0.804	2.061	0.715	2.208	0.628	2.360	0.545	2.514	0.465	2.670
24	1.273	1.446	1.188	1.546	1.101	1.656	1.013	1.775	0.925	1.902	0.837	2.035	0.750	2.174	0.666	2.318	0.584	2.464	0.506	2.613
25	1.288	1.454	1.206	1.550	1.123	1.654	1.038	1.767	0.953	1.886	0.868	2.013	0.784	2.144	0.702	2.280	0.621	2.419	0.544	2.560
26	1.302	1.461	1.224	1.553	1.143	1.652	1.062	1.759	0.979	1.873	0.897	1.992	0.816	2.117	0.735	2.246	0.657	2.379	0.581	2.513
27	1.316	1.469	1.240	1.556	1.162	1.651	1.084	1.753	1.004	1.861	0.925	1.974	0.845	2.093	0.767	2.216	0.691	2.342	0.616	2.470
28	1.328	1.476	1.255	1.560	1.181	1.650	1.104	1.747	1.028	1.850	0.951	1.959	0.874	2.071	0.798	2.188	0.723	2.309	0.649	2.431
29	1.341	1.483	1.270	1.563	1.198	1.650	1.124	1.743	1.050	1.841	0.975	1.944	0.900	2.052	0.826	2.164	0.753	2.278	0.681	2.396
30	1.352	1.489	1.284	1.567	1.214	1.650	1.143	1.739	1.071	1.833	0.998	1.931	0.926	2.034	0.854	2.141	0.782	2.251	0.712	2.363
31	1.363	1.496	1.297	1.570	1.229	1.650	1.160	1.735	1.090	1.825	1.020	1.920	0.950	2.018	0.879	2.120	0.810	2.226	0.741	2.333
32	1.373	1.502	1.309	1.574	1.244	1.650	1.177	1.732	1.109	1.819	1.041	1.909	0.972	2.004	0.904	2.102	0.836	2.203	0.769	2.306
33	1.383	1.508	1.321	1.577	1.258	1.651	1.193	1.730	1.127	1.813	1.061	1.900	0.994	1.991	0.927	2.085	0.861	2.181	0.796	2.281
34	1.393	1.514	1.333	1.580	1.271	1.652	1.208	1.728	1.144	1.808	1.079	1.891	1.015	1.978	0.950	2.069	0.885	2.162	0.821	2.257
35	1.402	1.519	1.343	1.584	1.283	1.653	1.222	1.726	1.160	1.803	1.097	1.884	1.034	1.967	0.971	2.054	0.908	2.144	0.843	2.236
36	1.411	1.525	1.354	1.587	1.295	1.654	1.236	1.724	1.175	1.799	1.114	1.876	1.053	1.957	0.991	2.041	0.930	2.127	0.868	2.216
37	1.419	1.530	1.364	1.590	1.307	1.655	1.249	1.723	1.190	1.795	1.131	1.870	1.071	1.948	1.011	2.029	0.951	2.112	0.891	2.197
38	1.427	1.535	1.373	1.594	1.318	1.656	1.261	1.722	1.204	1.792	1.146	1.864	1.088	1.939	1.029	2.017	0.970	2.098	0.912	2.180
39	1.435	1.540	1.382	1.597	1.328	1.658	1.273	1.722	1.218	1.789	1.161	1.859	1.104	1.932	1.047	2.007	0.990	2.085	0.932	2.164
40	1.442	1.544	1.391	1.600	1.338	1.659	1.285	1.721	1.230	1.786	1.175	1.854	1.120	1.924	1.064	1.997	1.008	2.072	0.952	2.149
45	1.475	1.566	1.430	1.615	1.383	1.666	1.336	1.720	1.287	1.776	1.238	1.835	1.189	1.895	1.139	1.958	1.089	2.022	1.038	2.088
50	1.503	1.585	1.462	1.628	1.421	1.674	1.378	1.721	1.335	1.771	1.291	1.822	1.246	1.875	1.201	1.930	1.156	1.986	1.110	2.044
55	1.528	1.601	1.490	1.641	1.452	1.681	1.414	1.724	1.374	1.768	1.334	1.814	1.294	1.861	1.253	1.909	1.212	1.959	1.170	2.010
60	1.549	1.616	1.514	1.652	1.480	1.689	1.444	1.727	1.408	1.767	1.372	1.808	1.335	1.850	1.298	1.894	1.260	1.939	1.222	1.984
65	1.567	1.629	1.536	1.662	1.503	1.696	1.471	1.731	1.438	1.767	1.404	1.805	1.370	1.843	1.336	1.882	1.301	1.923	1.266	1.964
70	1.583	1.641	1.554	1.672	1.525	1.703	1.494	1.735	1.464	1.768	1.433	1.802	1.401	1.838	1.369	1.874	1.337	1.910	1.305	1.948
75	1.598	1.652	1.571	1.680	1.543	1.709	1.515	1.739	1.487	1.770	1.458	1.801	1.428	1.834	1.399	1.867	1.369	1.901	1.339	1.935
80	1.611	1.662	1.586	1.688	1.560	1.715	1.534	1.743	1.507	1.772	1.480	1.801	1.453	1.831	1.425	1.861	1.397	1.893	1.369	1.925
85	1.624	1.671	1.600	1.696	1.575	1.721	1.550	1.747	1.525	1.774	1.500	1.801	1.474	1.829	1.448	1.857	1.422	1.886	1.396	1.916
90	1.635	1.679	1.612	1.703	1.589	1.726	1.566	1.751	1.542	1.776	1.518	1.802	1.494	1.827	1.469	1.854	1.445	1.881	1.420	1.909
95	1.645	1.687	1.623	1.709	1.602	1.732	1.579	1.755	1.557	1.778	1.535	1.803	1.512	1.827	1.489	1.852	1.465	1.877	1.442	1.903
100	1.654	1.694	1.634	1.715	1.613	1.736	1.592	1.758	1.571	1.780	1.550	1.803	1.528	1.826	1.506	1.850	1.484	1.874	1.462	1.898
150	1.720	1.747	1.706	1.760	1.693	1.774	1.679	1.788	1.665	1.802	1.651	1.817	1.637	1.832	1.622	1.846	1.608	1.862	1.593	1.877
200	1.758	1.779	1.748	1.789	1.738	1.799	1.728	1.809	1.718	1.820	1.707	1.831	1.697	1.841	1.686	1.852	1.675	1.863	1.665	1.874

$k' = k - 1$ is the number of regressors in the equation in addition to the constant term. This table was calculated by Dr R. W. Farebrother of the University of Manchester and is reproduced with his permission.

INDEX